DICTION
OF PARADOX

Glenn W. Erickson
John A. Fossa

University Press of America,® Inc.
Lanham • New York • Oxford

Copyright © 1998
University Press of America,® Inc.
4720 Boston Way
Lanham, Maryland 20706

12 Hid's Copse Rd.
Cummor Hill, Oxford OX2 9JJ

Library of Congress Cataloging-in-Publication Data

Erickson, Glenn W.
Dictionary of paradox / Glenn W. Erickson, John A. Fossa.
p.   cm.
Includes bibliographical references.
1. Paradox-Dictionaries. I. Fossa, John A. II. Title.
BC199.P2E75   1998   165—dc21   98-10526 CIP

ISBN 0-7618-1065-X (cloth: alk. ppr.)
ISBN 0-7618-1066-8 (pbk: alk. ppr.)

PREFACE

We have tried to write a dictionary that is both useful and intriguing, full of indications for further thought and providing the reader with the bibliographic resources to pursue those suggestions. Our search for material has been painstaking but hardly exhaustive, and we might, with some ingenuity and patience, have doubled the three to four hundred odd paradoxes named in this work. From Anscombe's and Arrow's to Zeno's and Zermelo's we have collected and summarized paradoxes as we found them; that is to say, the inclusion of a entry in this dictionary is not a sign of the importance or even coherence of the paradox reported. To be sure, we have not abstained from adding our own views when we saw fit. We have included cross-references and generic entries to guide the reader through the landscape of paradox. We are indebted to many people for their invaluable help in this work, and since there will inevitably be some mistakes in a book of this nature, it goes without saying that we and not they are responsible for them.

ABILENE PARADOX, THE. One of a series of paradoxical observations about management propounded by Jerry B. Harvey, its name derives from the example with with he illustrated it.

Formulation. Groups of people frequently act contrary to the desires of all of their members, thereby failing to achieve their goals.

Explanation. A family is relaxing on a hot Sunday afternoon when one of them suggests that they drive into Abilene, Texas, for dinner; no one in the family actually wants to face the four-hour round trip trek to Abilene, but each yields to his (mis)perception of the general will. It is important to see that the paradox does not arise from compromises that the group's members make in order to accommodate differing viewpoints. Rather, all the members implicitly agree on something (that is, not to go to Abilene), but the agreement is not recognized due to poor communications in the group. Indeed, by suppressing his own desires, each member contributes to the general misperception. In the corporate setting, the situation is further complicated by the multifarious power relationships involved. According to Harvey, the paradox reveals that the most serious obstacle to good management is not the inability to manage disagreement but the inability to manage agreement.

Resolution. In order to overcome the paradox, it is necessary to recognize its psychological roots: action anxiety, leading to a refusal to act at all; negative fantasies, depicting exaggerated consequences of proposing the desired action to the group; and fear of ostracism or separation from the group, including, in the corporate setting, loss of one's job. Once one realizes that the consequences of inaction may be just as momentous as those of action, however, these psychological roots may be undercut. Thus Harvey suggests two steps in coping with the paradox. First, one should make a realistic evaluation of the risks consequent upon both making one's desires known to the group and continuing to go along with the undesired proposal. Nevertheless, since by hypothesis the other members of the group are acting in such a manner as to enhance the undesired proposal, it may be extremely difficult to make this evaluation. Second, since other members of the group may in fact be acting contrary to their own desires, one should refrain from attributing any given feelings to the others and explain one's own position in a group setting. This step may expose the underlying agreement in the group and thereby prevent an unnecessary trek to Abilene.

READING

Harvey, Jerry B. *The Abilene Paradox and Other Meditations on Management.*
Lexington, MA: Heath, 1988.

ACHILLES, THE. Also known as Achilles and the Tortoise, the paradox is the second of Zeno's arguments against motion.
Formulation. "In a race the quickest runner can never overtake the slowest. Since the pursuer must first reach the point whence the pursuit began, the slower must always hold a lead" (Aristotle, *Physics*, 239b 15-18).
Explanation. A fast runner (say, brave Achilles) may be set the task of overtaking a slower one (say, a tortoise) that is given a head-start. In order to catch up to the tortoise, however, Achilles must first reach the point which the tortoise had attained when Achilles started after it. Yet during the interval it takes Achilles to reach this point, the tortoise will have advanced to a farther point. Thus Achilles must reach this new point, but by the time he does so the tortoise will have again moved to a new position. Hence there is always a residual interval between Achilles and the tortoise and the hero never catches the slow beast.
Resolution. Since we know from experience that Achilles catches the tortoise in short order, the point of resolving this paradox is to identify the fallacy that makes the paradox plausible. Aristotle distinguishes potential infinity from actual infinity. By the former, he means something like 'infinitely divisible'. Since space and time are only potentially infinite, the paradox, according to Aristotle, does not arise. The concept of infinity was troublesome to ancient Greek mathematicians because, in part, they did not have the concept of a limit. René Descartes, C. S. Peirce, and A. N. Whitehead are among those who have used the idea of a limit to resolve the paradox. According to this view, Achilles' predicament can be reduced to a convergent infinite series, such as

$$1/2 + 1/4 + 1/8 + \cdots + 1/2^n + \cdots$$

The limit of this series is simply one. Max Black argues, however, that the existence of a finite limit of an infinite series is not sufficient to resolve the paradox because it does not obviate the necessity of Achilles performing an infinite number of acts. J. M. Hinton and C. B. Martin contend that the paradox depends on an ambiguity. On the one hand, the description of the paradox merely requires Achilles to pass through all the intermediary points between his starting point and the point at which he overtakes the tortoise and this causes no further complications. On the other hand, the paradox may be interpreted as a series of commands restricting Achilles' movements in certain ways. The first interpretation, according to Hinton and Martin, verifies the premise of the paradox but invalidates the argument. In contrast, the second interpretation validates the argument, but falsifies the premise. See ZENO'S PARADOXES.

READINGS
Aristotle. *Physics.* VI-IX.
Black, Max. "Achilles and the Tortoise." *Analysis* 11.5 (1951): 91-101.
Hinton, J. M, and C. B. Martin. "Achilles and the Tortoise." *Analysis* 14.3 (1953): 56-68.
Taylor, Richard. "Mr. Wisdom on Temporal Paradoxes." *Analysis* 14.4 (1952): 15-17.
Whitehead, W. N. *Process and Reality.* Cambridge: Cambridge UP, 1929. 101-108.
Wisdom, J. O. "Achilles on a Physical Racecourse." *Analysis* 12.5 (1951): 67-72.

ACTING, PARADOX OF. Written by the *philosophe* and encyclopedist Denis Diderot (1713-1784), *The Paradox of Acting* is still frequently regarded as the single most significant statement about acting.
Formulation. The paradox is simply that in order to move an audience the actor must remain himself unmoved.
Explanation. If the stage actor is himself full of feeling, he will not be able to play the same part repeatedly with the same spirit and effectiveness. He would be emotionally drained after a few performances. Diderot observed "the unequal acting of players who play from the heart. Their playing is alternatively strong and feeble, fiery and cold, dull and sublime." It is not that actors should feel nothing at all; rather, what is needed is craftsmanship in order to achieve the fulfillment of auctorial design. Hence, the actor must strive for unity and consistency of performance regardless of his own emotional, mental, and even physical state. Further, the most artful acting does not give itself over to the passions being portrayed, but maintains its control and reserve. Like great poets, great actors must be fabulous puppets.
Resolution. This p1aradox is real enough. While actors who yield to their emotions may manage single great performances, they are liable to be uneven. They may have great expressive range and delicacy, but as a matter of nature rather than of art. They may thrive on film but fail to flourish on the more rigorous stage. It was in response to the present paradox that the various techniques for promoting inspiration in the actor were developed.
READINGS
Diderot, Denis. *The Paradox of Acting.* Trans. W. H. Pollock. New York: Hill, 1957.
Vartanian, Aram. "Diderot's Rhetoric of Paradox, or, The Conscious Automaton Observed." *Eighteenth-Century Studies* 14 (1981): 379-405.

ADVERBIAL SAMARITAN, THE. See the PARADOX OF GENTLE MURDER.

AESTHETICS, PARADOXES IN. Aesthetic paradoxes concern questions of the beautiful and other aesthetic effects, or problems in the philosophy of art. A few of the varieties of paradox in painting might be mentioned here. There are paradoxical positions and juxtapositions of bodily parts in painting from ancient Egypt to Cubism, the paradoxical effects of Trompe d'Oeil, the paradoxical geometries of the graphics of M. C. Escher. Again, there are Marcel Duchamps's paradoxical assignment of the status of art object on his ready-mades such as "Fountain," the urinal turned masterpiece; and Jasper Johns's American flags that play on a PERCEPTUAL PARADOXES such as retinal exaustion. See the PARADOX OF ANTI-ART, the PARADOX OF ACTING, LITERARY PARADOXES, the PARADOX OF TASTE, the PARADOX OF TRAGEDY, and the PARADOX OF THE UGLY.

ANALYSIS, PARADOX OF. According to G. E. Moore, the premises of philosophical analysis imply that an informative analysis is identical to a non-informative tautology. This paradox was apparently first noticed by C. H. Langford.

Formulation. "If you are to 'give an analysis' of a given concept, which is the *analysandum*, you must mention, as your *analysans*, a concept such that: (a) nobody can know that the *analysandum* applies to an object without knowing that the *analysans* applies to it, (b) nobody can verify that the *analysandum* applies without verifying that the *analysans* applies, (c) any expression which expresses the *analysandum* must be synonymous with any expression which expresses the *analysans*" (Moore, 663). Hence, the meaning of "*analysandum* is *analysans*" is the same as "*analysandum* is *analysandum*."

Explanation. Consider the concept of 'being a brother.' An adequate analysis of this concept, since it fulfils conditions (a)-(c) above, would be

(1) To be a brother is to be a male sibling.

Thus, according to Moore, 'brother' and 'male sibling' have identical denotations and we cannot employ the concept 'brother' without also knowing that the concept 'male sibling' applies. Neither can we verify that 'brother' is applicable to any given object without simultaneously verifying that 'male sibling' is also applicable, nor is there a synonym for the first term that is not synonymous with the second. Thus, there seems to be no way to distinguish the cognitive content of the aforementioned analysis from that of

(2) To be a brother is to be a brother.

The problem is not that the two propositions are merely logically equivalent, but that they have identical meanings. The second proposition, however, is plainly not an analysis of the concept brother'.

Resolution. Moore himself suggests that a statement of an analysis is partly about the concept being analyzed and partly about the verbal expressions used to express it, but he was never wholly satisfied with this response because he could not see how the statement of an analysis could be about the expressions rather than about the concept being analyzed. Max Black argues that, whereas proposition (2) above is an identity, proposition (1) is not an identity but a three-termed relation. Accordingly, the two propositions cannot be the same. Morton G. White, however, contends that Black's proposed three-termed relation is really an identity after all and thus Black's analysis does not dissolve the paradox. Ernest Sosa argues that from the point of view of Fregean semantics the terms 'brother' and 'male sibling' are co-designative but not synonymous; thus Sosa's proposed solution seems to contradict Moore's premise (c). Seemingly harking back to Black's position, but explicitly invoking a Kantian viewpoint, T. W. Schick equates the analysis of a concept with its decomposition into component concepts, thereby making explicit what was only implicit in the original concept. Again, Richard A. Fumerton denies that the psychological significance of proposition (1), as compared to the triviality of proposition (2), is sufficient reason for concluding that the two propositions differ in meaning.

READINGS

Ackerman, Diana F. "The Informativeness of Philosophical Analysis." *Midwest Studies in Philosophy* 6 (1981): 313-320.

——. "Two Paradoxes of Analysis." *Journal of Philosophy* 78 (1981): 733-735.

Anderson, C. Anthony. "Bealer's 'Quality and Concept'." *Journal of Philosophical Logic* 16 (1987): 115-164.

Bealer, George. "Remarks on Classical Analysis." *Journal of Philosophy* 80 (1983): 711-712.

——. *Quality and Concept.* Oxford: Clarendon, 1982. 69-77.

Black, Max. "The 'Paradox of Analysis.'" *Mind* ns 53 (1944): 263-267.

——. "The 'Paradox of Analysis Again: A Reply." *Mind* ns 54 (1945): 272-273.

Fumerton, Richard A. "The Paradox of Analysis." *Philosophy and Phenomenological Research* 43 (1983): 477-498.

Langford, C. H. "Moore's Notion of Analysis." *The Philosophy of G. E. Moore.* Ed. P. A. Schilpp. Evanston: Northwestern UP, 1942. 319-342.

Moore, G. E. "Reply to My Critics." *The Philosophy of G. E. Moore.* Ed.

P. A. Schilpp. Evanston: Northwestern UP, 1942. 660-667.

Schick, T. W., Jr. "Kant, Analyticity, and the Paradox of Analysis." *Idealistic Studies* 16 (1986): 125-131.

Sellars, Wilfrid. "The Paradox of Analysis: A Neo-Fregean Approach." *Philosophical Papers*. Springfield, IL: Thomas, 1967.

Sosa, Ernest. "Classical Analysis." *Journal of Philosophy* 80 (1983): 695-710.

Weitz, Morris. "Analysis, Philosophical." *Encyclopedia of Philosophy*. Ed. Paul Edwards. New York: Macmillan, 1967. Vol. 1, 97-105.

White, A. R. *Moore: A Critical Exposition*. Oxford, 1958.

White, Morton G. "A Note on the "Paradox of Analysis." *Mind* ns 54 (1945): 71-72.

— —. "Analysis and Identity: A Rejoinder." *Mind* ns 54 (1945): 357-361.

Zalta, Edward N. "Meinongian Type Theory and Its Applications." *Studies in Logic* 41 (1982): 297-307.

ANSCOMBE'S PARADOX. First noted by G. E. M. Anscombe in 1976, this is one of the PARADOXES OF VOTING.

Formulation. A set of proposals selected by simple majority rule may result in outcomes with which a majority of voters disagree in a majority of cases. Hence the majority may be frustrated by the majority's will being fulfilled.

Explanation. The following chart of five voters deliberating on three proposals illustrates the possibility just identified (based on Gorman, 46).

		P R O P O S A L S		
		A	**B**	**C**
	1	Yes	Yes	No
	2	No	No	No
Voters	3	No	Yes	Yes
	4	Yes	No	Yes
	5	Yes	No	Yes

A and **C** are both to be implemented since a majority of voters approves them. Yet the first three voters, who are also a majority, disagree with the results in a majority of cases: Voter One disagrees with the outcomes on proposals **B** and **C**; Voter Two with those on the proposals **A** and **C**; and Voter Three with those on proposals **A** and **B**.

Resolution. The paradox cannot arise when only a single proposal is considered. When a series of proposals (not necessarily voted on simultaneously) are considered, however, the paradox may occur either as a fortuitous result or as the result of deliberate manipulation by a "tyrant." In either case, the cumulative effect of the implemented proposals may well be a society repugnant to the majority of voters. M. P. T. Leahy's objection — that the total number of satisfied desires will always be in the majority — is irrelevant to this point. Consequently, two plausible arguments for democracy — that it is the best mode of decision-making because it insures the satisfaction of the will of the majority and that it is the fairest because it gives each person's desires equal weight — are undermined by the paradox. Carl Wagner points out that the paradox does not arise when the prevailing vote is at least three-fourths of the electorate on each proposal.

READINGS

Anscombe, G. E. M. "On the Frustration of the Majority by Fulfillment of the Majority's Will." *Analysis* 36.4 (1976): 161-168.

Gorman, J. L. "A Problem of the Justification of Democracy." *Analysis* 38.1 (1978): 46-50.

Leahy, M. P. T. "Lies, Damned Lies, and Miss Anscombe." *Analysis* 37.2 (1977): 80-81.

Wagner, Carl. "Anscombe's Paradox and the Rule of Three-Fourths." *Theory and Decision* 15 (1983): 303-308.

ANTI-ART, THE PARADOX OF. Anti-art was the fundamental concept of the Dada movement, which represented a radical repudiation of bourgeois art and culture. The more recent Pop Art and Kinetic Art movements also began as anti-art. Yet however shocking and destructive of traditional art anti-art is, the inevitable historical paradox has caught up with it and now anti-art is as celebrated, collectable and integrated into the tradition of bourgeois culture as any other artistic tendency.

ANTINOMIANISM. This doctrine holds that Christians are not bound to obey the law of God, especially as represented in the Old Testament legal system, but may continue in sin so that divine grace, that is, God's forgiveness of sin, may abound. The term was first applied by Martin Luther to John Agricola, and given to a Christian sect that appeared in Germany about 1535, but the argument was put forward as a rationale for moral licence since early Christian times. In colonial Massachusetts, Anne Hutchinson led antinomians in a controversy with John Winthrop. Antinomian doctrine has been seen in the sixteenth-century legend of the minnesinger Tannhauser, which Wagner made into an opera. Tannhauser spent a voluptuous year with Lady Venus at Venusburg, a magical land of sensuous delight accessible through a subterranean passage. Once he obtained permission to leave, he went straight to Pope Urban for absolution; but the Pope refused, "No, you can no more hope for atonement than this dry staff here can be expected to bud again." Tannhauser left, but three days later the staff burst into full bloom. Urban sent in every direction to call Tannhauser back, but by that time the poet had returned to spend his remaining days with Lady Venus. The miracle reminds the Pope that God's grace is not limited by the constraints of moral law.

ANTINOMY. An antinomy (Greek "opposing the law") is a logical contradiction, or extreme variety of paradox in which there is contradiction between two principles or inferences each of which seems equally necessary or reasonable but which cannot both be true. A frequently occurring distinction is that an antinomy is inconsistent, whereas a paradox may be only seemingly so. See DUMITRIU'S ANTINOMY OF THE THEORY OF TYPES, KANT'S ANTINOMIES, and ROSS'S ANTINOMY.

AQUIST'S PARADOX. See the EPISTEMIC OBLIGATION PARADOX.

ARROW, THE. Mentioned by Aristotle, Epiphanus, and Diogenes Laertius, this is the third of Zeno's arguments against motion.
Formulation. "An arrow in flight is motionless because it is always occupying a space equal to itself at each moment and because everything that occupies an equal space is at rest" (Aristotle, *Physics,* 239b 5-7). Zeno "argues thus: what is moving moves either in the place in which it is or in the place in which it is not. And it moves neither in the place in which it is nor in that which it is not. Therefore nothing moves." (Epiphanus, *Adversus Haereticos,* III.11; cited in Lear, n.1).
Explanation. Anything that occupies a space its own size is at rest. An arrow in flight, while it is in flight, exists in a present moment. Yet in that present moment the arrow occupies a space just its own size. Thus in the present moment the arrow is at rest. Yet that means that a moving arrow is also at rest, which is absurd.
Resolution. The present paradox is generally considered to be predicated upon the assumption that time consists of non-instantaneous atomic intervals. (For another view, see Vlastos.) Indeed, the paradox does not

seem to arise when time is conceived of as a succession of instantaneous moments since movement is dependent on velocity. But velocity is the ratio of distance (change in position) to elapsed time and there is no elapsed time at a point-like moment. Hence it would seem that the very concepts of rest and motion would not be applicable to an object at an instantaneous moment. Jonathan Lear is probably correct in asserting that the extension of the concept of velocity to instantaneous velocity by the concept of 'limit' is irrelevant to the paradox. Aristotle used the idea of velocity to argue that the concepts of rest and motion are not even applicable to atomic intervals since, by considering objects with different velocities, it would be possible to divide the atomic interval. Denying that motion is inconsistent with the atomicity of time, however, would seem to be but a hollow victory for, on the present view, that was Zeno's purpose anyway — moreover, Zeno is armed with other paradoxes purporting to show that motion is also inconsistent with instantaneous time. A possibility apparently not discussed in the literature is that a moving arrow might effectively fill a larger amount of space than an arrow at rest. Thus, the paradox would fail because it would contain a false (ambiguous) premise; nevertheless, motion and atomic time would not be contradictory. Lest this hypothesis be considered more paradoxical than the paradox itself, we hasten to add that the Lorentz-Fitzgerald contraction of Relativity Theory could be used to the same purpose. See ZENO'S PARADOXES.

READINGS

Aristotle. *Physics.* Bk. VI, ch. IX.

Hager, Paul. "Russell and Zeno's Arrow Paradox." *Russell* 7 (1987): 3-10.

Lear, Jonathan. "A Note on Zeno's Arrow." *Phronesis* 26 (1981): 91-104.

Vlastos, Gregory. "A Note on Zeno's Arrow." *Studies in Presocratic Philosophy.* Vol. 2. Ed. Allen, R. E., and D. J. Furley. London: Routledge, 1974. 184-200.

White, Michael J. "The Spatial Arrow Paradox." *Pacific Philosophical Quarterly* 68 (1987): 71-77.

ARROW'S IMPOSSIBILITY THEOREM. See ARROW'S PARADOX OF SOCIAL CHOICE.

ARROW'S PARADOX OF SOCIAL CHOICE. First proposed by the economist Kenneth Arrow, Arrow's Paradox is sometimes called Arrow's Impossibility Theorem or the Voter's Paradox. Related to ANSCOMBE'S PARADOX, this paradox of social choice theory purports to show that no rational, democratic mechanism is available for basing social policy on individual preferences.

Formulation. Arrow proved that no mechanism for instituting social choice on the basis of individual preferences can simultaneously satisfy the following four intuitively plausible principles:

(1)   Collective rationality: the mechanism should be applicable to any logically coherent finite set of individual preferences, over any finite set of choices.

(2)   Pareto principle: any preference unanimously shared by individual voters should be preserved by the mechanism.

(3)   Non-dictatorship: a mechanism cannot operate so as always to produce the choices of a single individual.

(4)   Independence of irrelevant alternatives: only the individual preferences with respect to the choices to be ordered may be considered by the mechanism.

Explanation. Arrow formalized principles (1)-(4) using first order predicate logic and then deduced the consequence that a single individual cannot determine the outcome of the social choice mechanism for any given pair of alternatives without determining it for all the choices and thereby being a dictator. But conditions (1), (2), and (4) imply that some individual must be decisive for some given pair of choices. Thus, conditions (1)-(4) are inconsistent. The following example captures the flavor of Arrow's demonstration. Let V_1, V_2 and V_3 be three voters who are to order the four social choices C_1, C_2, C_3, and C_4. Each ordering will be given by $\{a, b, c, d\}$, where each choice is preferred to all those to the right of it. This notation is possible since the assumption of collective rationality includes the provision that the orderings are logically well behaved; in particular, the orderings are connected (given any two choices, one is preferred to the other) and transitive (given any three choices, if the first is preferred to the second and the second is preferred to the third, then the first is preferred to the third). We now show that any mechanism satisfying Arrow's conditions will enforce one individual's choice against those of all the others for some pair of choices. By the principle of collective rationality, the mechanism should be applicable to the following preference ordering:

$$V_1: \ \{C_1, C_2, C_3, C_4\}$$
$$V_2: \ \{C_4, C_1, C_2, C_3\}$$
$$V_3: \ \{C_3, C_4, C_1, C_2\}$$

Since C_1 is preferred to C_2 by all the voters, the Pareto principle demands that C_1 be preferred to C_2 by the social choice mechanism. There are only twelve possible orderings ranking C_1 to the left of C_2 and for each one of these possible orderings there is at least one voter whose choice for some pair is preserved when the others chose the opposite order. If the mechanism produces the order $\{C_1, C_3, C_2, C_4\}$, for example, then only V_1 agrees that C_1 is preferable to C_4. The other eleven cases are similar and can be done by inspection. The result is paradoxical because it is hard to see how the apparently reasonable, and relatively weak, conditions (1)-(4) are mutually incompatible.

Resolution. Given the paradox, a consistent social choice mechanism must give up one of Arrow's four assumptions. Since conditions (2) and (3) have seemed unassailable to most commentators, attention has focused on conditions (1) and (4). One possible attack on the principle of collective rationality is that it cannot be taken for granted that individual preferences are logically well behaved in the requisite manner. In particular, Arrow's proof depends on the transitivity of the preference ordering. Another possibility is to deny that social preferences should be modeled on individual preferences, because the latter have an inherently psychological character that need not be reflected on the social level. Arrow himself suggested that the best point of attack is condition (4): if choices could be quantitatively assessed in a particular way rather than merely ordered, the paradox could be avoided.

READINGS

Arrow, Kenneth. *Social Choice and Individual Values.* New Haven: Yale UP, 1951; 2nd ed. 1963.

Davis, Michael. "Avoiding the Voter's Paradox Democratically." *Theory and Decision* 5 (1974): 295-311.

MacKay, Alfred F. *Arrow's Theorem: The Paradox of Social Choice; A Case Study in the Philosophy of Economics.* New Haven: Yale UP, 1980.

Rusciano, Frank Louis. *Isolation and Paradox: Defining 'The Public' in Modern Political Analysis.* New York: Greenwood, 1989.

Tullock, Gordon. "Avoiding the Voter's Paradox Democratically: Comment." *Theory and Decision* 6 (1975): 485-486.

AUTHOR'S PARADOX, THE. This is a case of the PARADOX OF NONEXISTENT OBJECTS applied to fictional characters. See the PARADOX OF NEGATION.

READINGS

Glannon, Walter. "The Author's Paradox." *British Journal Of Aesthetics* 28 (1988): 239- 247.

Pollard, D. E. B. "Authors without Paradox." *British Journal of Aesthetics* 29 (1989): 363-366.

BACKWARD INDUCTION PARADOX, THE. Suppose that two players are confronted with a finite number of PRISONER'S DILEMMAS. By a backward induction, each player will defect in every round of play even though a cooperative strategy is more advantageous to both players. Philip Pettit and Robert Sugden, however, argue that the players are not in a position to make the backward induction because the initial assumptions of game theory — that the players are rational and at the start of the game believe that the other players are also rational — "does not entitle him [the first player] to believe that in subsequent rounds his partner will still believe he is rational, irrespective of how he, the first player, has acted in the interim" (172). For a concrete example, see the CHAIN STORE PARADOX.

READING

Pettit, Philip and Robert Sugden. "The Backward Induction Paradox." *The Journal of Philosophy* 86 (1989): 169-182.

BALD MAN, THE. See EUBULIDES' PARADOXES and the SORITES.

BANACH-TARSKY PARADOX, THE. One of a series of paradoxical decompositions in measure theory, this paradox is related to the Hausdorff Paradox and other similar results.

Formulation. Any ball in $\mathbf{R}^3$ can be decomposed into a finite number of pairwise disjoint subsets that can then be recombined to form two balls of the same radius as the original ball. The result can be generalized to $\mathbf{R}^n$ for $n \geq 3$. The paradox is frequently, but fancifully, given as "a pea may be taken apart into finitely many pieces that may be rearranged using rotations and translations to form a ball the size of the sun" (Wagon, 3-4).

Explanation. Clearly, duplicating a ball or enlarging it are equivalent. In either case, the ball is cut into a finite number of pieces and then these pieces are rearranged in such a way as to obtain a set with a greater measure ("volume") than the original ball. The actions performed in this process are limited to the group of isometries on the metric involved; that is, they are limited to one-one functions from the metric onto itself that preserve distances (and, therefore, areas). Intuitively, the pieces of the original ball are not stretched by the rearrangement. Although the paradox does not arise in $\mathbf{R}^2$, a two dimensional example of a decomposition may be enlightening. We can find the area of a parallelogram, for example, by decomposing it into two pieces and rearranging them to form a rectangle:

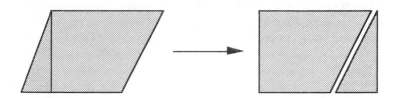

Although an analogous procedure has been used since the time of ancient Greece to find volumes of solid figures, the present paradox shows that the new figure may have a different volume than the original.

Resolution. The proof of the Banach-Tarski Paradox depends on the Axiom of Choice. This axiom allows one to form a new set by picking out an element from each set of a given collection of sets. A useful metaphor was adduced by Bertrand Russell. Given a collection of pairs of shoes, we can form a new set by picking the left shoe of each pair. If the original collection were pairs of socks, however, the above rule would not be applicable since we cannot distinguish between "left socks" and "right socks." Nevertheless, the Axiom of Choice allows us to form the new set by making an arbitrary choice from each pair of socks. A considerable number of mathematicians do not accept the validity of a procedure of set formation that depends on such nonconstructive methods as the Axiom of Choice and they thus are able to sidestep the paradox (although some paradoxical special cases still arise in the absence of this axiom). The majority of mathematicians, however, accept Choice and regard the present paradox and its near relations as proof of the nonexistence of the relevant finitely additive measures. Much mathematical activity has revolved around finding appropriate nonparadoxical measures.

READING

Wagon, Stan. *The Banach-Tarski Paradox.* Cambridge: Cambridge UP, 1985.

BARBER PARADOX, THE. This paradox is a humorous illustration of the more technical RUSSELL'S PARADOX.

Formulation. "In a certain village the barber shaves all, and only, the men who do not shave themselves. Who shaves the barber?" (Russell, *Principia Mathematica*, I 60).

Explanation. If the barber shaves himself, he must be one of those men who do not shave themselves. But if the barber does not shave himself, he must be shaved by the barber; that is, the barber must shave himself. In either case, we get a contradiction.

Resolution. Unless, of course, the barber turns out to be a woman, there cannot be any barber who satisfies the premises of the paradox; and, in fact, denying that any such barber could exist is the standard response to the paradox. It is evident that this response is satisfactory since, somewhat like a square circle, the barber has been defined by contradictory properties. The set theoretic analogue to the Barber Paradox is not so easily disposed of, however, because it is not intuitively evident what the source of the paradox is.

BARBER SHOP PARADOX, THE. Formulated by Lewis Carroll, this story involving three barbers was intended by Carroll to be an "ornamental" presentation of a problem in the interpretation of conditional propositions.

Formulation. Allen, Brown, and Carr are three barbers. They cannot all be out at the same time because someone has to mind the store. Furthermore, Allen is nervous about going out alone and always brings Brown along with him. If Carr were to go out, then Brown would have to stay in whenever Allen went out. This last, however, is impossible since Brown has to tag along with Allen. Hence, Carr can never leave the shop.

Explanation. We are given two premises:

(1) Allen, Brown, or Carr is in.
(2) If Allen is not in, then Brown is not in.

The argument proceeds by contradiction:

(3) Carr is not in.   (hypothesis)
(4) If Allen is not in, then Brown is in.   (from (1) and (3))
(5) Propositions (2) and (4) are contradictory.

Therefore,

(6) The hypothesis (3) is false and Carr is in.

The justification for proposition (5) is that "Allen is not in" is a sufficient condition for two contradictory results and, thus, both (2) and (4) cannot be true.

Resolution. The interpretation of conditional propositions has been problematical since the Stoics tried their hand at logic in Classical Antiquity. Thus, it is not surprizing that the various responses to the present paradox have invoked different interpretations of conditionals. Nevertheless, the overwhelming majority of respondents to the paradox have argued that it is falsidical since a contradiction only arises when, in conjunction with hypothesis (3), we assume that Allen is not in. Thus we are allowed to conclude only that whenever Carr is not in, Allen must be in. See the PARADOXES OF MATERIAL IMPLICATION.

READINGS

Burks, Arthur W., and Irving M. Copi. "Lewis Carroll's Barber Shop Paradox." *Mind* ns 59 (1950): 219-222.

Lewis Carroll [Charles Dodgson]. "A Logical Paradox." *Mind* ns 3 (1894): 436-438.

Jones, E. E. C. "Lewis Carroll's Logical Paradox." *Mind* ns 14 (1905): 146-8, 576-578.

Johnson, W. E. "A Logical Paradox." *Mind* ns 3 (1894): 583.

— —. "Hypotheticals in a Context." *Mind* ns 4 (1895): 143-144.

Sidgwick, A. "A Logical Paradox." *Mind* ns 3 (1894): 582.

— —. "Hypotheticals in a Context." *Mind* ns 4 (1895): 143.

"W." "Lewis Carroll's Logical Paradox." *Mind* ns 14 (1905): 292-293.

BEAKER PARADOX, THE. Called the wine and water problem by Richard Von Mises, this paradox is essentially the same as BERTRAND'S PARADOX.

Formulation. Given a mixture of water and wine that contains at least as much water as wine, there is a 50% probability that the water to wine ratio is between 1 and 3/2. But, by calculating the inverse ratio first, we find that there is also a 50% probability that the water to wine ratio is between 1 and 4/3. The two results are clearly incompatible.

Explanation. Let r be the ratio of the amount of water to the amount of wine in the given mixture. Clearly, if there is as much water as there is wine, $r=1$ and, if there is twice as much water as wine, $r=2$. Hence, we have

$$1 \leq r \leq 2.$$

It is, however, equally probable that r be at any point in the stated interval as at any other point in the interval. Thus, there is a 50% chance of r being in the upper half of the interval and a 50% chance of r being in the lower half of the interval. That is, there is a 50% chance that r is between 1 and 3/2. Consider, now, the ratio of wine to water; that is, $1/r$. Clearly, if there is twice as much water as wine, $1/r = 1/2$ and, if there are equal amounts of water and wine, $1/r = 1$. Hence, we have

$$1/2 \leq 1/r \leq 1.$$

Once again, it is equally probable that $1/r$ be at any point in the stated interval. Thus, there is a 50% chance of $1/r$ being in the upper half of the interval; that is, between 3/4 and 1. Therefore by taking the reciprocals, there is a 50% chance of r being between 1 and 4/3, which contradicts the previous result.

Resolution. The kind of problem illustrated by the present paradox may occur whenever continuous variables are used to characterize a given property. According to von Mises, however, the root problem of these paradoxes is the concept of equally possible alternatives based on intuitive (subjective) judgments or on a principle of indifference due to symmetry considerations. Thus, von Mises argues that it is necessary to establish the frequency distribution of the alternatives by empirical methods; this distribution is to be regarded as the initial conditions of any given problem and is thus independent of the probability calculus itself. In practice, the distribution is often determined by long-range frequency counts, that is, the experiment is iterated a large number of times and the results are then organized statistically. In cases such as the present problem, von Mises warns, it may be necessary to specify the actual procedure involved in determining the given collectives. See BERTRAND'S PARADOX and the INFINITE SERIES PARADOX.

READING

Von Mises, Richard. *Probability, Statistics and Truth.* New York: Macmillan, 1957. Ch. 1.

BELL-EPR PARADOX, THE. See the EINSTEIN-PODOLSKY-ROSEN PARADOX.

BERRY'S PARADOX. This paradox was first described by Bertrand Russell, who attributed it to the Cambridge librarian G. G. Berry. A logical paradox related to RICHARD'S PARADOX and ultimately to the LIAR, it has also been characterized as a semantic paradox.

Formulation. Consider the number specified by the phrase "the least natural number not specifiable by a phrase containing fewer than fifteen words," which phrase uses fewer than fifteen words. Variants include replacing "words" by "syllables" or "letters" with a corresponding adjustment to the number involved. Still other variants include Max Black's "the least integer not named in this book" and Robert E. Kirk's "the largest number definable by an English phrase containing . . . or fewer words."

Explanation. A few facts about the natural numbers and a natural language such as English make the paradox formally derivable. First, there is an infinite number of natural numbers. Second, any nonempty set of natural numbers has a least element. Third, the number of distinct words (letters, syllables) in English is finite. Thus, there is only a finite number of phrases restricted to a certain length which can be used to specify some member of the natural number sequence. Consequently, there will always be some numbers that are not specified by any phrase restricted to a given length. Yet this number is then specified by Berry's phrase, which is within the given length.

Resolutions. At first sight, the paradox would seem to be avoidable by outlawing phrases containing negatives. That such an approach does not suffice, however, is shown by Kirk's variant which generates the paradox without the use of negatives. Dorothy Grover attempts to give an account of reference according to which phrases such as Berry's fail to refer; but while promising, this approach does not explain why phrases such as Berry's generate the paradox whereas phrases such as "the least number not specifiable in English in less than three words" do not. Still another approach would be to order specifying phrases into a hierarchy of types (see the LIAR): wherein an attempt to state the paradox would involve specification$_1$ of the least number not specifiable$_2$ in fewer than n words and no paradox would arise.

READINGS

Black, Max. *The Nature of Mathematics.* London: Routledge & Kegan Paul, 1933. 97-101.

Brady, Ross T. Reply to Priest on the Berry Paradox." *Philosophical Quarterly* 34 (1984): 157-162.

Grover, Dorothy. "Berry's Paradox." *Analysis* 43.4 (1983): 170-176.

Kirk, Robert E. "A Negation-Free Version of the Berry Paradox." *Analysis* 41.4 (1981): 223-224.

Priest, Graham. "The Logical Paradoxes and the Law of the Excluded Middle." *Philosophical Quarterly* 33 (1983): 160-165. Discussion: 34 (1984): 157-63.

Russell, Bertrand. "Les Paradoxes de la Logique." *Revue de Métaphysique et de Morale* 14 (1906): 627-650.

BERTRAND'S PARADOX. First described by the French mathematician J. L. F. Bertrand, this is a PARADOX OF PROBABILITY THEORY.
Formulation. Classical probability theory, such as Laplace's, defines the probability of an event as the ratio of the number of times that an event

occurs to the number of "equally likely outcomes." Consider the probability that a chord, drawn at random in a circle, is longer than the side of the equilateral triangle inscribed in the circle. Since the midpoint of the chord is on the radius of the circle, the required probability must be 1/2. But since the chord is contained by two sides of the inscribed triangle, the probability must be 1/3. Moreover, since the midpoint of the chord is contained in the circle inscribed in the triangle, the probability must be 1/4.

Explanation. Given a chord, *c*, drawn at random in a circle, there are (at least) three different ways of calculating the probability that the length of *c* will be greater than the length of the side, *s*, of the inscribed equilateral triangle. First, draw the radius, *r*, containing the midpoint, **M**, of *c* and orient the inscribed triangle so that one side is parallel to *c* (fig. 1). Let **O** be the center of the circle and A be the intersection of the radius with the side of the triangle. Clearly, *c>s* if, and only if, **M** is between **O** and **A**. But **OA** = (1/2)*r* (since **OA** is 1/3 of the altitude of the triangle). By construction, **M** must be on *r*. Since the likelihood that **M** will be at any point on *r* is the same as that it will be at any other point on *r* and since half of these positions make *c* greater than *s*, the required probability must be 1/2. Another way of looking at the problem, however, gives a different result. Draw a tangent to the circle at one of the endpoints of the chord and orient the triangle so that one vertex is coincident with that endpoint (fig. 2). Clearly, *c>s* if, and only if, *c* is in the 60 degree angle made by the two sides of the triangle at the tangent. By construction, the chord must fall in the 180 degree angle on the same side of the tangent as the circle. Since the likelihood that *c* will be in any position in the 180 degree angle is the same as that it will be in any other position in that angle and since a third of these positions make *c* greater than *s*, the required probability must be 1/3. Although the paradox has already been established by the two contradictory results for the required probability, still another way of looking at the problem results in yet another value for this probability. Inscribe a circle in the triangle (fig. 3). Clearly, *c>s* if, and only if, **M** (the midpoint of the chord) is contained in the smaller circle (*c=s* when *c* is tangent to the smaller circle). By construction, **M** must fall somewhere in the larger circle. Since the likelihood that **M** will be at any point in the larger circle is the same as that it will be at any other point in that circle and since a fourth of these points make *c* greater than *s* (the radius of the smaller circle is half the radius of the larger circle — in fact, it is **OA** of Fig. 1 — therefore, the area is a fourth), the required probability is 1/4. It is evident that the results of these calculations are incompatible, but all three arise from a consideration of the ratio of successful outcomes to "equally likely outcomes." Consequently, a mathematical theory of probability cannot be based upon this intuitively appealing notion.

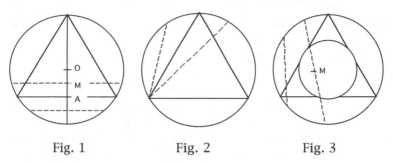

Fig. 1   Fig. 2   Fig. 3

Resolution. The problem here is that the phrase "equally likely outcomes" in the formulation of classical probability theory is not well enough defined to support unambiguous probability attributions. There are at least three approaches to resolving the paradox. First of all, Bertrand suggested that probabilities could not be well defined with respect to infinite sets of possible outcomes, so that probability theory should be restricted to situations in which the number of possible outcomes is finite. Since, however, it is often necessary to state probabilities for a range of values in a continuous distribution, this suggestion is too restrictive. Secondly, a more typical response is to abandon classical probability theory in favor of a long-range frequency count (see the BEAKER PARADOX). On this account, probabilities may not be derived *a priori*, but only through actual observation of the frequency of successful outcomes in a given sequence of trials (but see the INFINITE SERIES PARADOX for a difficulty with this view). Thirdly, it has been suggested that equally likely outcomes may be judged only relative to a particular procedure. There are, for example, particular procedures that produce each of the calculations in the formulation of the paradox: the chord in the first calculation could be generated, all other things being equal, by rolling a rod across the face of a circle; the chord in the second calculation could be generated by a rod attached at one end but free to spin around it; and the chord in the third, by selecting its center at random.

READINGS

Bertrand, J. L. F. *Calcul des Probabilités.* New York: Chelsea, 1972. Third Lecture.

von Mises, Richard. *Probability, Statistics and Truth.* New York: Macmillan, 1957. Ch. 1.

BISECTION PARADOX, THE. See the DICHOTOMY.

BODHISATTVA PARADOX, THE. This ethico-religious paradox was adduced by Arthur Danto. **Formulation.** The *bodhisattva* cannot pass over into Nirvana. He cannot because, were he to do so he would exhibit a selfishness that a *bodhisattva* cannot have. If he has the selfishness, he is not a *bodhisattva*, and so cannot enter into Nirvana. If he lacks the selfishness, again, he cannot enter Nirvana, for that would be a selfish act. So either way, the *bodhisattva* is impotent to enter Nirvana. Like God who, in the Christian teaching, cannot do evil because it is inconsistent with his nature, the *bodhisattva* cannot perform the ultimately selfish act. So no one can reach Nirvana: *we* cannot because we are not *bodhisattvas* and the *bodhisattva* cannot because he is a *bodhisattva*" (Danto, *Mysticism and Morality* 82; but see alternative formulation in his *Analytic Philosophy of Action 166*). **Explanation.** According to Danto, the *bodhisattva* is generally conceived of as someone who has attained enlightenment and can thus pass over into Nirvana; he nevertheless postpones doing so until all mankind can be brought to the same point so that everyone will pass over together. Danto's description of the *bodhisattva*, however, does not square with all interpretations of Buddhist doctrine. According to one main conception, the *bodhisattva* does not delay entering Nirvana until all mankind (better, all sentient creatures) can enter with him, but forebears only until they are secure in this prospect. But granting Danto his interpretation of the doctrine, the paradox would be that the *bodhisattva* cannot not enter Nirvana until all mankind enters with him because, if he tried entering before them, his selfishness would prevent him from entering Nirvana and, hence, he would not be a *bodhisattva* after all. If, however, he were indeed a *bodhisattva*, his lack of selfishness would prevent him from entering Nirvana ahead of everyone else. Thus, whether the *bodhisattva* is selfish or not, he is unable to pass over into Nirvana. But this result contradicts the conventional view that the *bodhisattva* 's delay is a postponement. **Resolution.** Perhaps Danto's (and our conventional) idea of what constitutes selfishness is not applicable at the point at which one is poised to enter Nirvana, because from that standpoint, even the distinction selfish/ unselfish is irredeemably fraught with egoistic identifications. It is even unclear whether the *bodhisattva* can be credited with a voluntary act of postponing his entry into bliss, because he would have had to have passed beyond any sort of willfulness to be a *bodhisattva*. Thus the decision to delay entering Nirvana is not made once the *bodhisattva* is a *bodhisattva*, but when the one who might be a *bodhisattva* enters into the path of the *bodhisattva*. This possibility, however, only resolves Danto's paradox by putting another paradox in its place — namely, that of how an act of will can place a being beyond willfulness and its opposite altogether.

READINGS

Danto, Arthur. *Analytic Philosophy of Action.* Cambridge: Cambridge UP, 1973.

——. *Mysticism and Morality: Oriental Thought and Moral Philosophy.* Harmondsworth, Eng.: Penguin, 1976.

Perrett, Roy. "The Bodhisattva Paradox." *Philosophy East and West* 36 (1986): 55-59.

BOOTS PARADOX, THE. The Russian geographer V. N. Bugromenko urges that the full potential of sophisticated mathematical techniques in geography, such as those pioneered by Barry N. Boots, are not being realized because "the methodological innovations that have been developed in English speaking geography often find themselves in a conceptual vacuum, so that it is difficult, if not impossible, to use these innovations for the resolution of concrete regional problems" (Bugromenko, 8). Bugromenko calls this situation the Boots Paradox and suggests that it is (partly) due to the fact that the innovations are due to university professors who have but little concern with practical applications.

READINGS

Boots, Barry N. "Using Explanatory Spatial Models in Planning Contexts." *Soviet Geography* 28 (1987): 10-13.

Bugromenko, V. N. "The Boots Paradox." *Soviet Geography* 28 (1987): 1-9.

BOTTLE IMP, THE. Citing "The Bottle Imp," a short story by Robert Louis Stephenson, Richard Sharvey proposed this paradox to the readers of *Philosophia* [Israel].

Formulation. "An indestructible bottle contains a powerful imp, and the owner of the bottle may command the imp to grant (almost) any wish. But if a person dies while he owns the bottle, he goes to hell and burns forever. An owner of the bottle may get rid of it only by selling it to someone else for less than he paid for it himself. Furthermore, he must inform the buyer of all these conditions, and the buyer must understand them and be rational (or else the bottle just comes back)."

Explanation. Sharvey argues that, even disregarding the risk of accidental death while in possession of the bottle, it would be irrational to buy the bottle for any finite amount of money. Obviously, it would be irrational to buy it for one cent since it could not then be resold, thereby condemning the buyer to burn in hell forever. (The imp cannot grant eternal life, nor create smaller currency units, nor grant any wish that would alter the conditions of the problem.) Furthermore, it is irrational to buy the bottle for $n+1$ cents, if it is irrational to by it for n cents, since, once again, it could not be resold. By induction, therefore, it is irrational to buy the bottle for any finite amount. The problem is to explain why such a bottle seems like a bargain at the price of, say, one thousand dollars.

Resolution. Many commentators have related the Bottle Imp to various other paradoxes. Roy A. Sorensen, for example, argues that it is a variation of the PREDICTION PARADOX. Michael J. Wreen, who relates the present paradox to various others, contends that the argument, as stated, is invalid since there are various scenarios that would seem to make buying the bottle for even one cent a rational act. Thus, a person who believes himself to be predestined to go to hell anyway may quite rationally buy the bottle in order to afford himself the temporary pleasures that it could provide; alternatively, as is the case in Stephenson's story, the bottle could be bought for various altruistic reasons without the buyer being thought irrational. Wreen then argues that even if these invalidating scenarios are eliminated, buying the bottle for a thousand dollars would indeed be rational, given that people are like they are. Such an argument evidently disrespects Sharvey's premise that the buyer be rational, but it also indicates that it is precisely Sharvey's definition of rationality that is responsible for the paradoxical result. Indeed, Saul Traiger observes that Sharvey's premises imply that any attempt to buy the bottle is a sufficient condition for irrationality; hence, no prospective buyer could effect the purchase since he would have to be rational to do so. Thus, according to Traiger, the purported paradox ceases to be an interesting argument.

READINGS

Margalit, A., and M. Bar-Hillel. "Expecting the Unexpected." *Philosophia* 13 (1983): 263-289.

Sharvey, Richard. "The Bottle Imp." *Philosophia* 12 (1983): 401.

Sorensen, Roy A. "The Bottle Imp and the Prediction Paradox." *Philosophia* 15 (1986): 424-424.

— —. "The Bottle Imp and the Prediction Paradox, II" *Philosophia* 17 (1987): 351-354.

Traiger, Saul. "The Problem of the Bottle Imp." *Philosophia* 15 (1986): 425-426.

Wreen, Michael J. "Passing the Bottle." *Philosophia* 15 (1986): 427-444.

BRADLEY'S PARADOX OF RELATIONS. Adduced by F. H. Bradley, this paradox produces an infinite regress of relations in a manner reminiscent of LEWIS CARROLL'S PARADOX OF ENTAILMENT, which is indeed a special case of the present paradox.

Formulation. Suppose that **A** and **B** are two terms that are connected by the relation **C**. Then, there must be a relation **D** connecting **A** and **C** and a relation **E** connecting **B** and **C**. By continuing to reason in this manner, an infinite regress of relations is generated.

Explanation. If **A** and **B** are two terms that are connected, they are connected by some relation **C**. Moreover, in order to explain the connection between **A** and **B**, the relation must be different from both of them (**A** and **B**). Yet **C** can only relate **A** and **B** if there is some connection between **A** and **C** and between **B** and **C**; thus, there must be new relations **D** and **E** to explain these connections. It would seem, then, that each new relation creates a need for still other relations in order to explain the connections between itself and its *relata*. Thus, we are propelled into an infinite regress, thereby leaving the original connection between **A** and **B** unexplained.

Resolution. Bradley used this paradox in defense of his idealism by concluding that external relations are not real, but only apparent. Eric Toms, however, argues that this conclusion is not necessary since the regress can be closed off by reflexive relations. A reflexive relation in this sense is not a reflexive relation in the usual ascription of the term (every object in the domain is related to itself by the relation). Rather a reflexive relation not only connects its *relata* to each other but also connects each of the *relata* to itself, obviating the need for a new relation to make the connection. Toms suggests that in the absence of a reflexive relation, the universe would be incomplete.

READINGS
Bradley, F. H. *Appearance and Reality.* Oxford: Clarendon, 1897. Ch. 2.
Toms, Eric. *Being, Negation and Logic.* Oxford: Blackwell, 1962. 54-55.

BRIDGE PARADOXES. A bridge paradox is one adduced as an intermediate between two other paradoxes in order to display their kinship. Roy A. Sorensen, for example, argues that Sharvey's BOTTLE IMP is a variation of the PREDICTION PARADOX by way of two "bridge paradoxes," the Last Buyer and the Designated Student.

BUDDHIST PARADOXES. Buddhism is a religion notable for its intellectual sophistication, and the role of paradoxes in the Buddhist tradition reflects this circumstance. Perhaps the most important use of paradoxes in both Buddhism and Taoism is to reveal the inherent inability of language to express ultimate reality. As such, the paradoxes are not there to be solved, but to be used as stepping stones to a better appreciation of the nature of knowledge and of reality. Once this better appreciation is attained, the paradoxes are no longer needed and may be discarded. The following example is from the Chinese Taoist Chuang Tzu (see Edward T. Ch'ien):

> The fish trap exists because of the fish; once you've gotten the fish, you can forget the trap. The rabbit snare exists because of the rabbit; once you've gotten the rabbit, you can forget the snare. Words exist because of meaning; once you've gotten the meaning, you can forget the words. When can I find a man who has forgotten words so I can have a word with him.

A slightly more technical example is that attributed to Bhartrkari, a fifth-century grammarian (see Hans G. and Radhika Herzberger):

> Consider the proposition "There are some things which are unnameable." Any attempt to verify this proposition by exemplification would be naming the unnameable.

Mark Siderits and J. Dervin O'Brien, for example, as well as I. W. Mabbett, have addressed the question of the kinship of Nagarjuna and ZENO'S PARADOXES, while Tyson Anderson compares Nagarjuna to Wittgenstein. Noteworthy, by the way, is how few paradoxes are actually discussed in this literature; the main topic seems to be paradox itself rather than paradoxes considered individually, but see the PARADOX OF NIRVANA.

READINGS

Anderson, Tyson. "Wittgenstein and Nagarjuna's Paradox." *Philosophy East and West* 35 (1985): 157-170.

Chung-Ying Chang. "On Zen (Ch'an) Language and Zen Paradoxes." *Journal of Chinese Philosophy* 1 (1973): 77-102.

Ch'ien, Edward T. "The Conception of Language and the Use of Paradox in Buddhism and Taoism." *Journal of Chinese Philosophy* 11 (1984): 375-399.

Herman, Arthur L. "Hedonism and Nirvana: Paradoxes, Dilemmas and Solutions." *Philosophica* [India] 10 (Ja-D 1981): 1-10.

Herzberger, Hans G. and Radhika Herzberger. "Bhartrhari's Paradox." *Journal of Indian Philosophy* 9 (1981): 1-17.

King-Farlow, John. "Anglo-Saxon Questions for Chung-ying Cheng." *Journal of Chinese Philosophy* 10 (1983): 285-298.
Mabbett, I. W. "Nagarjuna and Zeno on Motion." *Philosophy East and West* 34 (1984): 401-420.
Nishitani, Keiji. *Religion and Nothingness*. Berkeley: U of California P, 1982.
Sellman, James. "A Pointing Finger Kills 'The Buddha': A Response to Chung-Ying Cheng and John King-Farlow." *Journal of Chinese Philosophy* 12 (1985): 223-228.
Siderits, Mark, and J. Dervin O'Brien. "Zeno and Nagarjuna on Motion." *Philosophy East and West* 26 (1976): 281-299.
Slater, Robert. *Paradox and Nirvana*. Chicago: U of Chicago P, 1951.
Suzuki, D. T. "Reason and Intuition in Buddhist Philosophy." *Essays in East-West Philosophy*. Ed. Charles A. Moore. Honolulu: U of Hawaii P, 1951. 17-48.
— —. "Basic Thoughts Underlying Eastern Ethical and Cultural Practice." *Philosophy and Culture: East and West*. Ed. Charles A. Moore. Honolulu: U of Hawaii P, 1968. 428-447.
Tucker, John. "An Anglo-Saxon Response to John King-Farlow's Questions on Zen Language and Zen Paradoxes." *Journal of Chinese Philosophy* 12 (1985): 217-221.

BURALI-FORTI PARADOX, THE. A logical paradox arising in naive set theory, the Burali-Forti paradox was at one time mistakenly attributed to Georg Cantor (Moore and Garciadiego; Menzel,1984). CANTOR'S PARADOX is its analogue for cardinal numbers.
Formulation. The set of all ordinal numbers is well ordered and thus defines an ordinal number q. But since q is an ordinal number, q is an element of the set of all ordinal numbers and, therefore, q<q.
Explanation. For purposes of illustration, we may ignore the concept of well-ordering and consider an ordinal number to be an initial segment of the number sequence. Hence,

$$1 = \{0\}$$
$$2 = \{0,1\}$$
$$3 = \{0, 1, 2\}$$
$$\cdot$$
$$\cdot$$
$$k = \{0, 1, 2, \ldots, k-1\}$$
$$\cdot$$
$$\cdot$$
$$w = \{0, 1, 2, \ldots\}$$
$$w+1 = \{0, 1, 2, \ldots, w\}$$
$$\cdot$$
$$\cdot$$

As we can see from the examples listed above, every element of a set that defines an ordinal is less than the ordinal so defined. This is evident in the case of the so-called successor ordinals (for example, 3), since each new ordinal is the next number in the initial segment and thus is one more than the largest element of the set. But it is also true of the so-called limit ordinals; w, for example, is by definition greater than all the nonnegative integers. Thus,

(*)   if **a** and **b** are ordinals such that **a** is an element of the set **b**, then **a** is less than **b**.

Consider, then, **q** the entire sequence of ordinals. This will itself be an ordinal and, hence, by (*) **q** will be less than itself, which is a contradiction. **Resolution.** The Burali-Forti paradox is most commonly addressed by placing restrictions on the formation of sets so as to block the construction of the set of all ordinal numbers. In set theoretic terms, the collection of all ordinals is not a set, but a proper class; thus the purported ordinal q is not defined and the paradox does not arise. This resolution is closely related to that for RUSSELL'S PARADOX, though, as Suppes points out, it is important to realize that the devices for avoiding Russell's Paradox do not automatically work for the Burali-Forti.

READINGS

Dumitriu, Anton. "The Logico-Mathematical Paradoxes." *History of Logic.* Vol. 4. Tunbridge Wells, Eng.: Abacus, 1977.

Grattan-Guiness, I. *Dear Russell — Dear Jourdain.* New York, 1977. 24-51.

Hallett, Michael. *Cantorian Set Theory and Limitation of Size.* Oxford: Oxford UP, 1984. 176-185.

Hazen, A. "Logical Objects and the Paradox of Burali-Forti." *Erkenntnis* 24 (1986): 283-291.

Jourdain, P. E. B. "On the Question of the Existence of Transfinite Numbers." *Proceedings of the London Mathematical Society* 2, IV (1906-07): 266-283.

Menzel, Christopher. "Cantor and the Burali-Forti Paradox." *Monist* 67 (1984): 91-107.

— —. "On the Iterative Explanation of the Paradoxes." *Philosophical Studies* 49 (1986): 37-61.

Moore, G. H., and A. Garciadiego. "Burali-Forti's Paradox: A Reappraisal of Its Origins." *Historica Mathematica* 8 (1981): 319-350.

Suppes, Patrick. *Axiomatic Set Theory.* 2nd ed. New York: Dover, 1972. 8-9.

BURIDAN'S ASS. The medieval logician John Buridan is commonly credited with this paradox.

Formulation. An ass midway between two identical bales of hay will starve to death, because, having no reason to go toward one anymore than the other, and being incapable of going to both at the same time, he will remain where he is.

Explanation. In the event, the ass has no motivation to choose between the two courses of action that are equally attractive to him, so the result will be for him to chose neither and die.

Resolution. The idea that something is so evenly suspended between two alternatives that it finds itself incapable of coming down on either side has had various applications in the history of thought, especially for the question of how psychological agents choose between conflicting courses of action. The deadlock between the two equally attractive alternatives can be broken by making an arbitrary choice or by relying on an arbitrary decision procedure such as the toss of a coin.

READING

Makin, Stephen. "Buridan's Ass." *Ratio* 28 (1986): 132-148.

BYSTANDER PARADOX, THE. As suggested to Paul Woodruff by Bernard Katz, a theory of self-defence containing the following two principles falls prey to an existential paradox: first, if one is under attack and cannot save one's life from that attack without killing one's attacker, one is justified in killing one's attacker; second, one is not under any circumstances justified in killing an innocent person.

Formulation. "The paradox arises when, during a homicidal attack, an unarmed bystander occupies a position where he will be killed if the person attacked defends himself . . . Bystander hopes that Defender will consider him innocent under the theory of self-defence and prefer abandoning his defence to killing an innocent person. Defender knows all this, and tries to apply the theory of self defence to the case. Observing that Bystander's deliberate presence as an innocent blocks the defence, he concludes that Bystander is a direct supporter of the attack and may be justifiably killed as an attacker. Since Defender is not daunted by the prospect of killing an extra attacker, however, he no longer finds his defence obstructed by the presence of Bystander. So if he finds Bystander to be an attacker, then he must reconsider that finding; for by reaching his decision he has changed the relevant evidence in such a way that he ought to find Bystander innocent. But in doing so, he would alter the evidence once more, since he balks at killing an innocent" (Woodruff, 74-75).

Explanation. The problem is that on this theory of self-defence, the Bystander is an attacker only if he is judged to be an innocent, for it is only as an innocent that he can aid the attack by thwarting the defensive response. Similarly, the Bystander is an innocent only if he is judged to be an attacker, for then his presence is immaterial to both the attack and the defensive response. The argument does not issue in a formal contradiction, but it is paradoxical in that it places the Defender in an impossible situation. **Resolution.** Deeming it impossible to circumvent the paradox by qualifying the theory's account of 'attacker' and 'innocent', Woodruff suggests that the theorist either create a third category "for awkward victims like Bystander and declare that killing them is partially justified" (76-77) or else develop a theory of excuses that would exonerate Defender from the blame of killing Bystander. Dave Lovelace, however, argues that the paradox is falsidical in the first place, on the grounds that the Bystander who intends his presence to protect the Attacker is guilty, independently of how the Defender classifies him, because of his intention to further the attack.

READINGS

Lovelace, Dave. "A Note on the 'Bystander Paradox'." *Analysis* 38.4 (1978): 199-200.
Woodruff, Paul. "The Bystander Paradox." *Analysis* 37.2 (1977): 74-78.

CANTOR'S PARADOX. A logical paradox about cardinal numbers in set-theory discovered by Georg Cantor in 1899, its analogue for the ordinal numbers is the BURALI-FORTI PARADOX.
Formulation. For any set S, let |S| be the cardinal number of S and P(S) be the power set of S. Consider the set of all sets, U. By Cantor's Theorem, $|U| < |P(U)|$. But, P(U) is an element of U. Therefore, $|P(U)| \leq |U|$, contradicting the previous result.
Explanation. The cardinal number of a set S is the set of all sets which are the same size as S (two sets are the same size if their members can be put in one-to-one correspondence). The power set of S is the set of all subsets of S. Cantor proved that the cardinal number of a set is strictly less than the cardinal number of its power set. Now consider the set of all sets, call it U. Clearly the power set of U is a proper subset of U, so that its cardinal number is less than or equal to the cardinal number of U. Yet this finding contradicts the result that the cardinal number of any set is strictly less than the cardinal number of its power set.
Resolution. As with various other logical paradoxes, analysis of Cantor's Paradox leads to the conclusion that there is something wrong with the notion of the universal set, or the set of all sets. Various attempts have been made to formulate set theory in such a way that the logical paradoxes might be avoided; see RUSSELL'S PARADOX for further discussion.

READINGS

Mendelson, Elliott. *Introduction to Mathematical Logic.* New York: Van Nostrand Reinhold, 1979.

Suppes, Patrick. *Axiomatic Set Theory.* 2nd ed. New York: Dover, 1972.

CATCH-22. This colloquial name for one main kind of existential dilemma, namely the "damned-if-one-does-and-damned-if-one-doesn't" kind, comes from Joseph Heller's classic war novel, *Catch-22.* The dilemma does not actually issue in a contradiction. Rather, Orr is faced with the disagreeable prospect of continuing to fly more missions regardless of his mental well-being. Thus, the poignancy of the dilemma is not so much a matter of logical consistency as of the sense of unfairness and helplessness that it engenders. The sense of frustration is increased by the circumstance that certain of the regulations seem to support Orr's desires; yet other regulations make the first ones inoperable. Hence, the whole set of regulations on the relevant question is quite pointless.

READING

Heller, Joseph. *Catch-22.* New York: Simon and Schuster, 1961.

CHAIN STORE PARADOX, THE. Proposed by Reinhard Selten in 1978, the Chain Store Paradox concerns rational decision theory and is closely related to the PRISONER'S DILEMMA.

Formulation. The game has twenty-one players. Player A owns a chain of stores in twenty cities. At the first round of the game, Player 1 is to decide whether to open a rival store in city 1. If he chooses not to do so (OUT), the payoff to Player A for that round is five points while Player 1 gets one point. If he chooses to open a rival store (IN), then Player A must choose either a co-operative pricing strategy (CO-OP) or an aggressive one (AGG). If Player A selects CO-OP, the payoff to both players is two points; otherwise both get none. In the second round, the selection process is repeated with Player 2 in city 2, and so on until the twentieth round when the game is over. All players are completely rational and all choices are known to all players. The object for each player is to maximize his payoff. Although game theory dictates that player A always respond to IN with CO-OP, Selten reports that even mathematically trained players shun the valid game theory conclusion to opt for another strategy.

Explanation. The paradox arises from considering two different approaches to playing the game. The first of these is the game theoretical approach, which Selten calls the inductive theory. On this view, Player

20 should reason as follows: "if A is rational, then he will select CO-OP, because there are no more players after me to be deterred by an AGG strategy, and because CO-OP provides him with a higher payoff than AGG. But then my payoff for IN is 2, whereas for OUT it is only 1. Hence I select IN." A, being rational, then chooses CO-OP. Player 19 should reason as follows: "Player 20 is rational and should therefore reason as above. Hence, whatever passes between me and Player A can have no effect on Player 20's behavior. So I should choose IN, because A, being rational and knowing how Player 20 will behave, will choose CO-OP." The other players reason in a similar manner. The second approach, which Selten calls the deterrence theory, has A reasoning as follows: "While nothing can be done to influence Player 20, or perhaps Players 19 and 18, an AGG response to IN will deter others from choosing IN, resulting in a higher payoff when OUT is chosen." Selten maintains that though it cannot be decided exactly when Player A should stop choosing AGG, the deterrence theory is more intuitively appealing than the induction theory. The paradox is that rational players refuse to accept the valid conclusions of the inductive theory and opt for the deterrence theory as a guide to their practical behavior.

Resolution. Lawrence Davies argues that there is no paradox because the game theoretical approach depends upon certain unjustified assumptions — in particular, on a belief by Player A at round n that Player $n+1$ cannot be deterred by his choice at n. Davis points out that this belief presupposes a hierarchy of beliefs about beliefs about the rationality of other players, beliefs that may not be reliable. Given the information available to all players, it may indeed be rational for Player A to choose AGG. Walter Trockel also suggests that AGG is rational given the limits to the information possessed by the players. Selten himself believes that the paradox forces us to posit that there are different levels of rationality in human decision making. Since the game theoretical approach is no longer the uniquely rational one, decisions not made in accordance with it do not have the paradoxical character originally suggested by the game store paradox.

READINGS

Davies, Lawrence. "No Chain Store Paradox." *Theory and Decision* 18 (1985): 139-144.

Selten, Reinhard. "The Chain Store Paradox." *Theory and Decision* 9 (1978): 127-159.

Trockel, Walter. "The Chain Store Paradox Revisited." *Theory and Decision* 21 (1986): 163-179.

CHANGE, THE ANTIMONY OF. This puzzle, discussed in Antiquity by both Plato and Aristotle, challenges our conception of change. **Formulation.** Consider an object that is unchanging (in some respect) for a period of time and then undergoes a change (in that respect). At the precise instant that the change starts, is the object unchanging or changing? **Explanation.** The formulation given above is stated in general terms because, as Aristotle pointed out, the paradox applies to all forms of change. Nevertheless, it is probably most easily discussed in terms of motion. Thus consider an object that is originally at rest and at some instant begins to move. At that instant, is the object (still) at rest or (already) in motion? Neither alternative seems satisfactory. Nevertheless, as Joseph Wayne Smith observes,

> The real difficulty in our question is as follows. At the point of change it seems that the object is neither in motion or at rest. But if for all objects at all times, they are either at rest or in motion, a contradiction follows (101).

Resolution. One response to the paradox would be to agree with Parmenides that the very concept of change is contradictory and, thus, does not occur. Another response concedes the contradiction, but refuses to denigrate sense knowledge by denying change. In this view, however, our theoretical description of change is necessarily convoluted. Still another response, pioneered by Aristotle (*Physics*, VIII 8), is based on "cuts" in the continuum. Thus, the point of change can be seen in various ways as both (in the case of motion) the last point of rest and the first point of motion, or as the first point of motion whose antecedent period of rest has no last point. Smith argues that none of these solutions are satisfactory and that the only way out of the paradox is to recognize that "nature is arbitrary" (105). That is, in each particular case, one or other state is realized by chance, as it were. Smith claims further that this result is an incipient indication of free will in man.

Aristotle (*Physics*, VI 3 and 8), following Plato (*Parmenides* 156C-157A), however, gives another solution: at the point of change, the object is neither at rest nor in motion. To avoid the paradox, this view necessitates the denial of Smith's premise that "for all objects at all times, they are either at rest or in motion" (101). This denial is indeed intuitively satisfying because change is a process; that is, it is something that can only happen over time. "Instantaneous change" would seem, therefore, to involve a category mistake. We also need observe, however, that this discussion does not invalidate such mathematical concepts as "instantaneous velocity," which are technical concepts (involving limits) used to model physical situations.

READINGS

Kretzman, Norman. "Aristotle on the Instant of Change." *Aristotelian Society Supplement* 50 (1976): 91-114.

Smith, Joseph Wayne. *Reason, Science and Paradox: Against Received Opinion in Science and Philosophy*. London: Croom Helm, 1986. Ch.5.

Sorabji, Richard. "Aristotle on the Instant of Change." *Aristotelian Society Supplement* 50 (1976): 69-89.

CHISHOLM'S PARADOX. See the SLIPPERY SLOPE PARADOX.

CLARK'S PARADOX. Introduced by Romane Clark in 1978, this is an alleged problem for Hector-Neri Castañeda's Guise-Constantiation Theory. Since description of the paradox requires substantial background in Castañeda's theory of predication, we only note its existence here.

READINGS

Clark, Romane. "Not Every Object of Thought Has Being: A Paradox in Naive Predication Theory." *Nous* 12 (1978): 181-188.

Landini, Gregory. "Salvaging 'The F-er is F': The Lessons of Clark's Paradox." *Philosophical Studies* 48 (1985): 129-136.

CLOCK PARADOX, THE. The Clock Paradox is simply Albert Einstein's prediction that clocks and other temporal processes run more slowly from the standpoint of an observer moving relatively to them than do similar clocks and processes in the observer's own frame of reference. Such a prediction does not violate the principle of causality or the laws of logic. Einstein's prediction has received some empirical affirmation by experiments of J. C. Hafele and R. E. Keating, who measured small differences, consistent with the predictions of relativity theory, between the times indicated by clocks that had been flown around the world and those indicated by clocks that had stayed in the laboratory. Nevertheless, these experiments are not entirely convincing because they involve considerations of gravitational fields and thus transfer the paradox from its natural setting in the special theory to the general theory of relativity. The Clock Paradox is especially controversial in the narratively sharpened version called the TWIN PARADOX. Also see PARADOXES OF TIME TRAVEL.

COGNITION, THE PARADOX OF. Although this paradox is easily stated, full discussion would require an extensive background in connectionism. Hence, we will only state the paradox here and observe that the connectionist's response to the dilemma involved will strongly color his version of connectionism. As given by Smolensky the paradox is as follows: "In attempting to characterize the laws of cognition, we are pulled in two different directions: when we focus on the rules governing high-level cognitive competence, we are pulled towards structured, symbolic representations and processes; when we focus on the variance and complex detail of real intelligent performance, we are pulled towards statistical, numerical descriptions" (138).

READINGS

Fodor, J. A., and Z. W. Pylyshyn. "Connectionism and Cognitive Architecture: A Critical Analysis." *Cognition* 28 (1988): 2-71.

Gerken, L., and T. G. Bever. "Linguistic Intuitions are the Result of Interactions between Perceptual Processes and Linguistic Universals." *Cognitive Science* 10 (1986): 457-476.

Smolensky, Paul. "The Constituent Structure of Connectionist Mental States: A Reply to Fodor and Pylyshyn." *Southern Journal of Philosophy* 26 Sup. (1987): 137-161.

COGNITIVE RELATIVISM, PARADOXES OF. Jack W. Meiland identifies a number of attacks on a view he calls cognitive relativism, all of which reduce to the following basic dilemma. It is similar to a paradox identified by C. R. Kordig.

Formulation. Either relativism (subjectivism) applies to itself in which case it is only relatively (or subjectively) true, or it does not apply to itself, in which case it admits that some views are absolutely (or objectively) true.

Explanation. Either horn of the dilemma would seem to be distasteful to the relativist. On the one hand, if relativism is only relatively true, the relativist's position seems to be greatly undermined. But, on the other hand, if relativism is absolutely true, that in itself would seem to be a proof of the falsity of relativism.

Resolution. Meiland thinks that the cognitive relativist can grasp either horn of the dilemma without self-contradiction. The relativist can accept the relative character of relativism's own truth, or he can insist on its absolute character by distinguishing theses of its own kind (say, metaphilosophical theses), which are absolutely true, from the kind of theses it is about (say, philosophical theses), which are relatively true.

Nevertheless, the second horn of this dilemma makes relativism much less interesting, because it limits the scope of its validity and requires an account of how the special class of absolutely true doctrines escapes the considerations that leads to cognitive relativism in the first place. Still, many relativists hold that their view is neither self-contradictory nor self-defeating. A relevant metaphor, dating to Sextus Empiricus, is that of climbing a ladder to reach a point at which it might be kicked away. In other words relativists often claim that their arguments provide a means to an end that, once attained, allows disposal of the means. The proposed metaphor, however, is not very enlightening because accepting the apparent contradiction in relativism involves accepting just what the relativist is convinced is false.

READINGS

Galle, Peter. "Kordig's Paradox Objection to Radical Meaning Variance Theories." *Philosophy of Science* 50 (1983): 494-7.

Meiland, Jack W. "On the Paradox of Cognitive Relativism." *Metaphilosophy* 11 (1980): 115-126.

CONDORCET'S PARADOX. A paradox of voting adduced by the Marquis de Condorcet in 1785. It is a precursor of the recent PARADOXES OF VOTING.

Formulation. Suppose three voters, V_1, V_2, V_3, rank choices among three alternatives, A, B, C, as follows: V_1={A, B, C}; V_2={C, A, B}; V_3={B, C, A}. Then A is preferred to B by a two-to-one majority, B is preferred to C by a two-to-one majority, and C is preferred to A by a two-to-one majority. Therefore, no simple pairwise comparison can determine a preference among the three alternatives.

Explanation. William V. Gehrlein terms the described result a "no-winner" situation. The "no-winner" result depends on the existence of a "cyclical majority." Clearly, V_1, V_2, and V_3 may be equinumerous groups of voters instead of merely three individuals.

Resolution. Insofar as Condorcet's paradox shows a limitation of a particular voting mechanism, it is potentially worrisome for architects of democratic systems. The practical worry engendered by the possibility of cyclical majorities should be directly correlated to the likelihood of such an occurrence. Reviewing attempts to estimate the probability of cyclical majorities, Gehrlein finds that the probability of a cyclical majority increases as the number of choices increases, but decreases as the number of voters increases. He ultimately comes out with an estimate of from between one to twelve per cent probability for a "no-winner" situation.

Perhaps this probability is low enough for technicians of democracy to ignore, but see ARROW'S PARADOX OF SOCIAL CHOICE for a formal statement of the principles at stake when acquiescing in this situation.

READINGS

Condorcet, Marquis de. *Essai sur l'Appication de l'Analyse a la Probailité des Decisions Rendues a la Pluralité des Voix.* New York: Chelsea, 1973.

Gehrlein, William V. "Condorcet's Paradox." *Theory and Decision* 15 (1983): 161-197.

CONFIRMATION, PARADOXES OF. See HEMPEL'S PARADOXES OF CONFIRMATION, HUME'S PROBLEM OF INDUCTION, and GOODMAN'S PARADOXES OF CONFIRMATION.

CONFLICT-OF-DUTY PARADOX. See PARADOXES OF DEOTIC LOGIC, especially PLATO'S PARADOX and SARTRE'S PARADOX.

CONTINGENT LIAR CYCLES. Saul Kripke uses these problems to argue against Tarski's hierarchical semantics.

Formulation. Consider the following pair of statements:

(1) Most of Nixon's assertions about Watergate are false.
(2) Everything Jones says about Watergate is true.

The joint affirmation of (1) and (2) is paradoxical or not depending on the circumstances in which they are uttered. Tarski's semantics, therefore, is too radical.

Explanation. In most circumstances, the joint affirmation of (1) and (2) would be unexceptional. If, however, (1) was the only assertion about Watergate that Jones made and if Nixon made assertion (2) as well as an additional number of assertions about Watergate, half of which were true and half false, a paradox does arise. If (2) is true, then Jones's single statement about Watergate is true. But that statement is (1), so (1) is true. By (1), therefore, Nixon spoke falsely about Watergate more than half the time, so his assertion (2) must be false. Therefore, if (2) is true, it must be false. Suppose, then, that (2) is false. Then Jones must have asserted some falsehood about Watergate. His only assertion about the subject, however, was (1); hence, (1) is false. Thus, Nixon could not have spoken falsely about Watergate more than half the time; consequently, (2) must be true. Combining this result with the previous one, we find that — in the circumstances considered — (2) is true if, and only if, it is false. Kripke argues further that any semantics such as Tarski's that classifies sentences as meaningful or not by some property of the sentences themselves cannot deal adequately with this type of paradox. The only way for Tarski to avoid the paradox is to claim that the joint assertion of (1) and (2) violates his hierarchical distinctions. Nevertheless, the joint assertion of (1) and (2) is only paradoxical in exceptional situations. Thus Tarski's approach involves, so to speak, too much overkill to be a satisfactory response to the paradox.

Resolution. Kripke's own approach involves building up a series of models in a recursive fashion until a fixed point is reached when the next model does not differ from its predecessor. Since the details are too technical for reproduction here, we limit ourselves to observing that Kripke's approach has been quite influential in discussions of the LIAR and related paradoxes.

READINGS

Barwise, Jon, and John Etchemendy. *The Liar, An Essay on Truth and Circularity.* Oxford: Oxford UP, 1987. 85-89.

Kripke, Saul. "Outline of a Theory of Truth." *Journal of Philosophy* 72 (1975): 690-716.

CONTRADICTION, THE. This was Bertrand Russell's name for what is now known as RUSSELL'S PARADOX.

CONTRARY-TO-DUTY IMPERATIVE PARADOX, THE. Introduced in 1963 by Roderick Chisholm, this paradox poses problems for attempts to elaborate deontic logics capable of handling contrary-to-duty imperatives. The latter are imperatives that tell us what we should do when we neglect certain duties. They are analogous to contrary-to-fact conditionals, which tell us what would be true were certain facts other than they are. Contrary-to-duty imperatives are important because we sometimes falter, thereby incurring new duties.

Formulation. Deontic logics, which are logics that contain a modal operator, O, for "ought" or "is "obligatory," usually subscribe to the following two principles:

> (I) If it ought to be that some event, a, occurs and if it is obligatory that if a occurs then b occurs, then it ought to be that b occurs.
> That is: If [O (a) and O (if a, then b)], then O (b).

(II)   It is not true to say, of any *a*, both that *a* ought to occur and that *a* ought not to occur.
That is: Not [O (*a*) and O (not *a*)].

The following four (schematic) sentences are not consistent with principles (I) and (II):

    (1)   O (*a*)
    (2)   O (if *a*, then *b*)
    (3)   If not *a*, then O (not *b*)
    (4)   Not *a*.

Explanation. The sentences (1) - (4) capture contrary-to-duty situations. In particular, if *a* is an act that we are obliged to do, but which we forgo doing, sentence (3) is a contrary-to-duty imperative telling us what new obligation has been incurred by the failure to do *a*. Consider the following example (the sentences are numbered according to the corresponding schematic sentences above):

    (1)   I ought to visit my elderly mother.
    (2)   It ought to be that: if I go visit my mother, then I tell her that I am coming.
    (3)   If I do not go then I ought not to tell my mother I am coming.
    (4)   I do not go.

According to principle (I), (1) and (2) entail that I ought to tell my mother I am coming. Yet, (3) and (4) entail that I ought not to tell her that I am coming. What should be done? Ought I, or ought I not tell my mother I am coming? Intuitively, the answer is clear that I ought not, since, as Chisholm puts it, "most of us do neglect our duties from time to time yet it is reasonable to believe that we should make the best of bad situations to which our misdeeds have led" (33). In any case, the two results — that I ought to and that I ought not to tell my mother that I'm coming — are incompatible with principle (II). Thus, our intuition is at odds with the results of formal systems of deontic logic. For evaluations of specific formal systems in terms of this paradox, see Tomberlin and Decew.

Resolution. The paradox does not arise in von Wright's original version of deontic logic because it does not countenance sentences of the form "If *a*, then O(*b*)." But such logics, as Chisholm points out, are inadequate in that they cannot deal with contrary-to-duty imperatives. In logics that are rich enough to deal with such imperatives, there is at present no accepted resolution to the Contrary-to-Duty Imperative Paradox. The two principles (I) and (II) have not, however, gone unquestioned.

Chisholm observed that the sentence O(if *a*, then *b*) occasions paradoxical results parallel to the PARADOXES OF MATERIAL IMPLICATION. Also, it has been argued against principle (II) — by van Fraassen, for example — that it is not unreasonable to have conflicting obligations. Nevertheless, this approach is not entirely satisfactory if one accepts the notion of an all-things-considered duty that overrides conflicting obligations.

READINGS

Chisholm, Roderick M. "Contrary-to-Duty Imperatives and Deontic Logic." *Analysis* 24 (1963): 33-36.

Decew, Judith Wagner. "Conditional Obligation and Counterfactuals." *Journal of Philosophical Logic* 10 (1981): 55-72.

Mott, Peter. "On Chisholm's Paradox." *Journal of Philosophical Logic* 2 (1973): 197-211.

Tomberlin, James E. "Contrary-to-Duty Imperatives and Conditional Obligation." *Nous* 15 (1981): 357-376.

Von Fraassen, Bas. "Values and the Heart's Commands." *Journal of Philosophy* 70(1973): 5-19.

COPERNICUS' PARADOX. Perhaps the most notorious scientific paradox of the last millennium is that of Nicolaus Copernicus (1473-1543) to the effect that the earth revolves around the sun and not *vice versa*. Although we no longer refer to the heliocentric theory as paradoxical because it is nearly universally accepted as true in scientifically tutored nations, there still appears to be something paradoxical about the earth revolving around the sun because not only do we speak of the sun rising and setting but it actually appears to rise and set from our terrestrial vantage.

READING

Boorstin, Daniel J. *The Discoverers.* New York: Random,1983. Ch. 38.

CROCODILE'S DILEMMA, THE. This ancient puzzle is closely related to the LIAR. A crocodile steals a child and upon the mother's entreaties allows: "I will return your child if you guess correctly whether or not I will return your child". The mother replies: "You will not return my child." What should the crocodile do? If it returns the child, the mother has guessed incorrectly, so the child should not be returned. (The condition is understood to be both necessary and sufficient.) But if the crocodile does not return the child, it is bound to return it because the mother has guessed correctly. Perhaps Plutarch's report that the Egyptians worship God symbolically in the crocodile, for it is the only animal without a tongue, like Divine Reason, which does not need of speech (Isis and Osir*is* 381 B) bears on the significance of this dilemma.

READING

Suppes, Patrick. *Axiomatic Set Theory.* 2nd ed. New York: Dover, 1972. Ch. 9.

Plutarch's De Iside et Osiride. Ed. J. Gwyn Griffiths. Cambridge: U of Wales P, 1970.

CURRY PARADOX, THE. This paradox raises difficulties for the so-called axiom of abstraction (also called the comprehension principle) incorporated into early, naive versions of set theory.

Formulation. Any proposition, *p*, can be deduced from the axiom of abstraction. In particular, *p* may be a contradiction; thus, set theory containing an unrestricted axiom of abstraction is inconsistent.

Explanation. The axiom of abstraction holds that for any concept there is a set of things falling under that concept. In terms of set membership, an object belongs to the set determined by a given concept (property) if, and only if, the object falls under the concept (has the property). An object belongs to the set of artichokes, for example, if, and only if, it is an artichoke. Consider, then, the following complex concept (about sets):

(*) *p* is true whenever *x* e *x*.

By the axiom of abstraction, there is some set, C, that is determined by the concept (*):

(1) C is the set of sets *x* such that *p* is true whenever *x* e *x*.

Clearly, if C e C, then C falls under the concept (*); hence,

(2) *p* is true whenever C e C.

[Note that in the formal proof of (2), the antecedent is conditionalized so that (2) only depends on definition (*) and the axiom of abstraction.] Yet since C falls under the concept (*), C must belong to the set determined by the concept (*) — which, according to (1), is the set C itself. Thus,

(3) C e C.

But (2) and (3), by mo*dus ponens*, entail

(4) *p*.

Thus, since *p* is any proposition whatever, set theory with the axiom of abstraction is inconsistent.

Resolution. The artichoke example above shows the very great intuitive plausibility of the axiom of abstraction. Hence, there has been some reluctance to give it up. Nevertheless, the most successful attempts to resolve this paradox focus on ways to abandon or to restrict the abstraction principle so that the offending sets cannot be formed. Some commentators point out the self-referential element in its formulation, common to both the LIAR and RUSSELL'S PARADOX. The latter is a separate but related attack on the abstraction principle. For further discussion, see RUSSELL'S PARADOX.

READINGS

Curry, H. B., J. R. Hindley, and J. P. Seldin. *Combinatory Logic*, Vol. 2. Amsterdam: North Holland, 1972. Ch. 12.

Fitch, Frederick B. "A Method for Avoiding the Curry Paradox." *Essays in Honor of Carl G. Hempel: A Tribute on the Occasion of His Sixty-Fifth Birthday.* Ed. Nicholas Rescher. Dordrecht: Reidel, 1970. 255-265.

Goldstein, Laurence. "Epimenides and Curry." *Analysis* 46.3 (1986): 117-121.

Meyer, Robert K., Richard Routley, and J. Michael Dunn. "Curry's Paradox." *Analysis* 39.3 (1979): 124-128.

DAVIDSON'S PARADOX OF IRRATIONALITY. The paradox of irrationality is a problem described by Donald Davidson for his own theory of interpretation (or translation) and applies only to Davidson's theory or to others sharing its central features.

Formulation. "The underlying paradox of irrationality, from which no theory can entirely escape is this: if we explain [irrationality] too well, we turn it into a concealed form of rationality; while if we assign incoherence too glibly, we merely compromise our ability to diagnose irrationality by withdrawing the background of rationality needed to justify any diagnosis at all" (Davidson 303).

Explanation. Davidsonian views of interpretation require the assumption that the speakers of a language which is to be translated (the source language) are both rational and, on the whole, speakers of truth. The assumption is deemed necessary because the basic data for a translator consist in reactions of agreement and disagreement to specific utterances on the part of speakers of the source language. To establish correspondences between the truth conditions of the source language and the language into which the translation is made (the target language), such agreement and disagreement must be compared with the reactions of the speakers of the target language in the same environmental conditions.

According to this conception, too many irrational and/or false attributions will undermine the legitimacy of the proposed translation manual. Nevertheless, some allowance must be made for errors on the part of the source language speakers, and Davidson finds such errors acceptable insofar as they can be explained. Yet the consequence of this allowance is that the only kind of irrationality that is acceptable is that which can be explained and is hence rational after all.

Resolution. Davidson believes that some types of error can be allowed for within the process of translation, but that others absolutely undermine confidence in a given translation manual. Errors of logical consistency and of agreement with statements about directly observable features of the world would seriously jeopardize translation; but those arising from, say, shortcomings in perceptual systems will be explainable through empirical psychology. By distinguishing between acceptable and unacceptable error, Davidson believes that the paradox of irrationality may be largely accommodated. Nevertheless, Davidson's paradox might be avoided altogether if explanation can be distinguished from rationalization. Thus David Henderson suggests that the paradox arises because Davidson's theory only allows for explanation of the speaker's beliefs and actions "in terms of the rationality of those beliefs and actions" (365). Were, say, causal explanations allowed to support the translation manual, the paradox of irrationality might not threaten the translation project at all.

READINGS

Davidson, Donald. *Essays on Actions and Events.* Oxford: Clarendon, 1980.

Henderson, David. "A Solution to Davidson's Paradox of Irrationality." *Erkenntnis* 27 (1987): 359-69.

DEMOCRITUS' DILEMMA. This mathematical paradox was attributed to Democritus by Plutarch.

Formulation. In Heath's translation the paradox runs as follows. "If a cone were cut by a plane parallel to the base [by which is clearly meant a plane indefinitely near to the base], what must we think of the surfaces forming the sections? Are they equal or unequal? For, if they are unequal, they will make the cone irregular as having many indentations, like steps, and unevennesses; but, if they are equal, the sections will be equal, and the cone will appear to have the property of the cylinder and to be made up of equal, not unequal, circles, which is very absurd" (179-180).

Explanation. Democritus seems to think of the cone as being made up of many thin circular disks piled on top of each other. Whether he thought there were an infinite number of them is not altogether clear. In any case, if we choose two disks that are indefinitely close to each other, they must be either equal or unequal. If they are unequal, the cone would become tiered, like a wedding cake. But if they are equal, the cone would become a cylinder.

Resolution. Democritus' response to this problem is not known. Perhaps more importantly, however, Archimedes attributes to Democritus two theorems about volumes: (1) the volume of a cone is a third of that of the cylinder on the same base and of the same height and (2) the volume of a pyramid is a third of that of the corresponding prism. According to Heath, it is probable that Democritus used the idea of a solid being composed of an infinite number of plane sections in order to obtain these results, thereby anticipating Cavalieri's Principle.

READING

Heath, Thomas L. *A History of Greek Mathematics.* Oxford: Clarendon, 1921.

DEONTIC LOGIC, PARADOXES OF. Deontic logics are those that contain a modal operator for "ought" or "is obliged to," so these paradoxes concern the project of formalizing ethical thinking. See ÅQUIST'S PARADOX, CLARKE'S PARADOX, the CONFLICT-OF-DUTY PARADOX, the CONTRARY-TO-DUTY IMPERATIVE PARADOX, the EPISTEMIC OBLIGATION PARADOX, the EUALTHUS, the PARADOX OF GENTLE MURDER, the GOOD SAMARITAN PARADOX, the JEPHTA DILEMMA, the PARADOX OF THE KNOWER (IN DEONTIC LOGIC), PRIOR'S PARADOXES OF DERIVED OBLIGATION, the ROBBER'S PARADOX, ROSS'S ANTINOMY, SARTRE'S PARADOX, and the VICTIM'S PARADOX.

READINGS

Åquist, Lennart. *Introduction to Deontic Logic and the Theory of Normative Systems.* Naples: Bibliopolis, 1987.

Al-Hibri, Azizah. *Deontic Logic: A Comprehensive Appraisal and a New Proposal.* Washington: UP of America, 1978.

Castañeda, Hector-Neri. "Aspectual Action and Davidson's Theory of Events." In *Actions and Events.* Ed. Ernest LePore and Brian P. McLaughlin. Oxford: Blackwell, 1985. 294-310.

— —. "Tomberlin, Frege, and Guise Theory: A Note on the Methodology of Dia-Philosophical Comparisons." *Synthese* 61 (1984): 135-148.

Hilpinen, Risto, ed. *Deontic Logic: Introductory and Systematic Readings.* Dordrecht: Reidel, 1971.

DETERRENCE, THE PARADOX OF. This is an old quandary of nuclear deterrence strategy, expressed by David Gauthier as a paradox of game theory, in which all actors are assumed to be fully rational. **Formulation.** In order to dissuade the enemy from launching a nuclear first strike, it is best for the agent to adopt the policy of responding to a first strike with a retaliatory nuclear strike. Nevertheless, if the enemy does launch the nuclear first strike, the disastrous consequences of a retaliatory strike make it better for the agent not to retaliate. Yet, if it is better not to retaliate, the enemy may presuppose that the agent will follow the rational course and not retaliate, which makes it more rational for the enemy to initiate a nuclear first strike. **Explanation.** As long as no enemy attack has occurred, the policy of launching a retaliatory nuclear strike in response to a first strike is the best policy because it most reduces the enemy's reasons for launching such a strike. But once the enemy has attacked and, thus, the strategy for deterring the nuclear first strike has failed, the retaliatory policy is no longer rational. In fact, if the agent were to execute his policy of a nuclear retaliation, all that he would accomplish would be to complete the destruction of the world. Yet, if it would be irrational for the agent to execute his retaliatory policy and if the agent may be expected to act rationally, the putative threat of retaliation ceases to be a deterrent. Moreover, by symmetry of reasoning, in order to avoid being attacked himself and consequently put in a position where his own policy of retaliation would be irrational, the enemy has incentive to launch a first strike. Hence, the deterrent may actually cause an attack. **Resolution.** Gauthier resolves his own paradox by denying the premise that it is irrational for the agent to launch a retaliatory strike should the policy of nuclear deterrence fail. He argues that the costs and benefits of the retaliatory strike had already been evaluated by the agent at the time of the adoption of the retaliatory policy and, thus, need not be reconsidered after suffering the first strike. Indeed, according to Gauthier, one cannot evaluate one's activities from the perspective of the present moment, but must do so from as wide a perspective as possible. Hence, in order to insure the credibility of the deterrent, implementation of the retaliatory strike is rational. David Luban counters, however, that the rational agent cannot ignore the new state of affairs occasioned by the first strike. It is in fact counterintuitive that the agent would remain rational by performing the suboptimal act of completing the destruction of the world when he has better options available. Luban concludes that the paradox has no resolution and that either the utility of deterrence or the rationality of the agent has to be given up.

READINGS
Gauthier, David. "Deterrence, Maximization, and Rationality." *Ethics* 94
(1984): 474-495.
Luban, David. "The Paradox of Deterrence Revived." *Philosophical Studies*
50 (1986): 129-141.

DEVIL'S OFFER, THE. Proposed by Edward J. Gracely, this existential
dilemma involves a paradox of the infinite with some theological
presuppositions.

Formulation. Ms. C dies and unfortunately goes to hell, but a devil
approaches her with the opportunity to play a game of chance. If she
wins the game she can go to heaven and if she loses she must stay forever
in hell, but she can only play the game once. If she plays on the first day,
she has one half chance of winning, if she plays on the second day she has
two thirds chance of winning, on the third day three quarters chance, and
so on. The question is: When is it most rational for her to play?

Explanation. If she waits for a year before playing, her chances of winning
are .997268, but if she waits for a year and a day her chances will increase
by .000007. Although waiting this extra day increases the likelihood of
winning very little, the reward of winning is thought to be infinite. Indeed,
a finitely large extra chance of winning something infinite is worth more
than the presumably finite suffering of Ms. C's spending one more day in
hell. (More technically, the utility of waiting one more day — the extra
chance of winning times the infinite payoff — will always be infinite.)
Yet if it is always worthwhile waiting one more day, then there would be
no limit to how long she should wait and Ms. C would end up remaining
in hell forever in order to increase her chances of leaving it!.

Resolution. If hope of heaven lessens the suffering in hell, then whatever
the odds it might be foolish to play the game and risk losing that hope and
heaven too. Compared to waiting in hell forever without hope of escape,
deferring the playing of the game forever might be the wisest course. Heaven
itself may have no pleasure comparable to that of anticipating leaving hell
for heaven. Given the enormous probability of winning that is eventually
built up, however, such a solution seems like a perverse form of self-torment.
The root of the problem is that we are unable to discriminate among the
chances of winning because the infinite payoff makes each increase in our
chances infinitely desirable. Compare PASCAL'S WAGER.

READING
Gracely, Edward J. "Playing Games with Eternity: The Devil's Offer."
Analysis 48 (1988): 113.

DICHOTOMY, THE. Also called the Race Course and the Bisection Paradox, this is Zeno's first argument against motion. It was mentioned by Aristotle at *Physics* 239b11-13 and 263a4-6 as well as by Simplicius. **Formulation.** In order for a moving object to reach a distant point, it must always transverse half the remaining distance. Motion is thus impossible because it requires traversing an infinite series of distances one at a time. **Explanation.** Consider a runner heading toward the finish line on a race course. In order to finish the race, he must first reach a point midway between his present position and the finish line. The runner, once he has reached the midway point, still has half the race to complete; but he cannot do so without reaching the three-quarter point, which is halfway between the midpoint and the finish line. The process is repeated without end and, hence, there will always be a residual interval between the runner's position and the finish line, making it impossible for him to complete the race. The paradox is often formulated as a regression in the following manner: the runner must first reach the midpoint; but, in order to do so, he must first reach the quarter point; and so on without end. The conclusion would then be not that the runner cannot finish the race, but that he cannot even start. Gregory Vlastos has argued effectively that the original paradox was most likely to have been a progression, as we presented it above. Formulated as a progression, its basic affinity to the Achilles Paradox is readily seen. The argument can be summarized as follows:

(1)   Finishing any motion requires crossing an infinite sequence of successive distances.
(2)   The crossing of an infinite sequence of successive distances cannot be completed.
(3)   Therefore no motion can be finished.

Resolution. As may be expected, the responses to the paradox have been, in the main, similar to the responses to the Achilles. Aristotle, distinguishing between actual infinite and potential infinity, denied premise (1). Charles Chihara advances similar considerations. In contrast, the majority of modern interpreters deny premise (2), which they take to mean one of the following:

(a)   crossing the infinite sequence cannot be done because it would take an infinite amount of time;
(b)   crossing the infinite sequence cannot be done because the sequence has no final member.

In either case, the existence of convergent series (see the ACHILLES) is used to falsify the premise. Nevertheless, Leo Groarke argues that since

50Dictionary of Paradox

the runner must traverse the infinite sequence of distances one by one —
that is, he traverses them a finite number at a time — he is unable to get
beyond a finite number of intervals, regardless of the fact that the series is
convergent. Hence, according to Groarke, (b) has not been falsified and
the paradox remains a genuine puzzle. See ZENO'S PARADOXES.

READINGS

Aristotle. *Physics*. VI ix.
Chihara, Charles. "On the Possibility of Completing an Infinite Process."
  Philosophical Review (1965): 74-87.
Groarke, Leo. "Zeno's Dichotomy: Undermining the Modern Response."
  Auslegung 9 (1982): 67-75.
Thomson, James. "Infinity in Mathematics and Logic." *Encyclopedia of
  Philosophy*. Ed. Paul Edwards. London: Macmillan, 1967. Vol. 4, 183-
  190.
Vlastos, Gregory. "Zeno's Race Course." *Studies in Presocratic Philosophy*.
  Ed. R. E. Allen and D. I. Furley. London: Routledge, 1974. Vol. 2, 201-
  220.

DILEMMA. A lemma is something taken for granted (from Greek
lambanein, to take), and a dilemma is a "double lemma," or rather a kind
of "double-take" between two alternatives each of which issues in equally
undesirable consequences The dilemma has the following logical form:

> Either A or B.
> If A, then C.
> If B, then D.
> Therefore, C or D.

When C and D are identical, the argument is even more striking from a
psychological point of view. In Medieval philosophy, dilemmas were
called *argumentum cornutum*, because they are like bulls that will toss
one whichever horn one seizes; and we still speak of the alternatives A
and B as the "horns of a dilemma." Although modern logicians tend to
define the dilemma as any argument of the given form, regardless of the
repugnancy or not of the conclusion, the traditional conception of the
dilemma reveals its close connection with rhetoric and, like quandaries
and predicaments, requires us to choose between equally repugnant courses
of action. When one is caught in a dilemma, it is said that he is "impaled
on the horns" of the dilemma. "Escaping between the horns" destroys
the dilemma by showing that the alternatives propounded in the first
premise are not exhaustive; the third alternative, naturally, will be helpful

only in so far as it does not issue in undesirable consequences. "Taking the dilemma by the horns" is showing that at least one of the alternatives does not lead to the purported consequence; thus, it amounts to falsifying either the second or the third premise. Finally, the most rhetorically satisfying way to counter the dilemma is to "rebut" it (for an interesting example see THE EUALTHUS). This consists in constructing a new dilemma using the same alternatives, but issuing in consequences acceptable to the speaker and repugnant to his adversary (who had propounded the dilemma being rebutted). Many paradoxes are expressible as dilemmas and vice versa; in this regard. See BURIDAN'S ASS, DEMOCRITUS' DILEMMA, the PARADOX OF COGNITIVE RELATIVISM, the CROCODILE'S DILEMMA, the DEVIL'S OFFER, the JEPHTA DILEMMA, the PARADOX OF NAMING, PASCAL'S WAGER, the SANCHO PANZA, and ZENO'S DILEMMA.

READING

Eaton, Ralph M. *General Logic.* New York: Scribner, 1931. 191-200.

DOGMATISM PARADOX, THE. This epistemological paradox was first formalized by Gilbert Harman.

Formulation. "If I know that *h* is true, I know that any evidence against *h* is evidence against something that is true; so I know that such evidence is misleading. But I should disregard evidence that I know is misleading. So, once I know that *h* is true, I am in a position to disregard any future evidence that seems to tell against *h*. (Harman, 148)

Explanation. It is certainly a reasonable policy to disregard misleading evidence. Again, evidence against something that is true is bound to be misleading. Furthermore, if I know something to be true, it must be true. Hence all evidence against what I know to be true ought to be disregarded. Yet is seems overly dogmatic to ignore all evidence that runs counter to what one knows to be true.

Resolution. Both Norman Malcolm and Peter Unger support arguments of this kind, but with differing results. For whereas Malcolm thinks there are things so well known that countervailing evidence should be disregarded, Unger believes that the argument shows that claims to knowledge are intrinsically dogmatic. Since, however, dogmatism is irrational, so are claims to knowledge. Other philosophers try to resolve the paradox by establishing that there are flaws in Harman's argument. Carl Ginet, for example, uses the phenomenon of the acquisition of a piece of knowledge resulting in an overall loss of knowledge to show that in a non-deductive argument we may come to know the antecedent of a conditional and yet be unable to detach the consequent by *modus ponens*. This happens when the antecedent and the conditional are so related that not knowing the truth or falsity of the antecedent is a condition for asserting the conditional. Simplifying a bit, Ginet's claim is that the conditional

> If I know that *h* is true, I know that any evidence against
> *h* is evidence against something that is true.

can only be asserted if we do not know that *h* is true. Thus, by asserting the antecedent, we lose the conditional and, therefore, cannot progress by the familiar *modus ponens* argument. The very familiarity of the argument, however, leads us to disregard the exceptional character of the cited conditional and accept Harman's paradox. Roy A. Sorensen uses Frank Jackson's theory of the indicative conditional to argue that this type of "exceptional" conditional is in fact quite common.

READINGS

Ginet, Carl. "Knowing Less by Knowing More." *Midwest Studies in Philosophy V: Studies in Epistemology.* Ed. Peter A. French, Theodore E. Uehling, Jr., and Howard K. Wettstein. Minneapolis: U of Minnesota P,1980. 151-161.

Harman, Gilbert. *Thought* Princeton: Princeton UP, 1973.

Malcolm, Norman. "Knowledge and Belief." *Knowledge and Certainty.* Englewood Cliffs, NJ: Prentise-Hall, 1963. 67-68.

Sorell, Tom. "Harman's Paradox." *Mind* ns 90 (1981): 557-575.

Sorensen, Roy A. "Dogmatism, Junk Knowledge, and Conditionals." *Philosophical Quarterly* 38 (1988): 433-454.

Unger, Peter. *Ignorance.* Oxford: Clarendon, 1975. 105-114.

DONNE'S PARADOX OF THE HOLY GHOST. The scholarship that takes Donne's paradoxical thinking about religion as a theme is that extremely rare sort of literary study that uses paradox as a key word and actually identifies something like a paradox in it.

Formulation. In his study of paradox in Donne's thought, Jerome S. Dees cites four paradoxical formulations.

> (1)   There is no salvation but by faith, nor faith but by hearing, nor hearing but by preaching (Donne, VII 320).
> (2)   Here was a true Transubstantiation, and a new Sacrament. These few words, *Saul, Saul*, why persecutest thou me, are words of Consecration; After these words, *Saul* was no longer Saul but he was Christ. . . (VI 209).
> (3)   Knowledge cannot save us, but we cannot be saved without Knowledge (III 359).

(4) The Holy Ghost falls, through us, upon you also, so, as that you may, so, as that you must find it in yourselves (VIII 267).

Explanation. The paradox in the first statement lies in the circumstance that the preacher is necessary for salvation because the word can only be heard through preaching. Central to the reformed Protestant doctrine expostulated by Donne, however, is the idea that salvation is effected by the unmediated gift of grace given directly to the individual. Thus, according to Dees, the preacher is absolutely necessary for salvation, while being utterly useless as a causal agent in attaining that salvation. With regard to the second statement, Dees remarks: "What exercises Donne's imagination, thematically and structurally, is the paradox that the accusation is itself the transubstantiation, that the language of condemnation is itself the very means and seal of acceptance and union" (81). Donne resolves the paradox in the third statement by following Augustine's postulate of natural reason and regenerate reason. Finally, the last statement, whose paradoxicality subsumes that of the first three statements, asserts that although the Holy Ghost is present in each Christian by virtue of the sacrament of baptism, it is only through the ministrations of the preacher that the Holy Ghost's presence can be recalled by the faithful.

Resolution. From the standpoint of faith, this is a veridical paradox. The preacher, as bearer or vehicle of the Spirit, does not merely provide doctrine to be understood by reason but engages in a dialogue with his parishioners by which the memory of Holy Ghost residing in them since baptism is activated.

READINGS

Dees, Jerome S. "Logic and Paradox in the Structure of Donne's Sermons." *South Central Review* 4 (1987): 78-92.

Donne, John. *The Sermons of John Donne*. 10 vols. Ed. George R. Potter and Evelyn M. Simpson. Berkeley: U of California P, 1953-1962.

DUMITRIU'S ANTIMONY OF THE THEORY OF TYPES. The Theory of Types was elaborated in order to avoid certain paradoxes, foremost among which was RUSSELL'S PARADOX. The theory was proven consistent, originally by Jacques Herbrand and later by Gerhard Gentzen. Even so, Anton Dumitriu constructed a paradox in the Theory of Types, thereby purporting to show it to be inconsistent. Subsequently, however, Dumitriu argued that his paradox was not due to an inconsistency in the Theory of Types, but rather to its incompleteness and that the paradox could be avoided by invoking some well known conditions on definitions. It is perhaps this aspect of the paradox that is most interesting since the Theory of Types itself does not seem to be among the most favored ways of avoiding the original paradoxes such as Russell's.

READINGS

Church, A. "Review on A. Dumitriu's Antinomy of the Theory of Types." *Journal of Symbolic Logic* 37 (1972): 194.

Dumitriu, A. "The Antimony of the Theory of Types." *International Logic Review* 2 (1971): 51-54.

——. "The Antimony of the Theory of Types and the Solution of Logico-Mathematical Paradoxes." *International Logic Review* 5 (1974): 83-102.

Fehér, Marta, "Is There an Antinomy in the Theory of Types?" *International Logic Review* 3 (1972): 126-128.

EDEN, THE PARADOX OF. This religious paradox concerning the fall of man was suggested by Richard R. La Croix.

Formulation. Before eating the fruit of the tree of the knowledge of good and evil, Adam and Eve either knew that obedience to God is good and disobedience is evil or they did not know. If they did not know, they cannot be blamed for disobeying God by eating of the tree of the knowledge of good and evil, and God should not have punished them by casting them out of Eden. If they knew, then they already possessed knowledge of good and evil, and there would have been no temptation for them to eat the forbidden fruit. Furthermore, God would have known they possessed knowledge of good and evil, and he should not have made not eating the fruit and gaining what they already possessed a test of their righteousness. It was in fact unjust for him to put them under such an idle prohibition. Therefore, whether or not Adam and Eve knew that obeying him was good and disobeying was bad, God acted unjustly in the episode.

Explanation. By applying legal standards to the first two chapters of Genesis, it is argued that justice is not a necessary attribute of God.

Resolution. In response to La Croix, Allen Howard Podet makes three main points. First, the interpretation assumes that the expulsion from Eden was a punishment for disobedience, but the language of the text does not allow us this presupposition. Second, it assumes that knowing that it is good to obey God and evil to disobey Him is all that there is to know about good and evil, but there is much else that a knowledge of good and evil might involve. Third, the interpretation assumes that God was testing Adam and Eve's righteousness, but He might have been testing something else, such as their obedience, or even nothing at all.

READINGS
La Croix, Richard R. "The Paradox of Eden." *International Journal for the Philosophy of Religion* 15 (1984): 171.
Podet, Allen Howard. "La Croix's Paradox: An Analysis." *International Journal for the Philosophy of Religion* 18.1 (1985): 69-72.

EINSTEIN-PODOLSKY-ROSEN PARADOX, THE. First described in paper written jointly by Albert Einstein, B. Podolsky and Nathan Rosen, this is also called the EPR paradox and the Bell-EPR paradox. This paradox of quantum mechanics, like SCHRÖDINGER'S CAT, concerns difficulties in the concept of wave functions.

Formulation. "In a complete theory there is an element corresponding to each element of reality. A sufficient condition for the reality of a physical quantity is the possibility of predicting it with certainty, without disturbing the system. In quantum mechanics in the case of two physical quantities described by non-commuting operators, the knowledge of one precludes the knowledge of the other. Then either (1) the description of reality given by the wave function in quantum mechanics is not complete or (2) the quantities cannot have simultaneous reality. Consideration of the problem of making predictions concerning a system on the basis of measurements made on another system that had previously interacted with it leads to the result that if (1) is false then (2) is also false. One is thus led to conclude that the description of reality as given by a wave function is not complete." (Abstract, Einstein, Podolsky, and Rosen).

Explanation. In quantum mechanics the fundamental mode of description for a physical system is the "wave function" which gives probabilities for certain physical parameters of the system lying within specific ranges. Certain parameters (those described by "non-communicating operators," *i.e.*, those for which the order of their application may affect the result) are not independent and, according to Heisenburg's Uncertainty Principle, cannot be jointly measured without a combined degree of certainty. For instance, the velocity and position of a particle are not independent. Increased certainty about the position of a particle comes only at the cost of decreased certainty about its velocity, and vice versa. The EPR paradox considers two systems that interact with each other for a limited period. If the wave function of each individual system before the interaction is known, the wave function of the combined system can be calculated without further measurement. Thus, after separation, measurements of one or the other of the component systems enables the wave function for the other component system to be specified. Since the two systems are no longer interacting with each other, however, the measurements made on one system cannot effect a change in the other. Therefore, the derived wave function for the unmeasured system must describe the actual state of that system. In this way, we may obtain a complete description of the systems; hence, proposition (1) in the EPR abstract is false. But, then, we have joint certainty about quantities that are described by non-communicating operators, which result is incompatible with the Uncertainty Principle; hence, proposition (2) is also false. But, since the falsity of (2) follows from the falsity of (1) and since at least one of the pair must be true, proposition (1) must be true. Thus, the quantum mechanical wave functions do not completely describe reality.

Resolution. Niels Bohr provided the first and probably most influential attempt to resolve the paradox. He argued for rejecting the possibility of predicting a physical quantity, with certainty and without disturbing its system, as a sufficient condition for its reality. Reality at the quantum level just cannot be considered independently of measurement. Bohr sees this sort of consequence of quantum theory as compelling us to revise our naive views about the relationship of theory and reality. Instrumentalist views of scientific theory deny that theoretical terms must correspond to elements of reality. All that quantum theory need do is to make good predictions. Thus, no paradox arises from the assumption of incompatible wave functions, so long as each yields appropriate predictions. C. D. Cantrell and Marlan O. Scully maintain that EPR were correct to argue that wave function description is unacceptable, but they also suggest that the argument cannot be reformulated against quantum mechanical descriptions using "reduced density matrices," a technique used to describe systems whose initial conditions are not completely specified.

READINGS

Albert, David Z. "A Quantum-Mechanical Automaton." *Philosophy of Science* 54 (1987): 557-585.

Aerts, Dirk. The Missing Element of Reality in the Description of Quantum Mechanics of the E.P.R. Paradox Situation." *Helvetia Physica* 57 (1984): 421.

Bohr, N. "Can Quantum-Mechanical Description of Physical Reality Be Considered Complete?" *Physical Review* 48 (1935): 696-702.

Cantrell, C. D., and Marlan O. Scully. "The EPR Paradox Revisited." *Wallace R. Lamb, Jr.: A Festschrift on the Occasion of His Sixty-fifth Birthday*. Physics Report Book Series 3. Amsterdam: North-Holland, 1978. 499-508.

D'Espagnat, Bernard. *In Search of Reality*. New York: Springer, 1983.

Eberhard, P. H. "The EPR Paradox: Roots and Ramifications." *Quantum Theory and Pictures of Reality: Foundationalism, Interpretations and*

New Aspects. Ed. W. Schommers. Berlin: Springer-Verlag, 1989.

Einstein, A., B. Podolsky, and N. Rosen. "Can Quantum-Mechanical Description of Physical Reality Be Considered Complete?" *Physical Review* 47 (1935): 777-780.

Forster, Malcolm R. "Counterfactual Reasoning and the Bell-EPR Paradox." *Philosophy of Science* 53: 133-144.

Halpin, John F. "EPR Resuscitated: A Reply to Wessells." *Philosophical Studies* 40 (1981): 111-114.

Jammers, M. *The Philosophy of Quantum Mechanics.* New York: Wiley, 1974.

McGrath, James. "A Formal Statement of the Einstein-Podolsky-Rosen Argument." *International Journal of Theoretical Physics* 17(1978): 557.

Schoch, Daniel. "On the Formal Connection of the Einstein-Podolsky-Rosen Argument to Quantum Mechanics and Reality." *Erkenntnis* 29 (1988): 269-278.

Selleri, Franco, ed. *Quantum Mechanics Versus Local Realism: The Einstein-Podolsky-Rosen Paradox.* New York: Plenum, 1988.

Wessells, Linda. "The 'EPR' Argument: A Post-Mortum." *Philosophical Studies* 40 (1981): 3-30.

———. "EPR Resuscitated? A Reply to Halpin." *Philosophical Studies* 47 (1985): 121-130.

EINSTEIN'S CLOCK. See the PARADOX OF THE CLOCK.

ELECTRA, THE. See EUBULIDES' PARADOXES.

ENTAILMENT, PARADOX OF. This paradox of modal logic was introduced by C. I. Lewis. It is related to LEWIS CARROLL'S PARADOX OF ENTAILMENT, involving an infinite regress of entailments.

Formulation. An impossible proposition entails anything (everything).

Explanation. Dissatisfied with the PARADOXES OF MATERIAL IMPLICATION, Lewis intended to construct a modal logic formalizing the notion of entailment, which would not be heir to the mentioned paradoxes. "Possible" is taken as a primitive term and "P entails Q" is defined as "(P and Q) is impossible." Since Lewis was concerned with logical possibility, "possible" is intended to be understood as "self-consistent" and thus it turns out that "P is possible" is equivalent to "not: P entails its own negation." But, then, the paradox, entirely analogous to that of Material Implication, follows almost immediately:

(1)	P is impossible	
(2)	P and not-P	equivalent to (1)
(3)	P	from (2)
(4)	P or Q	from (3)
(5)	not-P	from (2)
(6)	Q	from (4) and (5).

Each line of the above proof (except the first) is entailed by previous lines and, since entailment is transitive, Q, which is an arbitrary proposition, is entailed by the impossible proposition P.

Resolution. There have been many attempts to sidestep the paradox by attacking the various steps in the given proof. For a summary of some of these attempts, as well as a cogent defense of the proof, see Bennett. One should observe, however, that the paradoxicality of Lewis's result is in no way due to a contradiction. Rather it is only paradoxical in that it does not accord with our intuitions about valid argumentation. Yet since we do not usually countenance (explicitly) impossible propositions as premises, counterintuitive results should not be disconcerting, which is indeed the view that Lewis eventually adopted.

READINGS

Bennett. "Entailment." *Philosophical Review* (1969): 197-236.

Lewis, C. I. and C. H. Langford. *Symbolic Logic.* New York: Dover, 1959.

Tennant, N. "Entailment and Proofs." *Proceedings of the Aristotelian Society* 79 (1978): 167-189.

EPIMENIDES, THE. According to Henry Alford (cited by Anderson, 2), the claim that Cretans are liars is attested to by a number of ancient sources including Polybius, Diogenianus, Psellus, Suidas, Diogenes Laertius and St. Paul.

Formulation. The King James version of Holy Writ gives St. Paul's report as follows: "One of them, even a prophet of their own, said, The Cretans are always liars, evil beasts, slow bellies. This witness is true" (*Titus* 1: 12-13).

Explanation. Some exegetes suggest that St. Paul was not cognizant of the possibility of any paradox in his report. Indeed, that the denigration of the Cretans attributed to their prophet constitutes a paradox is not at all apparent. For it is perfectly possible to be a liar without always lying. Indeed, as Kant pointed out, a necessary condition for lying is that telling the truth be the common practice. This is because lying is telling a falsehood with the intent to deceive and one could hardly intend to deceive anyone if nothing ever issued from one's mouth but untruths. On this account of what it is to be a liar, the claim that Cretans are always liars is just true if all of them practice verbal deceit sufficiently often to deserve the rebuke contained in the title of liar. That, of course, could be true even if the Cretan prophet had not lied on this one occasion. To generate a paradox, one has to take the term "liar" in the very strong sense according to which a liar never tells the truth about anything. Now this claim — that all Cretans always lie about everything — can be just straightforwardly false, if, for example, one Cretan ever told the truth about something. Indeed, if this is the thesis to which the Apostle to the Gentiles means to testify, his witness is undoubtedly false, for surely at least one member of the first civilized nation in Europe told the truth at least once. To generate the paradox, it has to be assumed as known that no Cretan ever told the truth about anything up to the time that the Cretan prophet — whose name Diogenes Laertius gives as Epimenides — claimed that all Cretans always lie. Now there is clearly a paradox. For if Epimenides's statement is true, then he told the truth when he said it, and hence at least one Cretan (Epimenides himself) told the truth once, so the statement is false; and if it is false, then it is true because all Cretans, including Epimenides in his own statement, have always lied. On this construction, the Epimenides is just a version of the LIAR paradox credited to the Megarian philosopher Eubilides: suppose that a man said, "I am lying" and nothing more. And indeed, medieval philosophers treated the Epimenides as equivalent to the liar. Even contemporary philosophers use the name "the Epimenides" for eloquent variation on "the Liar." But perhaps we have moved too fast, because, as Alonzo Church pointed out, there is something paradoxical about the Epimenides even if we do not assume that all Cretans had always lied up until the time Epimenides made his famous pronouncement. For if the statement is treated as true, then it follows immediately that it is false because at least one Cretan's statement — namely, Epimenides's own — is true. In contrast, however, if we treat it as false, there is no way of showing it to be true because we are no longer assuming that all Cretans had up to that time lied. Nevertheless, to treat it as false is to suppose that at least one statement by a Cretan other than Epimenides's own exists. A. N. Prior observes, "We thus reach the peculiar conclusion that if any Cretan does assert that nothing asserted by a Cretan is true, then this cannot possibly be the only assertion made by a Cretan — there must also be, beside this false Cretan assertion, some true one. Yet how can there be a logical impossibility in supposing that some Cretan asserts that no Cretan ever says anything true, and that this is the only assertion ever made by a Cretan?" (261).

Resolution. Recent interest in the Epimenides arises from L. Jonathan Cohen's claim that it is not equivalent to the Liar, because unlike the simple Liar it threatens the formalization of indirect rather than direct discourse. Prior argues that Cohen's statement, "If the policeman testifies that anything which the prisoner deposes is false, and the prisoner disposes that something which the policeman testifies is true, then something which the policeman testifies is false, and something which the prisoner says is true," is logically true only if another statement, "If the policeman testifies that anything which the prisoner disposes is false, and the prisoner disposes that something which the policeman testifies is true, then either the policeman or the prisoner must have said something else," is also true. The reason for this is that unless the policeman or the prisoner says something further, their testimony will not count as a proposition at all. On Prior's view, if Epimenides said, "Nothing asserted by a Cretan is true," and no Cretan had ever said anything before, what he said would be neither true nor false, because he would not be saying anything at all. See also PRIOR'S FAMILY OF PARADOXES.

READINGS

Anderson, Alan Ross. "St. Paul's Epistle to Titus." *The Paradox of the Liar*. Ed. Robert L. Matin. New Haven: Yale UP, 1970. 1-11.

Church, A. Review of *The Liar*, by A. Koyré. *Journal of Symbolic Logic* 12 (1946): 131.

Cohen, L. Jonathan. "Can the Logic of Indirect Discourse Be Formalized?" *Journal of Symbolic Logic* 22 (1957): 225-232.

Goldstein, Laurence. "Epimenides and Curry." *Analysis* 46.3 (1986): 117-121.

Mackie, J. L. *Truth, Probability and Paradox: Studies in Philosophical Logic*. Oxford: Clarendon, 1973.

Prior, A. N. "Epimenides the Cretan." *Journal of Symbolic Logic* 23 (1958). 261-266.

— —"On a Family of Paradoxes." *Notre Dame Journal of Formal Logic* 2 (1961): 16-32.

— —. "A Budget of Paradoxes." *Objects of Thought*. Oxford: Oxford UP, 1971.

EPISTEMIC OBLIGATION PARADOX, THE. This paradox, adduced by Lennart Åqvist, arises in epistemic extensions of deontic logic. The paradox consists in the fact that the following two intuitively consistent propositions actually lead to a contradiction:

(1)   Smith ought not rob Jones.

(2)   Wright ought to know that Smith robs Jones.

The paradox is very similar to the GOOD SAMARITAN PARADOX and the CONTRARY-TO-DUTY IMPERATIVE PARADOX.

READINGS

Åqvist, Lennart. "Good Samaritans, Contrary-to-Duty Imperatives, and Epistemic Obligations." *Nous* 1 (1967): 361-379.

Pörn, Ingmar. "A Note on Lennart Åqvist's Epistemic Obligation Paradox." In *Philosophical Essays Dedicated to Lennart Åqvist on his Fiftieth Birthday*. Ed. Tom Pauli. Uppsala: U of Uppsala P, 1982. 296-298.

EPISTEMIC PARADOXES. Epistemic paradoxes are those having to do with knowledge, belief and other related concepts. These include the PARADOX OF COGNITION, the PARADOX OF COGNITIVE RELATIVISM, the PARADOXES OF CONFIRMATION, the DOGMATISM PARADOX, THE PARADOX OF THE KNOWER, the PARADOX OF KNOWABILITY, HUSSERL'S PARADOX OF SUBJECTIVITY, MENO'S PARADOX, MOORE'S PARADOX, the PARADOX OF NAMING, the PARADOX OF THE PREFACE, the PARADOX OF SELF-REFERENCE IN SKEPTICISM, SOCRATIC PARADOX, PRIOR'S FAMILY OF PARADOXES AND WOLGAST'S PARADOXES OF KNOWLEDGE.

EPR PARADOX, THE. See the EINSTEIN-PODOLSKY-ROSEN PARADOX.

ETHICAL PARADOXES. On the view of the Utilitarian theorist, Henry Sidgwick, moral paradox arises whenever there are opinions that run counter to common sense morality (Marcus Singer "Common Sense and Paradox in Sidgwick's Ethics," *History of Philosophy Quarterly* 3 [1986];74). Human want in the midst of plenty is a paradox of this kind: "Unemployed purchasing power means unemployed labor and unemployed labor means human want in the midst of plenty. This is the most challenging paradox of our times" (Henry Agard Wallace, *Address* 1934). In another sense, a paradox is a proposition that appears absurd but is actually VERIDICAL. Common sense has its own paradoxes in this sense, as, for example, the one according to which sometimes we must be cruel in order to be kind. In a third sense, a paradox is a contradiction that is subtle enough to be intriguing, for example: "There is that glorious Epicurean paradox uttered by my friend the Historian [John Lothrop Motley (1814-1877)], in one of his flashing moments: 'Give us the luxuries of life, and we will dispense with its necessities'" (Oliver Wendell Holmes, *The Autocrat of the Breakfast Table* Ch. 6). Insofar it sounds as facetious as Marie Antoinettes's "Let them eat cake," seeking life's luxuries in lieu of its necessities is one of these. Our treatment of moral paradox, however, restricts itself to those arising in ethical and metaethical theory. These include the BYSTANDER PARADOX, Danto's BODHISATTVA PARADOX, the PARADOXES OF DEONTIC LOGIC, the PARADOX OF EXTREME UTILITARIANISM, the PARADOX OF FUTURE INDIVIDUALS, the PARADOX OF LOYALTY, the MERE ADDITION PARADOX, the PARADOX OF NIRVANA, the PARADOX OF PROMISING, the PARADOX OF UNSUCCESSFUL INTERVENTION, AND the UTILITARIAN PARADOX.

READINGS

Cunningham, Stanley B. "The Courageous Villain: A Needless Paradox." *Modern Schoolman* 62 (1985): 97-110.

Lebacqz, Karen. *Professional Ethics: Power and Paradox.* Nashville: Abington, 1985.

EUALTHUS, THE. Also called the Protagoras, this paradox of deontic logic harkens from ancient Greece and is indeed typical of the love of disputation and logical conundrums of that society.

Formulation. "Protagoras agreed to teach Eualthus rhetoric, on condition that Euathlus would pay him a certain sum of money when he won his first court case. But after completing the course, Eualthus did not engage in any lawsuits. Growing impatient, Protagoras sued Eualthus for payment of his fee. He argued: 'If I win this case Eualthus will be bound to pay me, for the court will have so decided; if I lose it, Euathlus will still be bound to pay, by our agreement, for he will have won his first case. So whatever happens Euathlus will be bound to pay; the court should therefore find in my favor'. But Euathlus, having learnt his lesson well, replied: 'If Protagoras wins this case, I shall not be bound to pay, for I need not pay until I win a case; but if Protagoras loses, this court will itself have decided that I need not pay; the court should therefore find for me.' What should the court have done?" (Mackie 297-298).

Explanation. Protagoras confronts Eualthus with a dilemma. Eualthus will either win the present suit or lose it. But, in either case, he is bound to pay: on the one hand, by his contractual obligation, or, on the other hand, by decision of the court. Eualthus rebuts the dilemma with one of his own. Protagoras will either win the present suit or lose it. But, in either case, he cannot collect payment: on the one hand, by his contractual obligation, or, on the other hand, by decision of the court.

Resolution. Like the SANCHO PANZA, the Eualthus is an existential version of the liar paradox. Also note that the dilemmas are so set up that the court's decision will become self-referential and, thus, the court becomes a LIAR. Hence, if the court is willing to disallow the self-referential implications of the original contract — by arguing, for example, that no private citizen can impose such conditions on the court — Protagoras's case would fall apart. Should the court decide not to avail itself of this argument, there may still be a practical solution. Unlike the Sancho Panza where it is a question of hanging and there is no room for compromise, here Eualthus can be made to pay half his putative debt. Such a resolution, in which the litigants split the difference of the conundrum, however, does not resolve the logical question of whether or not Euathlus should pay.

READING

Mackie, J. L. *Truth, Probability and Paradox: Studies in Philosophical Logic.* Oxford: Clarendon, 1973. Ch. 6.

EUBULIDES'S PARADOXES. Eubulides (c. 430-360 BC) was a student of and successor to Euclides, the slightly older contemporary of Plato who founded the Megarian school of philosophy. Along with Zeno, Eubulides was one of history's paramount paradoxers. Diogenes Laertius credits him with inventing seven paradoxes (ii.108), which William and Martha Kneale reduce to four basic kinds (*The Development of Logic*, 114).

First, there is the Liar: "A man says that he is lying. Is what he says true or false?" (Cicero, *De Divinatione*, ii.11; *Academica*, ii.96). This kind of paradox (see the EPIMENIDES, INSOLUBILIA, and the LIAR) plays on the strangeness of propositions that make claims about their own falsity. It is the archetypical semantical variety of logical paradox.

Second, there is the Hooded Man, also called the Unnoticed Man and the Electra: "You say you know your own brother. But that man who came in just now with his head covered is your brother, and you did not know him" (Lucian, *Vitarum Auctio*, 22). This kind of paradox not only points out that the word "know" has more than one sense, but also suggests that just because two things are the same thing is not always reason to assume that what can be said truly about one of them can be said about the other. This suggestion is the basis of the sense reference distinction invented independently in the late nineteenth century by the German logicians Edmund Husserl and Gottlob Frege.

Third, there is the Bald Man (*sorites*), or the Heap (*falakros*): "Would you say that a man was bald if he had only one hair? Yes. Would

you say that a man was bald if he had only two hairs? Yes. Would you. .
., etc. Then where do you draw the line?" (Diogenes Laertius, vii.82;
Cicero, Acade*mica*, ii.49; Horace, *Epistulae*, ii.1.45). This kind of paradox
establishes the vagueness of everyday words. For the recent discussion
of the Bald Man, see SORITES, RECENT and TRADITIONAL.

   Fourth, there is the Horned Man: "What you have not lost you still
have. But you still have horns" (Diogenes Laertius, vii.187). This type of
paradox reveals that statements that presuppose something may be negated
either in a restricted manner that accepts the presupposition or in an
unrestricted manner that rejects the presupposition. Consid the old
question, "Do you still beat your wife?" Whoever says either s or no
accepts the presupposition that he had formerly beaten her.   ly if he
says, "No, and I never did," or "Yes, I do now, but it is a q recent
practice with me," does one deny the presupposition that he d been
wont to do so.

EXCLUDED MIDDLE, THE PARADOX OF THE. This   ported
paradox, adduced by M. A. Makinde, attempts to show that for   l logic
cannot be completely separated from reality.
Formulation. Professor Popper is either a U-boat or not a U-b   . But,
we know that he is a philosopher and not a U-boat. The formal   ician,
however, is only entitled to assert that Professor Popper is a no   l-boat
thing. Thus, Professor Popper could just as well be, say, a kang o, for
that validates Professor Popper's non-U-boatness.
Explanation. The purported paradoxical element of Makinde's a   ment
is that a kangaroo can validate the truth of the Law of Excluded   iddle
when this is applied to Professor Popper and, hence, any tal   bout
kangaroos would seem irrelevant.
Resolution. In his exposition of the paradox, Makinde asserts that "No P
is U" follows from our knowledge that Popper is a philosopher and the
convention that P stands for Popper and U stands for U-boat. Hence, he
is using P and U as class terms. He then asserts "U or not-U," which is
either meaningless if U continues to be a class term, or no longer can
simply stand for the class U-boat if it is now a propositional term. Thus,
he seems to have made a category mistake, which might account for the
confusion. In any case, the question is what would count as a verification
of "(some) Popper is a non-U-boat thing." Clearly, if we are using 'Popper'
as a class term, we must find an instance of the class Popper that is not a
U-boat. Now, with apologies to Sir Karl, should we find a kangaroo that

is a Popper (and given that no kangaroo is a U-boat!), that would indeed suffice. But note, any old kangaroo won't do — it must be a Popper! But there is nothing paradoxical, or even counterintuitive, in all this. Just as clearly, if we are using 'Popper' as a singular term to refer to a given individual, then no reference to a kangaroo will verify the proposition "Popper is a non-U-boat thing." So once again no paradox arises. Makinde is nevertheless correct in pointing out that the proposition "Popper is a non-U-boat thing" tells us virtually nothing about what Popper is. Thus, if we can find a predicate attributable to Popper and exclusive of U-boats, the proposition would be verified. Thus, once again, if we know that no kangaroos are U-boats and if we can ascertain the truth of "Popper is a kangaroo," then we have the desired verification. But the intermediate links between Popper, kangaroos, and U-boats guarantee the logical relevance of kangaroos in the argument, so again there is no paradox.

READING

Makinde, M. A. "Formal Logic and the Paradox of the Excluded Middle." *International Logic Review* 8 (1977): 40-52.

EXISTENTIAL PARADOXES. Existential paradoxes are more often called DILEMMAS, quandaries, or predicaments. They place the agent in an impossible situation by making all of his options result in unacceptable consequences or by making it impossible for him to choose among the various alternatives. See BURIDAN'S ASS, the BYSTANDER PARADOX, CATCH-22, the CROCADILE'S DILEMMA, EUATHLUS, SMULLYAN'S PARADOX, the SANCHO PANZA, and the PARADOX OF THE SEEKER; also see PARADOXES OF GAME THEORY.

EXPERIMENTER EXPECTANCY PARADOX, THE. Proposed by Morris L. Shames, this paradox deals with the experimenter expectancy effect in psychological research. The experimenter expectancy effect, first noticed by R. Rosenthal and often referred to as the Pygmalion Effect, is that the experimenter's expectancies about the outcome of an experiment can influence that outcome.

Formulation. Experimentation on the experimenter expectancy effect is itself subject to the effect and, therefore, indeterminate.

Explanation. Suppose a researcher designs an experiment to try to detect the experimenter expectancy effect. If such an effect exists, then it would be operational in this experiment. Hence, the results will be determined by the researcher's own expectations and, therefore, will be biased and not constitute scientific evidence for the existence or non-existence of the effect. On the contrary assumption that the effect does not exist, it cannot, of course, be detected by scientific methods. Hence, in either case, the effect cannot be detected. **Resolution.** Shames argues that the paradox is a matter of degree. The more pervasive and the more inexorable is the evidence for the experimenter expectancy effect, the more pernicious is the paradox. In the "limiting case," in which the paradox is completely established, "investigations into the research process itself are impossibly hampered by the serious factor of indeterminacy" (Shames, 383). In reviewing the literature on the effect, however, Shames happily found that the size of the effect is usually relatively small and that it is not generalized to a large extent (apparently a large number of results originally thought to be instances of the experimenter expectancy effect were actually due to improper data analysis). Thus, argues Shames, the limited action of the effect reduces the indeterminacy involved and extricates us from the paradox. Shames warns, however, that a serious weakening of the evidence for the effect also carries a risk, namely that we may disregard the very real consequences of the effect and trivialize the paradox. We may also observe here that the effect is sometimes said to occur even when such precautions as "double-blind studies" are taken, so that these methodological techniques cannot be used to avoid the paradox. Presumably, Shames would argue that they lessen the effect of the effect and hence, make it more detectable. D. Primeaux, however, argues that Shames's procedure rests on a category mistake since scientific data cannot resolve the paradox. Indeed, given the paradox, the very studies that Shames cites would be indeterminate and could give us no scientific evidence as to the pervasiveness or to the inexorability of the effect. Moreover, according to Primeaux, the paradox can be generalized to any experiment — not just those undertaking to study the effect itself — and reveals that "the naive presumption that the existence of these effects is scientifically demonstrable and their extent measurable" (636) is not justified.

READINGS

Primeaux, D. "On Shames' Experimenter Expectancy Paradox." *Philosophy of Science* 47 (1980): 634–637.

Shames, Morris L. "On the Metamethodological Dimension of the Expectancy Paradox." *Philosophy of Science* 46 (1979): 382-388.

EXTREME UTILITARIANISM, THE PARADOX OF. Related to Kroon's UTILITARIAN PARADOX, this paradox, introduced by Marcus G. Singer, appears to be a genuine paradox in one form of Utilitarianism. **Formulation.** According to one main version of extreme, or act, utilitarianism, the rightness or wrongness of an action is a matter of the consequences of the action. Yet since judging an action to be right or wrong is itself an action, the act of judging an action right or wrong is a matter of the consequences of judging that action right or wrong. Therefore it is right to judge some right actions to be wrong actions. **Explanation.** Central to the theoretical elegance of utilitarianism is that it reduces the question of the approbation and disapprobation of agents to the question of the rightness and wrongness of approving or disapproving of them. Yet this maneuver puts the advocates of act utilitarianism in the following predicament. If the consequences of judging that an action is right (wrong) is better than the consequences of judging that an action is wrong (right), then the act utilitarian is obliged to judge the act right (wrong) even if the consequences of the action being judged are worse (better) than one of its available alternatives. It is to be judged a right (wrong) action even though by the terms of the theory itself, it is a wrong (right) action. **Resolution.** The extreme utilitarianist would be able to avoid the paradox by claiming that judging an action to be right or wrong is not itself an action. Singer, however, counters that the consequences of doing so would be overwhelmingly high and that a more reasonable response would be to move away from extreme utilitarianism toward a more pragmatic stance, such as that of John Dewey, where the paradox does not arise.
READING
Singer, Marcus G. "The Paradox of Extreme Utilitarianism." *Pacific Philosophical Quarterly* 64 (1983): 242-248.

FALSIDICAL PARADOX. See VERIDICAL AND FALSIDICAL PARADOX.

FORTUNATE FALL, PARADOX OF THE. Named by Arthur O. Lovejoy, the paradox of the fortunate fall (*felix culpa*) has been traced by Lovejoy and Herbert Weisinger from John Milton's *Paradise Lost* back to ancient times. The paradox is that if Adam had not fallen and been expelled from Eden, there would not have been the good fortune of the redemption story with its conclusion in the coming of the New Jerusalem. In other words, without man's failure the world would not be saved. As W. B. Yeats puts it in *Leda and the Swan*, "Nothing can be sole or whole that has not been rent." Although the skeptic may scoff that had man not stumbled the world would not need salvation, from the standpoint of Judeo-Christian faith, this is one of the most fundamental and veridical paradoxes and is clearly related to man's finitude and fallibility, as well as God's infinite mercy.

READINGS

Johnson, Courtney. "John Marcher and the Paradox of the 'Unfortunate' Fall." *Studies in Short Fiction* 6 (1969): 121-135.

Kauffman, Corinne E. "Adam in Paradox." *The Arlington Quarterly* 1 (1968): 111-117.

Lovejoy, Arthur O. "Milton and the Paradox of the Fortunate Fall." *Essays in the History of Ideas.* Ed. Arthur O. Lovejoy. New York: George Braziller, 1955. 277-95.

Weisinger, Herbert. *Tragedy and the Paradox of the Fortunate Fall.* London: 1953.

FREEDOM, PARADOX OF. According to Hans Jürgen Eysenk,"the notion of a motive-less action is difficult to give any meaning to, and is probably not what most people mean when they talk about 'freedom of will,' or freedom of choice.' But if we are not talking about a complete lack of motivation, then surely the action is determined by the preponderance of motivating factors one way or the other, and there is no freedom involved" (369). Since the notion of freedom is thus paradoxical, Eysenck continues, it must be rejected for scientific determinism. It is not clear, however, that "motive" and "cause" are synonymous terms; in fact, we generally claim to be able to weigh conflicting motives and choose among them. Hence, Eysenck's claim that a motivated action is determined by the motives involved is doubtful and, unless this claim can be substantiated, the paradox fails.

READING

Eysenck, Hans Jürgen. "The Paradox of 'Freedom' and the Social Function of Psychiatry." *Metamedicine* 3 (1982): 367-374.

FUTURE INDIVIDUALS, PARADOX OF. Discovered independently by Robert M. Adams, Derek Parfit, and Thomas Schwarz, this paradox was first named by Michael D. Bayles. It seeks to show that we have no moral obligations to future individuals beyond, say, the next few generations. **Formulation**. Let us assume that in a few generations from now a certain set of individuals will exist if we adopt no controlled growth policies. Let us assume that this set of individuals will be no worse off than if they did not exist at all. Do we have an obligation to improve the quality of their lives by adopting a policy of controlled growth? It appears that we do not on the following assumptions. First, an individual is who he or she is partly because of their specific genetic endowment. Second, certain broad-scale policies, such as controlled growth policies, have the power of bringing about mass changes in future events through ripple effects. Since controlled growth policies have the effect of changing the specific conditions under which a very large number of people are conceived, the result of adopting such policies would not be to improve the lot of the future generations of individuals that were to come anyway, but rather to substitute for those generations generations filled with other individuals. **Explanation**. If obligations are always to individual people and not to people under some generic description, certain obligations toward future individuals can never be fulfilled because in trying to fulfill them we will bring about the appearance of other individuals than those to whom we were obliged. **Resolution**. The paradox is more threatening to an individualistic construction of obligation than to obligations to future generations. It would seem that the membership of a family or a nation or a species at one phase of its unfolding might have obligations to its membership at a later phase without those obligations being owed to specific individuals members. Alternatively, the obligation might be owed to each individual, but not depend on his individuality.

READINGS

Adams, Robert M. "Existence, Self-Interest, and the Problem of Evil." *Nous* 13 (1979): 53-65.

Kavka, Gregory S. "The Paradox of Future Individuals." *Philosophy & Public Affairs* 11 (1981): 93-112.

Parfit, Derek. "On Doing the Best for Our Children. *Ethics and Population*. Ed. Michael Bayles. Cambridge, MA: Schenkman, 1976. 100-115.

— —. "Future Generations: Further Problems." *Philosophy & Public Affairs* 11 (1981): 113-172.

Schwarz, Thomas. "Obligations to Posterity." *Obligations to Future Generations*. Ed. Richard Sikora and Brian Barry. Philadelphia: Temple UP, 1978. 3-13.

GAME THEORY, PARADOXES OF. Game theory is the study of games and, more specifically, the strategies involved in playing them. As elsewhere in mathematics, game theory considers formalized models which are idealizations of concrete situations. Among the simplifying assumptions usually imposed on these models is that all players are rational and are completely informed about the rules and about the other players "moves." Thus all players are expected to make optimal choices, that is they choose the move that will maximize their own positions. Game theory gives rise to many paradoxes, among which see the BACKWARD INDUCTION PARADOX, the BOTTLE IMP, the CHAIN STORE PARADOX, the PARADOX OF DETERENCE, the DEVIL'S OFFER, GIDEON'S PARADOX, the LOTTERY PARADOX, NEWCOMBE'S PARADOX, PASCAL'S WAGER, the PREDICTION PARADOX, the PRISONER'S DILEMMA, and the ST. PETERSBURG PARADOX.

READING
Owen, Guillermo. *Game Theory.* 2nd ed. New York: Academic, 1982.

GEACH'S PARADOX. A semantic paradox that apparently allows the valid derivation of any statement whatsoever. First announced by P. T. Geach as an example of negation-free INSOLUBILIA, Allen Hazen later noted it independently. We follow Hazen's presentation here.

Formulation. Let q be an arbitrary statement. Consider the sentence

(*):   If (*) is true, then q.

Since (*) asserts its own truth, (*) cannot be false. Hence q follows by *modus ponens.*

Explanation. If we interpret conditional propositions as the material implication of classical logic, the only way that the conditional can be false is for the antecedent to be true and the consequent false (see the PARADOXES OF MATERIAL IMPLICATION). But the antecedent of (*) is just (*) — alternatively (although many logicians claim that this amounts to the same thing), the antecedent of (*) asserts the truth of (*). In either case, if we assert the antecedent, we can assert the whole conditional (since the antecedent asserts the whole conditional) and, hence, we may detach the consequent q by *modus ponens.* What will happen on the hypothesis that the antecedent is false? The negation of the antecedent is that the whole conditional (*) is false; but we already know that (*) can only be false if its antecedent is true, which contradicts the hypothesis. Hence, according to classical logic, the antecedent must be true. The paradox, however, does not depend on classical logic. Hagen cites, for example, the following derivation in Intuitionist Logic, due to Raymond Smullyan:

(1)	(*) is true	premise
(2)	If (*) is true, *q*.	(2) is just (*), which we may assert from (1)
(3)	*q*	(1), (2), *modus ponens*
(4)	If (*) is true, *q*.	(1), (3), the Deduction Theorem
(5)	(*) is true.	restatement of (4)
(6)	*q*	(4), (5), *modus ponens*.

Observe that lines (2) and (3) are dependent on the premise (1) — they have been indented to reflect this — but line (4) eliminates the premise by incorporating it into a conditional. Since (5) and (6) only depend on (4), they too are independent of (1). Also observe that, since *q* is an arbitrary proposition, we apparently have a valid deductive method for establishing any conclusion whatsoever, including false or even contradictory ones. This result challenges the usefulness of deductive logic as a truth-preserving inference system.

Resolution. The Smullyan proof reveals that this paradox is similar to the CURRY PARADOX and, thus, admits of similar responses. We merely note here that Geach, following Moh Shaw-kwei, would focus on the inference allowing the discharge of assumption (*) at step (4), while Hazen favors an approach, suggested by John Myhill, using levels of implication. The self-referentiality of this paradox also makes it similar to the LIAR and to RUSSELL'S PARADOX.

READINGS

Geach, P. T. "On Insolubilia." *Analysis* 15.3 (1955): 209-211.

Hazen, Allen. "A Variation on a Paradox." *Analysis* 50.1 (1990): 7-8.

Myhill, John. "Levels of Implication." *The Logical Enterprise*. Ed. A. R. Anderson, R. B. Marcus, and R. M. Martin. New Haven: Yale UP, 1975. 179-185.

— —. "Paradoxes." *Synthese* 60 (1984). 129-143.

Shaw-kwei, Moh. "Logical Paradoxes for Many-Valued Systems." *Journal of Symbolic Logic* 19 (1954): 37-40.

GEACH'S PARADOX OF THE 1,001 CATS. Reminiscent of the SHIP OF THESEUS, this puzzle about identity was formulated by P. T. Geach.

Formulation. Suppose that there is exactly one cat sitting on a mat. The cat has at least 1,000 hairs. But for each one of these hairs, there is a cat that differs from the first cat by exactly that hair. Therefore, there are 1,001 cats sitting on the mat.

Explanation. Consider a single hair of the cat sitting on the mat. Clearly, the animal that consists of all the parts of the cat, except the designated hair, is a cat. Just as clearly, this second cat is different from the first one since we can distinguish the two by the criterion of the designated hair (one has that hair, while the other does not). Hence, there are two different cats sitting on the mat. This is already paradoxical for there cannot be only one cat sitting on the mat and two cats sitting on the mat at the same time.

Resolution. Geach argues that the paradox reveals that the relation of absolute identity cannot be maintained without contradiction. Nevertheless, each of the 1,001 cats is the same cat as the original one, according to Geach, where "is the same cat as" expresses an equivalence relation weaker than identity. E. J. Lowe, however, counters that none of Geach's 1,001 "cats" is really a cat at all because, in essence, having identical physical parts is not a criterion for identity in cats.

READINGS

Geach, P. T. "Reply to Lowe." *Analysis* 42.1 (1982): 30.
— —. "Reply to Lowe's Reply." *Analysis* 42.1 (1982): 32.
Lowe, E. J. "The Paradox of the 1,001 Cats." *Analysis* 42.1 (1982): 27-30.
— —. "Reply to Geach." *Analysis* 42.1 (1982): 31.
— —. "On Being a Cat." *Analysis* 42.3 (1982) 174-177.

GENTLE MURDER, PARADOX OF. Also known as the Adverbial Samaritan, this strengthened version of the GOOD SAMARITAN PARADOX of deontic logic was formulated by James William Forrester. We give a variant of the version given by Barry Loewer and Marvin Belger.

Formulation. Certainly, Arabella ought not murder Barbarella. Nevertheless, it ought to be that if she does murder Barbarella, she should do so gently. As a matter of fact, she does commit the murder. Hence, she ought to murder Barbarella gently. But this last implies that she ought to murder Barbarella. Therefore, Arabella ought to murder Barbarella and she ought not murder Barbarella.

Explanation. The premises in the above story do not seem exceptional — in particular, a gruesome murder is generally considered to be more shocking and more reprehensible than a "gentle" murder. But, more importantly, the reasoning seems intuitively correct. In particular, if one ought to do something gently, the adverb can be separated in the following manner: we ought to perform the act and we ought to do so gently. Hence, it follows that we ought to perform the act. In fact, the story is formalizable in most systems of deontic logic and the conclusion is a valid consequence. Nevertheless, in most systems the conclusion is regarded as contradictory.

Resolution. Hector-Neri Castañeda observes that the crucial step permitting the deduction of the contradiction is the removal of an antecedent containing no free variables from the scope of the ought operator. Thus, whenever a deontic system asserts that "ought (X does A, if *p*)" is equivalent to "if *p*, then (X ought to do A)," the paradox will arise. Nevertheless, Castañeda thinks the equivalence so plausible that he is unwilling to give it up. Walter Sinnott-Armstrong, however, argues that a more detailed consideration of the logical structure of the propositions involved in the paradox (using Davidson's theory of action sentences) reveals that the contradiction is due to problems with the scope of the intensional operator, just as in the case of the GOOD SAMARITAN.

READINGS:

Forrester, James William. "Gentle Murder, Or the Adverbial Samaritan." *Journal of Philosophy* 81 (1984): 193-197.

Loewer, Barry, and Marvin Belzer. "Help for the Good Samaritan Paradox." *Philosophical Studies* 50 (1986): 117-127.

Sinnott-Armstrong, Walter. "A Solution to Forrester's Paradox of Gentle Murder." *Journal of Philosophy* 82 (1985): 163-168.

GIBBS'S PARADOX. This is a paradox in the theory of chemical thermodynamics. When two substances are mixed, the entropy remains the same throughout the process and collapses to zero only at its completion. The paradox is that no matter how close the substances come to being an ideal mixture, no attendant change in the entropy occurs until the mixing is completed. The responses to this paradox are too excessively technical to be presented here.

READING

Denbigh, K. G. and M. L. G. Redhead. "Gibbs' Paradox and Non-Uniform Convergence." *Synthese* 81 (1989): 283-313.

GIDEON'S PARADOX. Attributed by Maya Bar-Hillel and Avishai Margalit to their friend Gideon Schwarz, this paradox concerns the concept of economic rationality.

Formulation. Mary is given a choice between two gifts, say $1000 and $5. A bystander promises to reward Mary with $1,000,000 if she chooses irrationally. This second offer throws Mary into a quandary. She would prefer $1000 to $5, and so should select the former. Yet she would then be acting rationally and would lose out on the $1,000,000. In order to receive the $1,000,000 payoff, she should select the $5. But then her selection of the smaller gift is the rational choice with regard to the ultimate payoff and will not be rewarded after all.

Explanation. Mary's problem is that any attempt to make an irrational choice will itself be rational because she is trying to be irrational in order to secure the biggest payoff. Should she try to make a rational choice, however, she would be irrationally foregoing the largest payoff. Hence, her choice will be irrational if, and only if, it is rational.

Resolution. Perhaps we should first observe that it is not impossible for Mary to act irrationally in the given situation. She could stomp her feet in genuine frustration and just refuse to choose, thereby foregoing even the minor gift of $5 (depending on how we fill in the details, even this could be considered rational; but we simply suppose that it is an irrational, emotional reaction). Mary could even choose irrationally: she may choose the $1000 because she took an immediate irrational dislike to the bystander, or she may choose the $5 because she superstitiously believes five to be a lucky number. When, however, we assume that Mary is completely rational and has as a goal the maximization of her payoff (see the PARADOXES OF GAME THEORY), the paradox does arise. Bar-Hillel and Margalit argue that the paradox arises because the attribution of rationality or irrationality to Mary's choice is only made subsequently to her act of choice and, hence, any theory of rationality cannot make rationality depend on the outcome of the act to be judged. Nevertheless, the temporal aspects of the situation seem but incidental to the story as told. The real logical problem, also noted by Bar-Hillel and Margalit, would seem to be rather the self-referentiality of the conditions imposed by the bystander. Thus, perhaps surprisingly, the present paradox is akin to the Liar and RUSSELL'S PARADOX.

READING
Bar-Hillel, Maya, and Avishai Margalit. "Gideon's Paradox — A Paradox of Rationality." *Synthese* 63 (1985): 139-155.

GÖDEL'S PARADOX OF UNDECIDABILITY. Attempts to prove the consistency of mathematics by reducing it to logic were frustrated by the discovery of the PARADOXES OF SET THEORY. Especially notable in this regard was RUSSELL'S PARADOX. David Hilbert thus set up the goal, called Metamathematics, of showing the consistency of a first order system of logic entirely by finite means. Gödel's results are generally regarded as entailing the futility of Metamathematics.

Formulation. Gödel demonstrated the following two theorems for certain logical systems:

(1) Consistency implies incompleteness.
(2) Consistency implies that there is no proof of consistency formalizable within the system.

Explanation. Gödel's argument was originally about the system elaborated by Alfred North Whitehead and Bertrand Russell in their *Principia Mathematica*, but it is generally considered to hold in any system rich enough to express elementary arithmetic. He proceeded by associating a unique natural number to all the expressions of the system and then enumerated the formulas of the system. By using Cantor's diagonal method, Gödel was able to find a formula, G, that asserts its own unprovability. Simplifying a bit, we may assert that if the system is consistent, G cannot be false, for if it were, then G would be a false, provable formula. Theorem (2) is a corollary of (1).

Resolution. Gödel's results are extremely paradoxical in that they were highly unexpected and counterintuitive. Some logicians, however, claim that his results are paradoxical in a more pernicious sense. Gödel himself observed that his argument was closely related to the LIAR, and Graham Priest argues that what the argument really shows is that some contradictions are true, thereby making logic paraconsistent; indeed, for Priest, it is exactly the logical paradoxes that are these true contradictions.

READINGS

Broyles, James E. "Paradox and Argument." *International Logic Review* 8 (1977): 160-169.

Chihara, Charles S. "Priest, the Liar, and Gödel." *Journal of Philosophical Logic* 13 (1984): 117-124.

Dowden, Bradley H. Accepting Inconsistencies form the Paradoxes." *Journal of Philosophical Logic* 13 (1984): 125-130.

Priest, Graham. "The Logic of Paradox." *Journal of Philosophical Logic* 8 (1979): 219-241.

— —. "The Logic of Paradox Revisited." *Journal of Philosophical Logic* 13 (1984): 153- 179.

Smullyan, Raymond. *Forever Undecided: A Puzzle Guide to Gödel*. Oxford: Oxford UP,   1987.

GOODMAN'S PARADOXES OF CONFIRMATION. In 1954, Nelson Goodman posed "a new riddle of induction" as a successor to HUME'S PROBLEM OF INDUCTION and HEMPEL'S PARADOXES OF CONFIRMATION.

Goodman's riddle concerns the question of what predicates or properties of objects are suitable subjects for inductive generalization. **Formulation.** Define the predicate 'grue' as 'green if observed before time *t*, and blue otherwise'. Now if *t* is some time in the future, all emeralds observed thus far are both grue and green. So either hypothesis — that all emeralds are grue, and that all emeralds are green — are equally well supported. **Explanation.** The difficulty is how to determine which predicates are legitimate terms for inductive generalization; or, as Goodman puts it, which are the "projectible" predicates. While it is intuitively obvious that 'grue' is less projectible than 'green', Goodman's argument challenges us to find an objective basis for our preference. **Resolution.** The present paradox has been widely discussed since the time of its introduction. Many philosophers have followed Rudolf Carnap's suggestion that 'gruc' is less acceptable than 'green' because it makes essential reference to a point in time. Goodman's response to this suggestion is to show how to make 'green' and 'blue' relative to time. He defines 'bleen' as 'blue if observed before time *t*, and green otherwise.' He then argues that our terms 'green' and 'blue' can be defined respectively as 'grue if observed before time *t*, bleen otherwise', and 'bleen if observed before time *t*, grue otherwise.' Michael Anthony Slote proposes that 'green' is a differential property in the sense that if something is green then it can be distinguished on this basis from something that is not green. But it is not always logically possible to distinguish relevant objects using the property 'grue'. John O'Connor has challenged this solution by recalling the interdefinability of the blue-green and the grue-bleen pairs and R. G. Swinburne claims that Slote's solution is vague. Goodman's own solution to the problem is to argue that 'green' is preferable to 'grue' because the former term is better "entrenched," that is, has featured in more successful inductions than the latter. It does not, however, seem satisfactory to hold that a practice is justified just because it is what has been practiced. Nathan Stemmer claims that the paradox can only be resolved by adducing a further premise. He suggests the following: "The nature of the world will continue to be intuitively uniform" (181), recognizing that his proposal is only a partial solution to the paradox because the new premise is itself only partially justified. Nevertheless, we may observe that a premise of this kind is akin to our naive judgment that we have direct empirical evidence for the proposition "all emeralds are green," whereas we have no direct empirical evidence that they will some day be perceived as blue.

READINGS

Bunch, B. L. "Rescher on Goodman's Paradox." *Philosophy of Science* 47 (1980): 119-123.

Chao-Tien, L. "Solutions to the Paradoxes of Confirmation, Goodman's Paradox and Two New Theories of Confirmation." *Philosophy of Science* 45 (1978): 415-419.

Goldstick, D. "The Meaning of 'Grue'." *Erkenntnis* 31: 139-141.

Goodman, Nelson. *Fact, Fiction, and Forecast.* Cambridge: Harvard UP, 1983. Ch. 3, Sec. 4, 73-80.

Konyndyk, Jr., Kenneth. "Solving Goodman's Paradox: A Reply to Stemmer." *Philosophical Studies* 37 (1980): 297-305.

O'Connor, John. "Differential Properties and Goodman's Riddle." *Analysis* 28.2 (1967): 59.

Schlesinger, George N. "Is It True What Cicero Said About Philosophers?" *Metaphilosophy* 19 (1988): 282-293.

Slote, Michael Anthony. "Some Thoughts on Goodman's Riddle." *Analysis* 27.4 (1967): 128-132.

——. "A General Solution to Goodman's Riddle?" *Analysis* 29.2 (1968): 55-58.

Stemmer, Nathan. "A Partial Solution to the Goodman Paradox." *Philosophical Studies* 34 (1978): 177-185.

Swinburne, R. G. "Grue." *Analysis* 28.4 (1968): 123-128.

GOOD SAMARITAN PARADOX, THE. This is one of the PARADOXES OF DEONTIC LOGIC.

Formulation. "Suppose that Arabella (the good Samaritan) ought to help Barbarella who has asked her to spare a dime. Now, Arabella will kill her husband's mistress next week and this person, unbeknownst to Arabella, happens to be Barbarella. Barbarella is the only person Arabella will kill next week. The paradox is that when these sentences are paraphrased into standard deontic logic . . . they seem to entail that Arabella ought to kill someone" (Loewer and Belzer 117).

Explanation. The paradox, of course, is first of all that Arabella be obliged to kill anyone at all, which goes against all our moral intuitions. Secondly, the premises

Arabella ought to help Barbarella.
Arabella will kill someone.

do not seem to warrant the conclusion that she ought to kill anybody.

Resolution. This is a falsidical paradox due to the failure of the substitutivity of identity in contexts governed by an intensional operator (here, the operator "ought"), which makes the present paradox resemble the MORNING STAR PARADOX in quantified modal logic. Thus, the paradox is dispelled by observing proper scope distinctions on the logical operators. But that is not the end of the story, because Forrester has gone on to invent the PARADOX OF THE GENTLE MURDER, a strengthened version of the Good Samaritan.

READINGS

Åqvist, Lennart. "Good Samaritans, Contrary to Duty Imperatives and Epistemic Obligations." *Nous* 1.4 (1967).

Loewer, Barry, and Marvin Belzer. "Help for the Good Samaritan Paradox." *Philosophical Studies* 50 (1986): 117-127.

GRELLING PARADOX, THE. See the HETEROLOGICAL PARADOX.

HEAP, THE. See EUBULIDES' PARADOXES and the SORITES.

HEDONISTIC PARADOX, THE. That a person who insistently seeks pleasure for himself will not find it, but that the person who helps others find pleasure will in the end find pleasure himself (or has a greater chance of finding it), is sometimes called the hedonistic paradox. Related to this paradox is that fact that pleasure is not to be sought for itself, that it is not an end in itself separate from the activity or experience of which it is an aspect. Pleasure is attainable only as an attitude or feeling accompanying other things. For a related paradox in Buddhism, see the PARADOX OF NIRVANA.

HEGELIAN PARADOXES. Among the many philosophers who have a penchant for paradox, Hegel is one of the foremost. There are many specific paradoxes in Hegel's work, such as his contention that the Master is held in thrall by his dependence on the Slave while the latter's work sets him free. Beyond these individual paradoxes, however, Hegel's whole dialectical logic, which incorporates contradiction as an essential element, is paradoxical. According to Howard P. Kainz, "Hegel's system as a whole is a true paradox, not only involving a complex network of simultaneous recursions, but simultaneously holding together the overarching, architectonic oppositions of being and thought, along with numerous corollary and subsidiary oppositions, whose dialectical connections with the originary paradox will be . . . necessitated in the unfolding of the overall system-paradox" (97). The "originary paradox" to which Kainz refers is the experience of self-consciousness, which Hegel generalizes to the "unity-in-distinction of being and thought" (Kainz, 84).

READING

Kainz, Howard P. *Paradox, Dialectic, and System.* University Park: Penn State UP, 1988.

HEMPEL'S PARADOXES OF CONFIRMATION. Related to other problems of inductive logic, such HUME'S PROBLEM OF INDUCTION and GOODMAN'S PARADOXES OF CONFIRMATION, these paradoxes are also called the Ravens Paradox. We will consider only a single version of the paradoxes here.

Formulation. Scientific hypotheses generally take the form

All Fs are Gs.

An hypothesis is confirmed whenever we observe an instance of an F with the property G. We may, however, rewrite the hypothesis in the following, logically equivalent form:

All non-Gs are non-Fs.

Therefore, the observation of an instance of a non-G, no matter how irrelevant it may seem to the original hypothesis, will confirm the hypothesis if it has the property non-F.

Explanation. Consider, for example, the hypothesis

All ravens are black.

Each time we observe a raven and find it to be black, we count that as a confirmation of the hypothesis. When we happen upon a green shamrock, however, we believe that we are leaving zoology behind for botany. Nevertheless, the green shamrock is a non-black thing that has the property of being a non-raven. Thus, it confirms the hypothesis

All non-black things are non-ravens.

But, since this hypothesis is logically equivalent to the first hypothesis, we seem forced to accept the intuitively repugnant conclusion that the observation of a green shamrock is a confirmation instance of the hypothesis "All ravens are black." Hempel's paradoxes thus bring into question the entire practice of confirming scientific hypotheses.

Resolution. The present paradox is among the most widely discussed paradoxes of the twentieth century, yet no commonly accepted solution has been found. One approach is to deny that"all ravens are black" is equivalent to "all non-black objects are non-ravens." Such a position seems too radical, however, and R. G. Swinburne argues that it would be contrary to accepted scientific procedure. Another approach is to attempt to develop a notion of relevance of evidence to hypotheses. Even though it would complicate the underlying logic of science, this could be a promising approach; nevertheless, it has proven extremely difficult to formulate adequate generalized relevance conditions. A third suggestion, due to Karl Popper, is to abandon the goal of confirmation altogether; on this view, the only legitimate scientific approach to a hypothesis is to attempt to disconfirm it, by searching for counter-instances. Popper's position has been extremely influential and perhaps will be incorporated in any final solution to the problem. Even so, it seems almost perverse to deny that our vast experience with black ravens has no bearing on the confirmation of the hypothesis that "all ravens are black." Still another response is to accept the paradox by agreeing that the observation of green shamrocks does confirm the stated hypothesis and then try to downplay, in some manner, the importance or the degree of confirmation obtained thereby.

READINGS

Alexander, H. G. "The Paradoxes of Confirmation." *British Journal for the Philosophy of Science*. 9 (1958): 227-233.

Aronson, Jerrold L. "The Bayesians and the Raven Paradox." Nous 23 (1989): 221-240.

Black, M. "Notes on the Paradoxes of Confirmation." *Aspects of Inductive Logic*. Ed. J. Hintikka and P. Suppes. Amsterdam: 1966. 175-197.

Gaifman, H. "Subjective Probability, Natural Predicates and Hempel's Ravens." *Erkenntnis* 14 (1979): 105-147.

Cooke, Roger M. "A Paradox in Hempel's Criterion of Maximal Specificity." *Philosophy of Science* 48 (1981): 327-328.

Eriksen, Leif. "Confirmation, Paradox, and Logic." *Philosophy of Science* 56 (1989): 681-687.

Fisch, Menachem. "Hempel's Ravens, the Natural Classification of Hypotheses and the Growth of Knowledge." *Erkenntnis* 21 (1984): 45-62.

Hempel, C. G. "Studies in the Logic of Confirmation (I)." *Mind* ns 54 (1945): 1-26.

——. "Studies in the Logic of Confirmation (II)." *Mind* ns 54 (1945): 97-121.

Hintikka, J. "Inductive Inferences and the Paradoxes of Confirmation." *Essays in Honor of Carl G. Hempel: A Tribute on the Occasion of His Sixty-Fifth Birthday.* Ed. Nicholas Rescher. Dordrecht: Reidel, 1970. 24-46.

Huggett, W. J. "On Not Being Gulled by the Ravens." *Australasian Journal of Philosophy* 38 (1960): 48-50.

Humburg, Jürgen. "The Solution of Hempel's Raven Paradox in Rudolf Carnap's System of Inductive Logic." *Erkenntnis* 24 (1986): 57-72.

Lawson, Tony. "The Context of Predication (and the Paradox of Confirmation)." *British Journal for the Philosophy of Science* 36 (1985): 393-407.

Mackie, J. L. "The Paradox of Confirmation." *British Journal for the Philosophy of Science* 13 (1963): 265-277.

Rody, Phillip J. "(C) Instances, the Relevance Criterion, and the Paradoxes of Confirmation." *Philosophy of Science* 45 (1978): 289-302.

Schwartz, R. "Paradox and Projection." *Philosophy of Science* 39 (1972): 245-248.

Stemmer, Nathan. "'Justificatory' Solutions to Hempel's Raven Paradox and Goodman's "New Riddle of Induction'." *Philosophical Studies* 34 (1978): 177-185.

Stove, D. "Popperian Confirmation and Not the Paradox of the Ravens." *Australasian Journal of Philosophy* 37 (1959): 149-151.

——. "A Reply to Watkins." *Australasian Journal of Philosophy* 38 (1960): 51-54.

Suppes, P. "A Bayesian Approach to the Paradoxes of Confirmation." *Aspects of Inductive Logic.* Ed. J. Hintikka and P. Suppes. Amsterdam: 1966. 198-207.

Swinburne, R. G. "The Paradoxes of Confirmation: A Survey." *American Philosophical Quarterly* 8.4 (1971): 318-329.

Watkins, J. W. N. "Confirmation, Paradoxes and Positivism." *The Critical Approach.* Ed. M. Bunge. New York: 1964. 92-115.

——. "Reply to Stove." *Australasian Journal of Philosophy* 37 (1959): 240-241.

——. "Reply to Mr. Stove's Reply." *Australasian Journal of Philosophy* 38 (1960): 54-58

Weintraub, Ruth. "A Paradox of Confirmation." *Erkenntnis* 29 (1988): 169-180.

Whitely, C. H. "Hempel's Paradoxes of Confirmation." *Mind* ns 54 (1945): 156-158.

von Wright, G. H. "The Paradoxes of Confirmation." *Aspects of Inductive Logic.* Ed. J. Hintikka and P. Suppes. Amsterdam: 1966. 208-218.

HERACLITUS' PARADOXICAL APHORISMS. A native of Ephesus, Heraclitus died sometime between 478 and 470 B.C. He spoke in such an obscure manner that the ancients called him "the dark." Sometimes the fragments of his book are paradoxical because they attribute contradictory attributes to things, or because they identify opposites. Here are several paradoxes representative of Heraclitus.

(1)   God is day, he is night; winter and summer, war and peace, satiety and hunger; he changes form even as fire when mixed with various incenses is named according to the pleasant perfume of each.
(2)   Immortals are mortal, mortals immortal, each living and dying the life of the other.
(3)   The way up and the way down are one and the same.
(4)   The living and the dead, the waking and the sleeping, the young   and the old, these are the same; the former are moved about and become the latter, the latter in turn become the former.

In these remarks Heraclitus is not trying to confuse us but merely to state the truth as he understands it. Sometimes he explains the contradiction in such a manner that it is clearly only apparent.

(5)   Sea water is the purest and the foulest. For fish it is drinkable and life-preserving, for men it is undrinkable and deadly.

At other times his remarks are paradoxical because they contradict accepted notions.

(7)   You could not step twice in the same rivers; for other and yet other waters are ever flowing on.
(8)   In the same rivers we step and we do not step. We are and are not.

Plato characterizes Heraclitus' idea that all things are in perpetual change by the phrase "Everything flows." We do not step into the same river twice not only because the river changes between the steps, but because we ourselves change in a similar manner. The circumstance that not only does the river change the very movement we step into it, but that we do also, was expressed by a student of Heraclitus, "You cannot step into the same river once."

READINGS
Kirk, G. S. *The Cosmic Fragments.* Cambridge: 1954.
Mackenzie, Mary Margaret. "The Moving Posset Stands Still: Heraclitus

Fr. 125." *American Journal of Philology* 107 (1986): 542-551. Discussion: 109 (1988): 397-401.
Williams, Howard. "Heraclitus' Philosophy and Hegel's Dialectic." *History of Political Thought* 6 (1985): 381-404.

HETEROLOGICAL PARADOX, THE. Also called the Grelling, or Grelling-Nelson, Paradox, this is a set-theoretical paradox, related to RUSSELL'S PARADOX.

Formulation. "Some adjectives have meanings which are predicates of the adjective word itself; thus the word 'short' is short, but the word 'long' is not long. Let us call adjectives whose meanings are predicates of them, like 'short', autological; others heterological. Now is 'heterological' heterological? If it is, its meaning is not a predicate of it; that is, it is not heterological. If it is not, its meaning is not a predicate of it, and therefore it is heterological." (Ramsey, *Foundations of Mathematics* 27)

Explanation. Since we can easily find many examples of autological and heterological adjectives, it would seem that the classification of adjectives using these concepts would be quite natural. But 'heterological' is itself an adjective and so should be heterological or not. Nevertheless, this apparently innocuous predicate turns out to apply to itself if, and only if, it does not apply to itself.

Resolution. Russell thought that the heterological paradox was further support for the hierarchy approach to the logical paradoxes (see the LIAR and RUSSELL'S PARADOX). According to this view, which is the basis for Russell's Theory of Types, the proper formulation of the statement, "'Heterological' is heterological," would include a device such as subscripts to show that the second use of 'heterological' makes a metalinguistic claim about the first. "Hierarchy" solutions remain, however, controversial because there seems little reason for them except for the purpose of avoiding paradox; in other words, such solutions appear irredeemably *ad hoc*. Other attempted solutions have focused on the meaningfulness of the claim that "'Heterological' is heterological." For example, Gilbert Ryle argued that statements such as "'x' is y" can only be meaningful when there are established criteria for determining when the predicate y applies to 'x'. In the sentence, "'Long' is heterological," such criteria are available, since we know what it is for a word to be long or short. But in the paradoxical sentence, there are no such criteria since we do not know what it is for a word to be heterological in the absence of any other relevant properties. That is to say, 'heterological' is appropriately applied to words only when those words indicate the appropriate philological properties by which they should be judged. Attempts to resolve the paradox by claiming that the paradoxical sentence is meaningless, however, can be met by constructing the following paradox. Define M-heterological as any "adjective whose meaning is not a predicate of itself, or which is meaningless when applied to itself". Then consider the sentence, "'M-heterological' is M-heterological."

READINGS

Bowden, Leon. "Heterologicality." *Analysis* 12.4 (1952): 77-81.

Fitzpatrick, P. J. "'Heterological' and Namely-Riders." *Analysis* 22.1 (1961): 18-22.

Geach, P. T. "Ryle on Namely-Riders." *Analysis* 21.3 (1961): 64-67.

— —. "Namely Riders Again." *Analysis* 22.3 (1962): 92-94.

Goldstein, Lawrence. "Categories of Linguistic Paradox and Grelling's Paradox." *Linguistics and Philosophy* 4 (1981): 405-421.

— —. "Linguistic Aspects, Meaninglessness and Paradox: A Rejoinder to John David Stone." *Linguistics and Philosophy* 4 (1982): 579-592.

Lawrence, Nathaniel. "Heterology and Hierarchy." *Analysis* 10.4 (1950): 77-83.

Mackie, J. L., and J. J. C. Smart. "A Variant of the 'Heterological Paradox' — A Further Note." *Analysis* 14.6 (1954): 146-148.

— —. "A Variant of the 'Heterological' Paradox." *Analysis* 13.3 (1953): 61-65

Martin, Robert L. "On Grelling's Paradox." *Philosophical Review* 77 (1968): 321-330.

Meager, Ruby. "Heterologicality and the Liar." *Analysis* 16.6 (1956): 131-138.

Ramsey, F. P. "The Foundations of Mathematics." In *The Foundations of Mathematics*. Ed. R. B. Braithwaite. London: Routledge, 1931. 1-61.

Ryle, Gilbert. "Heterologicality." Analysis 11.3 (1951): 61-69.

Stone, John David. "Meaninglessness and Paradox: Some Remarks on Goldstein's Paper." *Linguistics and Philosophy* 4 (1981): 423-429.

von Wright, G. H. *Philosophical Papers: Philosophical Logic II.* Ithaca: Cornell UP, 1983. 1-24

HILBERT'S HOTEL. Ever since the days of ancient Bethlehem, travelers have been frustrated by arriving at their destinations only to find that all the hotels have been booked solid. The management of Hilbert's Hotel has taken a big step toward eliminating this problem: the hotel has an infinite number of rooms. Given the great increase of late in the number of travelers, even this vast number of rooms is completely occupied during peak travel times. The beauty of Hilbert's Hotel, however, is that it is able to defy our finitistic expectations. For example, should a guest arrive when all the rooms are occupied, he would not have to be turned away. The management would simply ask each of the guests to move into the room with the next highest number to that of their present room. The guest in room 1 would move into room 2; the guest in room 2 would move into room 3; and so on. Now, clearly, each guest would still be accommodated since there is no end to the number of rooms different from room 1. In fact, if we knew a guest's old room number, we could figure out exactly what his new room would be. Yet just as clearly, room 1 has been freed so that the new arrival can also be accommodated. Should a group of n new arrivals appear at the hotel, the first *n* rooms could be freed by reassigning each guest to room number *k+n*, where *k* was the original assignment. The capabilities of Hilbert's Hotel, however, have yet to be really tested. Even if an infinite number of new arrivals were to arrive at the already full hotel, the old guests could be transferred to the even numbered rooms (since there are an infinite number of even numbers, all these guests would still be accommodated), which would free the infinite number of odd numbered rooms for the infinite number of new arrivals. In fact, supposing that there are an infinite number of planets, Hilbert's Hotel could host a convention, to which each planet sent an infinite number of delegates!

HOLLIS'S PARADOX. This is a PREDICTION PARADOX.
Formulation. Two people, A and B, think of positive integers and whisper the numbers chosen in a third's, C's, ear. C then asserts that neither A nor B can work out whose number is greater. He also adds that they did not both choose the same number. A reasons as follows: "Clearly, B did not choose 1 since, if he had, he could deduce that my number would be greater than his. Further, B can reason similarly about me, which is correct since I picked 157. Hence, 1 was not picked by either of us. But then B did not choose 2 since, now that 1 has been eliminated, B could again deduce that my number was the greater. Once again, B can reason analogously about me. Therefore, 2 could not have been picked by either of us. By continuing this chain of reasoning, it follows that 157 was not chosen by either of us, even though I chose it!"
Explanation. Hollis claims that the assertion that C was wrong about A and B's ability to decide which number is greater is also paradoxical, since, if he was, A must conclude that both numbers are greater than each other, which is obviously absurd. C's assertion thus eliminates the

possibility that 1 was chosen by either A or B since, it being the smallest number, whoever chose 1 would know that the other's number was larger. But, then 2 becomes the smallest number that can be chosen and so the same argument applies to it. After 157 steps, A is forced to conclude that he could not have chosen the very number (157) that he did choose and an induction argument results in the conclusion that no number could have been chosen by either A or B.

Resolution. Doris Olin suggests that, even if B had picked 1, he could only infer that A's number was smaller if he was sure of the correctness of C's statement. Hollis, however, argues that a slight modification in the story line (substitute "at least equal" for "greater") would save the paradox. Michael Kingham argues, among sundry other things, that the paradox depends on the fallacy of epistemic distribution: "A knows that (if p, then q)" implies (fallaciously) that "if p, then A knows q." George Rea claims that Olin and Kingham are correct if by "work out whose number is greater," we mean "infer from premises known to be true." But, Rea also claims that the paradox can be reformulated to avoid these objections, although the reformulation itself — which involves inference without knowledge or conditional inference — also eventually succumbs to an analysis revealing that C's statement cannot be true.

READINGS

Hollis, Martin. "A Paradoxical Train of Thought." *Analysis* 44.4 (1984): 205-6.

— —. "More Paradoxical Epistemics." *Analysis* 46.4 (1986): 217-218.

Kingham, Michael. "A Paradox Derailed: Reply to Hollis". *Analysis* 46.1 (1986): 20-24.

Olin, Doris. "On a Paradoxical Train of Thought." *Analysis* 46.1 (1986): 18-20.

— —. "On an Epistemic Paradox." *Analysis* 47.4 (1987): 216-17.

Rea, George. "A Variation of Hollis's Paradox." *Analysis* 47.4 (1987): 218-220.

HOODED MAN, THE. See EUBULIDES'S PARADOXES.

HORNED MAN, THE. See EUBULIDES'S PARADOXES.

HUI SHIH'S PARADOXICAL APHORISMS. In Chapter 33 of the *Chuang Tsu* appear the ten paradoxes of Hui Shih (c. 370-c. 310 BC), all that remains of the five cart loads of books this Chinese logician is reputed to have written. Some of these paradoxes resemble Heraclitus'. We cite the following from Vincent Shih's translation:

> (1) The heavens are as low as the earth; and mountains are as level as marshes.
> (2) The moment the sun reaches its zenith it declines; and the moment a thing is born it dies."
> (3) The south has no limit and has a limit.
> (4) I go to Yüeh today and arrived there yesterday.

These oracular utterances are meant to suggest the mutability and relativity of all things.

READING

Shih, Vincent Y. C. "Hui Shih." *The Encyclopedia of Philosophy*. Ed. Paul Edwards. New York: Macmillan, 1967. Vol. 4, 69.

HUMANISM, THE PARADOX OF. This veridical paradox of culture criticism was analyzed by the literary critic Joseph Wood Krutch.

Formulation. "It would appear, then, that the complex of ideas and preferences which passes current under the name of humanism may be separated into two distinct parts. The complex includes on the one hand a tendency to stress the importance of the social virtues set up in opposition to the destructive, anarchic tendencies of what it mistakenly calls the 'natural' man, and it includes on the other hand a sympathy with the attempt to create human, as opposed to natural, values. Yet these social virtues are, as we have seen, themselves animal, and among men they flourish most in those societies where the genuinely human tendencies — both virtuous and vicious — are least prominent. 'Humanism' in this popular sense is thus obviously at war with itself, for the simple reason that the closer it comes to realization of one half its ideal the further it is bound to be from the possibility of achieving the other, since the second demands a detachment from the aims of nature and the first a harmony with them" (Krutch 34-35).

Explanation. In the chapter of which this passage is the conclusion, Krutch exposes two contradictory tendencies in the popular conception of humanism: humanism is seen to favor "communitarian" values (in the sense now associated with philosophers such as Alasdair MacIntyre) and "expressive individualism" (in Robert N. Bellah's sense). Yet, as MacIntyre and Bellah's group argue so compellingly, the incompatibility of the communitarian and individualistic orientations in America, and in the Occident in general, has grown even more acute since Krutch identified it.

Resolution. The popular conception of humanism must be revised in order to better recognize the dramatic tensions that it masks. Just how this is to be done, however, and whether the tensions can be adequately resolved are still open questions.

READINGS

Bellah, Robert N., and others. *Habits of the Heart: Individualism and Commitment in American Life.* New York: Harper, 1985.

Krutch, Joseph Wood. "The Paradox of Humanism." *The Modern Temper: A Study and a Confession.* New York: Harcourt, 1929. 27-55.

MacIntyre, Alasdair. *After Virtue: A Study in Moral Theory.* 2nd ed. Notre Dame: U of Notre Dame P, 1983.

HUMAN SCIENCES, PARADOXES IN THE. This heading comprises paradoxes having to do with the character of human being and and its scientific investigation. Psychological paradoxes are especially prominent in our list: the ABILENE PARADOX, the PARADOX OF ACTING, the BODHISSATTVA PARADOX, BURIDAN'S ASS, the EXPERIMENTER EXPECTANCY PARADOX, the PARADOX OF FREEDOM, the HEDONISTIC PARADOX, the PARADOX OF LOGICAL PSYCHOLOGISM, MEEHL'S METHODOLOGICAL PARADOX, the PARADOX OF PAIN, PARADOXICAL SLEEP, PERCEPTUAL PARADOXES, the PRODUCTIVITY PARADOX, the SEEKER PARADOX, the PARADOX OF SELF-DECEPTION, the PARADOX OF SINCERITY, the PARADOX OF THE THINKING BEHAVIORIST, the PARADOX OF TRUST, and the PARADOX OF UNSUCCESSFUL INTERVENTION.

HUME'S PROBLEM OF INDUCTION. Raised by David Hume in 1777, this is the origin of the problem of justifying non-deductive reasoning and is the predecessor of HEMPEL'S and GOODMAN'S PARADOXES OF CONFIRMATION.

Formulation. "We have said that all arguments concerning existence are founded on the relation of cause and effect; that our knowledge of that relation is derived entirely from experience; and that all our experimental conclusions proceed upon the supposition that the future will be conformable to the past. To endeavor, therefore, the proof of this last supposition by probable arguments, or arguments regarding existence, must be evidently going in a circle, and taking that for granted, which is the very point in question." (Hume sec. 30)

Explanation. Valid deductive arguments guarantee the truth of their conclusions, given the truth of their premises; the reliability of valid deductive arguments can be readily established. The reliability of inductive arguments is, however, more problematical. Suppose one establishes that all crows observed thus far are black, and conclude that the next crow to be observed will also be black. The conclusion is not guaranteed by the observational premise, because the color of the next crow is logically independent of the color of the previous ones. Yet the form of the argument seems inherently reliable and it is tempting to argue that the conclusion is justified in virtue of the previous reliability of arguments just like it. Yet why should the next argument of this form be reliable, just because previous examples have been? Hume points out that this justification of inductive reasoning itself relies on inductive reasoning, and is therefore circular.

Resolution. The most accepted response to Hume is to point out that he apparently requires a deductive standard of reliability for what it is, after all, not a deductive argument. Inductive argumentation should perhaps be held to a different standard. There have been innumerable subsequent attempts to develop suitable "inductive logics." Prominent among early schemes is that held by John Stuart Mill.

READING

Hume, David. *Enquiries Concerning Human Understanding*. Oxford: Oxford UP, 1975.

HUSSERL'S PARADOX OF SUBJECTIVITY. Edmund Husserl, the founder of the phenomenological movement, poses "the paradox of human subjectivity": How can the objective world depend for its character on finite human subjectivity?

Formulation. "Universal intersubjectivity, into which all objectivity, everything that exists at all, is resolved, can obviously be nothing other than mankind; and the latter is undoubtedly a component part of the world. How can a component part of the world, its human subjectivity, constitute the whole world, namely, constitute it as its internal formation, one which has always already become what it is and continues to develop, formed by the universal interconnection of intentionally accomplishing subjectivity, while the latter, the subjects accomplishing in cooperation, are themselves only a partial formation within the total accomplishment?" (Husserl 179).

Explanation. Humanity is held to be a collective subjectivity that constitutes (not in a causal sense but through the projection of meaning-structures) the world as the whole of beings, and yet humanity is incorporated in the world, which seems absurd.

Resolution. Husserl tries to resolve the paradox of human subjectivity by clarifying an equivocation in its formulation. Humanity as a component part of the world must be sharply distinguished from the extramundane subjectivity that is the constituting ground of the world. The collective subjectivity of mankind is part of the world, and is bracketed, along with the rest of the world in the transcendental reduction that reveals transcendental subjectivity. After Husserl, there was a fundamental break with his transcendental phenomenology by thinkers, such as Martin Heidegger, Maurice Merleau-Ponty, and Hans-Georg Gadamer, who denied that the reduction to transcendental subjectivity was possible. For these so-called existential phenomenologists the paradox of human subjectivity remains a paradox unless the phenomenologist envisions something, such as Heidegger's *Dasein* or Merleau-Ponty's *Chiasma*, that is more fundamental than the distinction between subjectivity and objectivity.

READINGS

Hopkins, Burt C. "Husserl's Account of Phenomenological Reflection and Four Paradoxes of Reflexivity." *Research in Phenomenology* 19 (1989): 180-194.

Husserl, Edmund. *The Crisis of European Philosophy and Transcendental Phenomenology*. Trans. David Carr. Evanston: Northwestern UP, 1970.

HYDROSTATIC PARADOX, THE. Containers of different shapes and sizes, connected with each other at the bottom are known as Pascal's vases. If we (partially) fill a set of Pascal's vases with a liquid, the height of the liquid will be the same in all the containers:

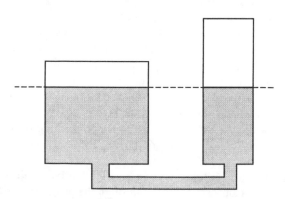

This implies that the pressure at the bottom of each container will be the same even though the weight of the liquid in each container may be different. That different weights of the same liquid can cause the same pressure is known as the Hydrostatic Paradox. It is resolved by observing that the greater weight is distributed over a greater area, so that the pressure per unit area of the base is the same in each container.

INCARNATION, THE PARADOX OF THE. Søren Kierkegaard claims that one must face this absolute paradox in order to arrive at true Christian belief.

Formulation. One of the central tenets of the Christian faith is the incarnation. But the concept of the God-man is inherently absurd.

Explanation. Luis Pojman interprets Kierkegaard's paradox as founded on the fact that the meaning of God as an infinite, unchanging being is radically incompatible with the finite, constantly changing nature of man. Hence, "God-man" is an oxymoron, a contradiction in terms.

Resolution. There seem to be two basic responses (other, of course, than the denial of the incarnation) to this paradox. The first, and perhaps most widespread, is that Kierkegaard is claiming that Christian belief is opposed to reason and that the latter must be abandoned in order that the believer embrace on faith alone what reason tells him is impossible. C. S. Evans, however, argues that Kierkegaard does not mean to imply that the incarnation involves a logical paradox because that would imply that it is meaningless. The absurdity of the incarnation does not stem from meaninglessness, however, but rather from our inability to comprehend the nature of God — and, for that matter, our inability to comprehend the nature of man. This interpretation, according to Evans, is supported by the fact that Kierkegaard argues that it is impossible to remain neutral in face of the paradox: faith and taking offense are the only two options. A purely rational reaction is really naught but a disguise for offense, which is grounded in the pride of the supposedly unlimited powers of human reason.

READINGS

Evans, C. S. "Is Kierkegaard an Irrationalist? Reason, Paradox and Faith." *Religious Studies* 25 (1989): 347-362.

Gurrey, C. S. "Paradox, Will and Religious Belief." *Philosophy* 66 (1991): 503-511.

Pojman, Louis. *The Logic of Subjectivity.* University, AL: U of Alabama P, 1984.

INDOCTRINATION, THE PARADOX OF. Suggested by Ludwig Wittgenstein's pedagogical remarks in *On Certainty*, the paradox of indoctrination was formulated by C. J. B. Macmillan in 1983.
Formulation. "The problem of indoctrination is this: in a modern democratic society, the desired goal of education is that each student develop a set of beliefs that are rationally grounded and open to change when challenged by better-grounded beliefs. In order to develop such students, however, it would seem that they must acquire a belief in rational methods of knowing which must itself be beyond challenge, *i.e.*, held in a manner inconsistent with its own content. Thus, students must be indoctrinated in order not to be indoctrinated: a pedagogical dilemma or paradox" (Macmillan 370).
Explanation. According to Wittgenstein, intellectual development depends upon imparting some beliefs that "stand fast with regard to all others" (370); unless the child trusts the context of learning, it cannot learn anything. Yet if that trust is not merited, the "chaos of doubt" should follow (371).
Resolution. Macmillan suggests that the way out of the paradox is to recognize that the basic system of beliefs and practices imparted through indoctrination makes possible a more advanced learning through evidence and reasoning, and that these critical activities "provide ways of avoiding indoctrination" (371). James E. Garrison develops this answer more fully. Indoctrination is necessary, even desirable, both for the well-being of the individual and the community, but there is a way around the pernicious aspects of the paradox if there is, in the words of John Dewey, "at least a self-correcting indoctrination, not one that demands the subordination of critical discrimination and comparison" (267). This program of liberal education is expressible in the slogan "n*o indoctrination without inoculation* " (268) by the introduction of doubt directed at the basic system of beliefs. Thus, although a certain amount of indoctrination is needed to instill a rational outlook in our children and make them autonomous, functional members of society, they must eventually be brought to confront the fact that rationality is not self-grounding. Perhaps an effective way of doing so, is to come to grips with the present paradox itself.

READINGS

Garrison, James W. "The Paradox of Indoctrination: A Solution." *Synthese* 68 (1986): 261-273.
Macmillan, C. J. B. "On Certainty and Indoctrination." *Synthese* 56 (1983): 363-372.

INDUCTIVE PROBABILITY, THE PARADOX OF. This paradox of probability theory was propounded by Stephen Spielman.
Formulation. Given a set of statements, one of which must be true, and given that the probability of some claim given one member of the set is the same as the probability of that claim given any other member of the set, a contradiction arises because the probability of the claim is not unique. More formally, let $P(a|b)$ stand for "the probability of a, given b." Then,

b_1 or b_2 or . . . or b_n
and $\quad\quad P(a|b_1) = P(a|b_2) = \ldots = P(a|b_n)$
imply that $\quad P(a|b_1) = P(a) = P(a|\,b_1\text{ or }b_2\text{ or}\ldots b_n) \neq P(a|b_1)$.

Explanation. Consider the probability that the roll of two dice will total 7. We know that each one of the numbers from 1 to 6 have an equal probability of being thrown on the first die and that one, and only one, of these six numbers will be thrown. Furthermore, no matter what number is rolled on the first die, there is only one favorable result on the roll of the second die. Hence the probability that the dice will total 7, given that 1 is rolled on the first die, is equal to the probability that the dice will total 7, given that 2 is rolled on the first die, is equal to *etc.* Thus the final result is independent of the number rolled on the first die because the probability of totaling 7 does not change for different throws of the first die and, hence, this probability is 2/11. That is,

$P(a) = P(a|b_1) = P(a|b_2) = P(a|b_3) = P(a|b_4) = P(a|b_5) = P(a|b_6)$
$= 2/11.$

Since one of the six numbers must be rolled on the first die, however, the probability that 1 or 2 or 3 or 4 or 5 or 6 is rolled on that die is certainty (=1). Thus, the probability of totaling 7, given that one of the six numbers is rolled on the first die, is just the probability that the two dice will total 7, which is 1/6. That is,

$P(a|\,b_1\text{ or }b_2\text{ or }b_3\text{ or }b_4\text{ or }b_5\text{ or }b_6) = P(a) = 1/6.$

Thus, probability theory implies two different results for the same event, which is, of course, contradictory.
Resolution. Spielman argues that the paradox is due to the principle that the probability of a claim, based on the totality of available evidence, determines the odds of the claim. Kenneth S. Friedman, however, counters that the principle is indeed valid and that the source of the paradox is that,

even when the disjuncts are mutually exhaustive, assuming any one of them does actually constitute new information and that affects the probability of the original claim.

READINGS

Friedman, Kenneth S. "Resolving a Paradox of Inductive Probability." *Analysis* 35.6 (1975): 183-185.

Speilman, Stephen. "Assuming, Ascertaining, and Inductive Probability." *AmericanPhilosophic Quarterly Monograph #3: Studies in the Philosophy of Science.* 1969. 143-161.

INFINITE, PARADOXES OF THE. Along with semantical and set-theoretical paradoxes, paradoxes of the infinite are one of the most important classes of paradox for the development of logic and mathematics. Many of them are due to the fact that our mental habits, thought strategies, and intuitions, all of which were developed in finite settings, do not carry over to the infinite. Included in this class are, among others, the DEVIL'S OFFER, the PARADOX OF ENTAILMENT, HILBERT'S HOTEL, the INFINITE SERIES PARADOX, KANT'S COSMOLOGICAL ANTINOMIES, the LAMP PARADOX, LEWIS CARROLL'S PARADOX OF ENTAILMENT, OLBER'S PARADOX, PASCAL'S WAGER, THE THIRD MAN, and ZENO'S PARADOXES.

READINGS

Bolzano, Bernard. *Paradoxes of the Infinite.* Trans. Fr. Prihonsky. London: Routledge and Kegan Paul, 1950.

Hughes, Patrick, and George Brecht. *Vicious Circles and Infinity: A Panoply of Paradoxes.* Garden City, NY: Doubleday, 1975.

Smith, Joseph Wayne. *Reason, Science and Paradox: Against Received Opinion in Science and Philosophy.* London: Helm, 1986. Ch. 3.

Thomas, Ivo. "A Twelfth-Century Paradox of the Infinite." *Journal of Symbolic Logic.* 23 (1958): 133-134.

INFINITE SERIES PARADOX, THE. This paradox, originally adduced by Bertrand Russell, is proffered to show that the von Mises-Reichenbach theory of probability is inconsistent.

Formulation. Let n_i be non-prime and p_i prime and arrange the natural numbers in a sequence in the following two ways:

(1) $n_1 \, p_1 \, n_2 \, p_2 \, n_3 \, p_3 \cdots$
(2) $n_1 \, p_1 \, n_2 \, n_3 \, p_2 \, n_4 \, n_5 \, n_6 \, p_3 \cdots$

By using sequence (1), the probability that an integer chosen at random will be prime is 1/2; by using sequence (2), this probability is zero.

Explanation. The von Mises-Reichenbach theory of probability is based on the relative frequency of the favorable event occurring in a large number of trials. Any specific number of trials, however, can give only an approximation of the probability. In order to get the exact probability, as well as to insure the uniqueness of the result, it is necessary to find the limit of these favorable occurrences as the number of trials approaches infinity. Hence, the trials are arranged as a sequence and the required limit is found. In sequence (1) each non-prime is followed by a prime, so that the relative frequency of the primes for each initial segment ending in a prime is 1/2. But the limit of a constant is just that constant, so the probability of picking a prime at random is 1/2. In sequence (2), the ith prime is preceded by i non-primes. Hence, each initial segment ending in a prime will contain i primes and $1/2\ i(i+1)$ non-primes. Thus, the relative frequency of the primes will be

$$i/[1/2\ i(i+1)+i]$$

which reduces to

$$2/(3i+1).$$

The limit of this ratio as i approaches infinity is zero. Hence, the probability of picking a prime at random is zero. Now, the absolute number of both primes and non-primes is the same in both sequences and, hence, the probability must be unique. Thus, $1/2 = 0$, which is a contradiction.

Resolution. Joseph Wayne Smith argues that the paradox reveals that the von Mises-Reichenbach theory of probability is inconsistent. Arthur Pap, however, has shown that the two sequences used in deducing the paradox are not random sequences and thus violate a presupposition of the theory; hence, no paradox is engendered.

READINGS

Pap, Arthur. *An Introduction to the Philosophy of Science.* New York: Free P, 1962. 180-181.

Smith, Joseph Wayne. *Reason, Science and Paradox: Against Received Opinion in Science and Philosophy.* London: Croom Helm, 1986. 124-127.

INFORMATION, PARADOX OF. David Miller formulated this paradox to show that Reichenbach's "straight rule" of induction is inconsistent.

Formulation. Let $p(a)$ be the frequency-based probability of a and $P(A,B)$ the logical probability of the statement A, given the statement B. Let $-a$ be the event that occurs when a does not occur. Miller's derivation is then as follows, where a is the event of rolling a 5 on a fair die:

(1) $P(A, p(a) = r) = r$
(2) $p(a) = 1/2$ if, and only if, $p(a) = p(-a)$
(3) $P(A, p(a) = 1/2) = P(A, p(a) = p(-a))$
(4) $P(A, p(a) = 1/2) = 1/2$
(5) $P(A, p(a) = p(-a)) = p(-a)$
(6) $p(-a) = 1/2$
(7) $p(a) = 1/2$
(8) $1/2 = 1/6$

Explanation. Line (1) is a statement of Reichenbach's "straight rule" and may be translated as "if the frequency of rolling a 5 has been found to be r, then the probability of rolling a 5 on the next roll of the die is also r." Given that the frequency has been established by extensive investigations, this is a reasonable assumption. (For the purposes of the paradox, the existence of small margins of error are immaterial.) Line (2) results from the fact that if $p(a) = 1/2$, then $p(-a) = 1 - p(a) = 1/2$ and (3) is the result of the substitution of equivalent propositions. Lines (4) and (5) are instances of (1). Line (6) follows from (4) and (5), while (7) follows from (6) by arithmetic (as in (2)). But we know from statistics that $p(a) = p(\text{rolling } 5$ on a fair die) $= 1/6$; hence, this fact and (7) give us (8).

Resolution. Miller's notation is poorly formulated. It led J. L. Mackie to object that Miller's derivation depends on an illicit generalization over the variable a. Miller countered that a is a constant, standing for "5 is rolled on the next roll of the die" and thus Mackie's objection was not pertinent. Even if the exact formulation of Mackie's objection was flawed, however, his point is well taken because line (4) of the derivation, if it is to be regarded as true, is a conditional probability and this condition is lost in Miller's notation [similar remarks apply to (5)]. The condition is that the statistics has given p(a) = 1/2, but later [line (8)] Miller asserts that the statistics gives $p(a) = 1/6$. Thus, the source of the contradiction would seem to be Miller's equivocation on the statistics, rather than Reichenbach's rule.

READINGS

Bub, J., and M. Radner. "Miller's Paradox of Information." *British Journal for the Philosophy of Science* 19 (1968): 63-67.

Mackie, J. L. "Miller's So-Called Paradox of Information." *British Journal for the Philosophy of Science* 17 (1966): 144-147.

Miller, David. "A Paradox of Information." *British Journal for the Philosophy of Science* 17 (1966): 59-61.

———. "On a So-Called Paradox: A Reply to Professor J. L. Mackie." *British Journal for the Philosophy of Science* 17 (1966): 147-149.

———. "The Straight and Narrow Rules of Induction: A Reply to Dr. Bub and Mr. Radner." *British Journal for the Philosophy of Science* 19 (1968): 145-157.

Popper, Karl. "A Comment on Miller's New Paradox of Information."
British Journal for the Philosophy of Science 17 (1966): 61-69.
— —. "A Paradox of Zero Information." *British Journal for the Philosophy
of Science* 17 (1966): 141-143.
Smith, Joseph Wayne. *Reason, Science and Paradox: Against Received
Opinion in Science and Philosophy.* London: Helm, 1986. Ch. 7.

INSOLUBILIA. The Insolubilia, or "Unsolvables," are for the most
part medieval variations of the LIAR paradox, called the *Mentiens.*
Medieval logicians collected at least fourteen different versions of the
paradox, as in Albert of Saxony's *Perutilis logica* (1522) and developed
over a dozen different solutions to it, as in Paul of Venice's *Logica magna*
(1499). One version goes as follows:

> Plato says: What Aristotle is about to say is false.
> Aristotle says: What Plato just said is true.

Assume that Plato has spoken truly. What Plato said was that Aristotle will
speak an untruth, so — as per Plato's dictum — Aristotle's statement is
false. But Aristotle's statement was that Plato had indeed spoken truly and
the only way that this can be false is for Plato's statement to be false. Hence,
if Plato's statement is true, it is false. Assume, then, that Plato's statement is
false. This means that Aristotle must have spoken truly. But his statement
was that Plato had spoken truly, which must indeed be true. Hence, if Plato's
statement is false, it is true. The upshot is that Plato's statement is true if,
and only if, it is false, which, of course, is a contradiction. A. N. Prior's
solution to this kind of paradox is discussed in PRIOR'S FAMILY OF PARADOXES.
Joseph R. Jones outlines Paul of Venice's presentation of another version of
the Liar, called the Bridge, as follows (187):

> Let us establish as a true principle that those who speak truly
> will cross the bridge and those who speak falsely will not.
> Now Sortes says, 'Sortes will not cross the bridge.' If this is a
> true statement, then according to the above principle, he will
> cross; but he says that he will not cross; hence either the prin-
> ciple (that all truth-sayers cross) is false, or Sortes is lying: in
> which case he will not cross the bridge, as he (truthfully) says.

On Jones's view, the Bridge is the source of the Sancho PANZA, and the same
resolutions apply to both. See also EUBULIDES' PARADOXES and the LIAR.

READINGS
De Ruk, L. M. "Some Notes on the Medieval Tract *De Insolubilibus.*"
Vivarium 4 (1966): 84.

Herzberger, H. G. "Truth and Modality in Semantically Closed Languages." *The Paradox of the Liar.* Ed. R. Martin. New Haven: Yale UP, 1970. 25-46.

Moody, E. A. *Truth and Consequence in Medieval Logic.* Amsterdam: North-Holland, 1973. 103-110.

Prior, A. N. "Some Problems of Self-Reference in John Burridan." *Proceedings of the British Academy* 48 (1962): 281-296.

Spade, Paul Vincent. "The Origins of Medieval *Insolubilia*-Literature." *Franciscan Studies* 33 (1973): 292-309.

— —. *The Medieval Liar: A Catalogue of the Insolubilia Literature.* Toronto: , 1975.

— —. "Ockham on Terms of First and Second Imposition and Intention, with Remarks on the Liar Paradox." *Vivarium* 19 (1981): 47-55.

— —. "Five Early Theories in the Medieval *Insolubilia*-Literature." *Vivarium* 25 (1987): 24-46.

— —, and Gordon Anthony Wilson. *Johannis Wyclif: Summa In*solubilium. Binghamton, NY: Medieval and Renaissance Texts, 1986.

INTERESTING NUMBERS, PARADOX OF. Let the set of positive integers be divided into two disjoint, nonempty subsets — the interesting numbers and the uninteresting numbers — using any criterion we wish. Then consider the set of uninteresting numbers. It must have a least element, say x. But, since x has this unique property of being the least uninteresting number, x is indeed interesting after all, so we move it into the interesting set. The resulting uninteresting set will again have a least element, which in turn makes it interesting. By reiterating the argument a sufficient number of times, we find that there are no uninteresting numbers! This is, of course, a falsidical paradox, depending as it does for its plausibility on the ambiguous use of "interesting."

IRRATIONAL NUMBERS, THE PARADOX OF. To the man on the street, it is the Pythagorean belief that the world exhibits an intrinsically rational structure that is paradoxical, not the discovery of irrational number that so scandalized the Pythagorean school. The early Pythagoreans thought that "all is number and harmony." By numbers they meant the positive integers; by harmonies, the ratios and proportions between these integers. Yet not all geometrical relationships can be expressed as ratios between whole numbers. For example, the isosceles right triangle with the two equal sides of one unit has a hypothenuse equal to the square root of two. Indeed, this became the standard example of an "incommensurable" quantity (more precisely: two quantities are incommensurable if they cannot be measured by a common unit), although the original discovery may have been made in the regular pentagon. In any case, geometry played a central role, since line segments are continuous, as opposed to the discrete system of natural numbers. Hence, the Pythagoreans were faced with an example of something that (for them) really existed, but which could not be explained by numbers and harmonies. Thus the discovery of such "irrational numbers" seriously threatened the Pythagorean conception of the cosmos, their existence being a flaw in an otherwise elegant universe. Report has it that when one of their members made the existence of irrational numbers public, he was taken out to sea by the brothers and drowned.

READING

von Fritz, Kurt. "The Discovery of Incommensurability by Hippasus of Metapontum." *Annals of Mathematics* 46 (1945): 242-264.

JEPHTA PARADOX, THE. Taken from the *Book of Judges* by Georg Henrik von Wright as a test case for deontic logic, this paradox involves the substitution of identity in deontic contexts and, thus, is similar to the MORNING STAR PARADOX in modal logic:

> Jephta promises God that he will sacrifice the first being that he meets on his way home. The first being that he meets, however, is his daughter Miriam. Therefore, he ought to sacrifice his daughter.

Since the present paradox is structurally similar to the Good SAMARITAN, we will not discuss it further here. See also the PARADOX OF GENTLE MURDER.

READINGS

van Eck, Job A. "A System of Temporally Relative Modal and Deontic Predicate Logic and its Philosophical Applications." *Logique et Analyse* 24 (1982): 249-290 and 339-381.

von Wright, Georg Henrik. "A Correction to a New System of Deontic Logic." *Danish Yearbook of Philosophy* 2 (1965): 103-107.

KANT'S ANTINOMIES. Immanuel Kant (1724-1804) was the propounder of a series of paradoxes that he styled "antinomies." These included his four COSMOLOGICAL ANTINOMIES, his ANTINOMY OF TELEOLOGICAL JUDGMENT, his antinomy of taste (see the PARADOX OF TASTE), his ANTINOMY OF PRACTICAL REASON, and his antinomy of bipolar duality.

Samuel Fleischacker adduces yet a "fifth antinomy," which he claims to be Kantian in style.

READING
Fleischacker, Samuel. "A Fifth Antinomy." *Philosophia* [Israel] 19 (1989): 23-27.

KANT'S ANTINOMY OF PRACTICAL REASON. This is a religious and an ethical paradox. **Formulation.** The *summum bonum*, or highest good, has two elements, the supreme good, which is virtue, and the complete good, which includes not only virtue but also happiness. The highest good demands then the union of virtue and happiness, but how is this union to be effected? Either the desire for happiness must motivate the maxims of virtue, or else the maxims of virtue must be the efficient cause of happiness. Yet neither of these alternatives is possible, because, on the one hand, if happiness is made the end of action, it destroys the morality of action, and because, on the other, virtue is neither a necessary nor a sufficient condition of happiness, but only the condition for deserving happiness. **Explanation.** It appears that if the world had a coherent structure, happiness and virtue would be related to each other in some fundamental manner, either insofar as acting from duty must help to bring about happiness, or insofar as the pursuit of happiness facilitates acting from duty. Yet acting from duty does not issue in happiness but only in being worthy of happiness, and acting from prudence is incompatible with acting from duty. Thus, the highest good does not seem to be a well wrought whole. **Resolution.** Although no finite, and hence sensible, being has sufficient knowledge and power to secure an absolute happiness consistent with its duty, there is no reason to presume that the world of sensible experience — that is, the world of phenomena — is the the only one there is. In a nonsensible (that is, intelligible) world — a noumenal world — virtue and happiness might be united. The demand of practical reason for a union of virtue and happiness might be satisfied then by the ideal of an intelligent Author of nature, who would reward virtue with eternal happiness.

READINGS
Cassirer, H. W. *A Commentary on Kant's Critique of Judgment.* New York: Barnes, 1938. Sec. 70.
Kant, Immanuel. *The Critique of Practical Reason.* Trans. Thomas K. Abbott. London: Longmans, Green, 1909. 209-216.

KANT'S ANTINOMY OF TELEOLOGICAL JUDGMENT. In Kant's day, science — especially physical science — had already propounded the goal of identifying causality with efficient causality. Kant nevertheless proposed that understanding things through final causality does not in principle conflict with mechanistic explanation. The present paradox supports this contention.

Formulation. The thesis is that all production of material objects is possible in accordance with purely efficient causality. The antithesis is that some production of material objects is not possible in accordance with purely efficient causality.

Explanation. The thesis and antithesis are generated by taking as constitutive of the natural world two maxims that play a role in guiding the empirical investigation of nature in a systematic manner. The thesis above results from taking as a principle constitutive of nature the regulative principle that all material objects should be judged in accordance with purely efficient causality. In turn, the antithesis issues from taking as constitutive the regulative principle that not all material objects can be judged in accordance with purely efficient causality, but require instead to be judged in accordance with teleological, or final, causality.

Resolution. The antimony of teleological ascription arises from taking as determinative of the natural world principles that arise from and have their validity in the empirical investigation of nature. So long as these principles are not absolutized in this way there is no contradiction. The principle of determinant judgment, which seeks explanation through purely mechanical laws, need not contradict the principle of reflective judgement, which tries to understand things in their purposive organization. For in the end it might be determined that the validity of both principles is to be comprehended through a single underlying principle.

READINGS

Cassirer, H. W. *A Commentary on Kant's Critique of Judgment*. New York: Barnes, 1938. Sec. 70.

Kant, Immanuel. *The Critique of Judgment*. Trans. J. H. Bernard. New York: Hafner, 1951. Pt. 2, Div. 2.

KANT'S COSMOLOGICAL ANTINOMIES. In the Transcendental Dialectic of the *Critique of Pure Reason*, Kant put forward four "cosmological" antinomies. The first two of these were called mathematical antinomies, the last two dynamical antinomies; and each consists of a rationalist thesis and an empiricist antithesis. In the First

Antinomy, the thesis is that the world has a beginning in time, and in respect of space it is enclosed in limits. The antithesis is that the world has no temporal beginning, and no limits in space; it is infinite in respect to both space and time. In the Second Antinomy, the thesis is that every composite thing in the world consists of simple parts and nothing anywhere exists except the simple or that which is formed by composition of it. The antithesis is that no composite thing in the world consists of simple parts and there exists nothing simple anywhere in the world. In the Third Antinomy, the thesis is that causality in accordance with the laws of nature is not the only causality from which the world as a whole is derivable, but it is necessary to accept a causality by freedom as an explanation of them. The antithesis is that there is no freedom — everything in the world happens according to the laws of nature. In the Fourth Antinomy, the thesis is that there belongs to the world either as part of it or as its cause an absolutely necessary being. The antithesis is that there nowhere exists an absolute being either in the world or outside it as its cause.

Explanation. Together with the paralogisms, the four antinomies are meant to establish the Principle of Critical Philosophy, namely, that concepts are validly employed only insofar as they are applied to possible experience. Application of ideas beyond possible experience inevitably results in the pernicious contradictions of Transcendent Metaphysics.

Resolution. The details of the arguments for the antinomies are hard to follow, and commentators rarely find them convincing. For example, in *The World as Will and Representation,* Arthur Schopenhauer finds in each case the arguments for the theses invalid and those for the antitheses valid (see Vol. I, "Criticism of the Kantian Philosophy"). Most philosophy since Kant has joined in his desire to limit the sway of metaphysics, the common complaint being that he did not go far enough in this direction.

READINGS

Baldacchino, Lewis. "Strawson on the Antimony." *Mind* 93 (1984): 91-97.

Ewing, A. C. *A Short Commentary on Kant's Critique of Pure Reason.* Chicago: U of Chicago P, 1938.

Gram, M. S. "Kant's First Antinomy." *Kant Studies Today.* Ed. Lewis White Beck. La Salle, IL: Open Court, 1969. 210-229.

Greenwood, John D."Kant's Third Antinomy: Agency and Causal Explanation." *International Philosophical Quarterly* 30 (1990): 43-57.

Kant, Immanuel. *Immanuel Kant's Critique of Pure Reason.* Trans. Norman Kemp Smith. New York: St. Martin's P, 1929. 384-484.

Moore, A. W. "Aspects of the Infinite in Kant" Mind ns 97 (1988): 205-223.

Schopenhauer, Arthur. *The World as Will and Representation.* 2 vols. Trans. E. F. J. Payne. New York: Dover, 1969.

Strawson. *The Bounds of Sense: An Essay on Kant's Critique of Pure Reason.* London: Methuen, 1966. 34-36, 133-140.

Welton, T. D. *Kant's Critique of Pure Reason.* Oxford: Clarendon, 1958. 203-217.

Wolfe, Julian. "On the Impossibility of an Infinite Past: A Reply to Craig." *International Journal for Philosophy of Religion* 18 (1985): 91.

KNOWABILITY, PARADOX OF. Frederick B. Fitch presented this argument purporting to show that the idea of a truth that is unknown is problematical.

Formulation. The two principles upon which the argument rests are:

(1)   If a proposition is true, then it is knowable.

(2)   There is at least one truth, say p, that is never known.

Applying principle (2) to (1), we obtain

(3)   It is known that: p and (p is not known).

Yet since the knowledge of a conjunction entails knowledge of each conjunct, we have

(4) p is known and it is known that p is not known.

Clearly, if something is known, it is true; hence we may drop the "it is known that" operator from the second conjunct, resulting in

(5) p is known and p is not known.

But (5) is a contradiction. For ease of exposition, we have ignored the modal operator that appears in the original argument. Hence, we now reformulate (1) - (5), using 'P' to stand for logical possibility and 'k' for "it is known by someone at sometime that."

(1)   For all q: if q, then PKq.

(2) p and not-(Kp).

(3)   PK(p and not-(Kp)). letting $q = (p$ and not-(Kp)) in (1)

(4)   P[Kp and K(not-(Kp))].

(5)   P(Kp and not-(Kp)).

Line (5) now asserts that a certain contradiction is logically possible.

Explanation. Principle (1) asserts that all truths are knowable. This assertion is actually relatively weak for it merely asserts that there is nothing self-contradictory about having knowledge of a true proposition. Principle (2) is obviously meant to be relativized to human knowers. Both seem intuitively plausible. Nevertheless, we are led to conclude that a certain contradiction is not contradictory (logical possibility is the absence of contradiction), which is itself a contradiction.

Resolution. Of the principles (1) and (2), the second seems more secure; thus, the first has received more attention. Dorothy Edgington proposes a reformulation of (1) to block the paradox. She holds that the correct expression of (1) is that for any actual truth it is possible to know that it is actually true. In other words, there exists some world, *w*, such that someone in *w* knows that the proposition '*p* and not-(K*p*)' is true in the actual world. No contradiction is derivable from this expression provided that *w* is distinct from the actual world. A problem with this solution is that the requisite knowledge of the actual world can only exist in a different possible world, which requirement seems to run counter to the intuition underlying (1) — namely, that there are no truths about our own world or situation which, in principle, we are blocked from knowing. Another approach is to question the applicability of principle (1) to truths such as (2). Support for (1) is derived from consideration of simple facts about the world, together with the idea that with some hard work and serendipity we can discover those facts. Of course, there may be facts that are sufficiently remote in space and time to make them undiscoverable in practice, but which could have been discovered by an agent in the right place in the right time. Sentences such as (2), which bring in knowledge as their own subject matter, are not the stuff on which such intuitions are built.

READINGS

Edgington, Dorothy. "The Paradox of Knowability." *Mind* ns 94 (1985): 557-568.

Fitch, Frederick. B. "A Logical Analysis of Some Value Concepts." *Journal of Symbolic Logic* 28 (1963): 135-142.

Williamson, Timothy. "On the Paradox of Knowability." *Mind* ns 96 (1987): 256-261.

KNOWER, THE PARADOX OF THE. Not to be mistaken for the PARADOX OF THE KNOWER IN DEONTIC LOGIC, this epistemic version of the LIAR was first adduced by Richard Montague and David Kaplan. It seems to jeopardize the status of the concept of omniscience, for if the paradoxical statement S were in fact true, there could be no all-knowing being. The reasoning is reminiscent of that of the Paradox OF KNOWABILITY.

Formulation. The sentence

> (S)   No one knows that this sentence is true

cannot be false.

Explanation. Suppose S to be false. Then someone does know it to be true. Yet if someone knows it to be true, then it is true. Therefore the supposition that it is false must be incorrect. Hence, we ourselves now know S to be true, since we have just demonstrated it. Yet if someone knows S to be true, it must be false because S asserts that nobody knows it. Therefore, S must be both true and false, which is contradictory. **Resolution.** Perhaps the most common response to the present paradox is to claim that S is meaningless. S can be branded as meaningless by asserting that no reasonable sentence can include self-reference, making it nothing more than a trivial variant of the Liar. Another approach is to claim that propositions and not sentences are proper objects of knowledge; thus, S would be ill-formed because it presupposes that sentences are objects of knowledge. Still another approach would be to affirm that the predicate "knows" is meaningless. Thomas Tymoczko, however, argues that all these alternatives are too extreme. According to Tymoczko, a closer examination of the paradox reveals that it rests on four epistemological principles:

> The Veracity Principle: If someone knows a sentence it is true.
> The Completeness Principle: If someone demonstrates a sentence, he knows it.
> The Extension Principle: If someone knows both a conditional and its antecedent and uses *modus ponens* to detach the consequent, then he knows the consequent.
> The Metaveracity Principle: We know the Veracity Principle.

Although all four of these principles are intuitively plausible, they have all been challenged on independent grounds.

READINGS

Anderson, C. Anthony. "The Paradox of the Knower." *Journal of Philosophy* 80 (1983): 338-355.
Montague, Richard, and David Kaplan. "A Paradox Regained." *Notre Dame Journal of Formal Logic* 1.3 (1960): 79-90.
Smullyan, Raymond. *Alice In Puzzle-Land.* New York, 1982.
Tymoczko, Thomas. "An Unsolved Puzzle about Knowledge." *Philosophical Quarterly* 34 (1974): 437-458.

KNOWER (IN DEONTIC LOGIC), THE PARADOX OF. This problem of deontic logic is somewhat similar to the PARADOX OF THE KNOWER. The example is due to James E. Tomberlin.

Formulation. Given certain reasonable systematic principles, the following three sentences are inconsistent:

(1)   X set fire to the store during Y's watch.
(2)   If X set fire to the store during Y's watch, Y ought to
know about it.
(3)   X ought not set fire to the store.

Explanation. From (1), (2), and *modus ponens*, we get

(4)   Y ought to know that X set fire to the store.

Moreover, given that knowledge entails truth (see also the PARADOX OF KNOWABILITY and the PARADOX OF THE KNOWER), we conclude that

(5)   (Y knows that X set fire to the store) entails (X set fire
to the store).

Finally, given the principle that whatever is entailed by an obligatory statement is itself obligatory, we obtain

(6)   X ought to set fire to the store.

Lines (3) and (6), however, are contradictory.

Resolution. **Fred Feld**man argues that the paradox can be avoided by relativizing the ought operator to temporal states and taking certain precautions in formulating conditional obligations.

READINGS

Feldman, Fred. "The Paradox of the Knower." *Philosophical Studies* 55 (1989): 93-100.

Tomberlin, James E. "Obligation, Conditionals, and the Logic of Conditional Obligation." *Philosophical Studies* 55 (1989): 81-92.

KRIPKE'S PIERRE. See the PARADOX OF NAMING.

LAMP PARADOX, THE. Proposed by J. F. Thompson, this puzzle is a spin-off of considerations relating to ZENO'S PARADOXES.

Formulation. A lamp, originally off, is turned on and off an infinite number of times. Will it then be on or off?

Explanation. It is assumed that the infinite number of switchings can be done in a finite amount of time. This can be done as follows: the switch is thrown at time zero, again at one minute, again at one minute and thirty seconds, and so on. After two minutes have elapsed, the switch will have been thrown an infinite number of times. When the two minutes are up, the lamp is certainly either on or off. It cannot, however, be on because each time it was turned on it was subsequently turned off. Likewise, it cannot be off because each time it was turned off it was subsequently turned on.

Resolution. J. F. Tompson concludes that the task, which is one example of what is often called a "super-task," is logically impossible. Another approach is to deny that the final state of the lamp is determined by the infinite number of switchings effected.

READINGS

Berresford, Geoffrey C. "A Note on Thompson's Lamp 'Paradox'." *Analysis* 41.1 (1981): 1-3.

Thompson, J. F. "Tasks and Super-Tasks." *Analysis* 15.1 (1954): 1-13.

Ray, Christopher. "Paradoxical Tasks." *Analysis* 50.2 (1990): 71-74.

LAWYER, THE. See the EUALTHUS.

LEGAL PARADOXES. Legal paradoxes may occur when different, but equally binding laws impose conflicting obligations upon the citizen. A generally more interesting type of legal paradox, however, results when an apparently innocuous legal principle puts the citizen (or the State) in an impossible position. Legal paradoxes are often Catch-22s or DILEMMAS, and may be considered to be a subspecies of DEONTIC PARADOXES, although the latter designation usually implies that the paradox is being considered in the framework of deontic logic. See, for example, the EUATHLUS, the PARADOX OF NATURAL RIGHTS, SANCHO PANZA, the PARADOX OF SELF-AMENDMENT, and SMULLYAN'S PARADOX.

LEWIS CARROLL'S PARADOX OF ENTAILMENT. This problem purports to be a serious challenge to the notion of entailment.

Formulation. Let (A and B) entail C. But one may refuse to accept C unless the proposition "If A and B, then C" is true. Adding this as a premise, we obtain (A, B, and (If A and B, then C)) entail C. Proceeding in this manner, an infinite regress is generated.

Explanation. Let A and B be the premises of a valid argument that has C as its conclusion. It is possible that someone accept both A and B and yet not accept C if he does not accept the proposition "If A and B, then C." Hence, the latter must be added as a premise to the argument. The same reasoning can be applied to the new, three-premised argument; and, indeed, each new argument generates a need for a new premise thereby generating an infinite regress.

Resolution. W. J. Rees argues that "If A and B, then C" is a meta-premise and, thus, is not on the same level as the premises A and B. Thus, it should not be added as a new premise to the argument and the regress is avoided. The import of Ree's argument is well taken, though it seems to lose its plausibility in the simplified form of the paradox given above. (Carroll originally used Euclid's first theorem as an example.) In any case, the plausibility of Carroll's paradox seems to rest on viewing logic in terms of psychology, that is in terms of an individual's "acceptance" of the propositions involved in the argument. For the logician, if the argument is valid, that's the end of the story. If someone accepts the premises but not the conclusion, either he is implicitly denying the validity of the argument or has not understood that the argument is valid. In neither case is it necessary to add a new premise to the argument to insure its validity and, hence, no regress arises. We may also observe that, at least in classical logic, we have a result that states that (A and B) entail C if, and only if, "If A and B, then C" is a theorem.

READINGS

Carroll, Lewis [Charles Dodgson]. "What the Tortoise Said to Achilles." *Mind* ns 4 (1895): 278-280.

Rees, W. J. "What Achilles Said to the Tortoise." *Mind* ns 60 (1951): 241-246.

LIAR, THE. Known since antiquity, this is perhaps the paradox that has most exercised the occidental mind.

Formulation. There are many versions of this paradox, including:

What I am now saying is false.
[The sentence printed in brackets on this page is false.]
'Yields a falsehood when applied to its own quotation' yields a falsehood when applied to its own quotation. (Quine, The *Ways of Paradox,* 9.)

There are also indirect versions, such as

Plato says: What Aristotle is about to say is false.
Aristotle says: What Plato just said is true.

There are even imperative variants, for example,

Disobey this order!

Apparently, the inhabitants of the isle of Crete were once known for their skill at prevarication, for one of the most widely known literary sources of the paradox affirms that

> One of them, even a prophet of their own, said, The Cretans are always liars, evil beasts, slow bellies. This witness is true. (*The Epistle to Titus*, 1:12-13.)

Explanation. Perhaps one of the sources of the perennial popularity of this paradox is that it is very easy to understand since it requires no specialized knowledge for its formulation. Consider, for example, the straightforward version

> What I am saying now is false.

If this statement is true, what it states must be the case. But it states that it itself is false. Thus, if it is true, it is false. On the contrary assumption, if the statement is false, then what it states must not be the case and, thus, it is true. Therefore, the statement is true if, and only if, it is false. One of the essential elements in this paradox is self-reference, be it direct or indirect. In the present version, the paradoxical proposition predicates falsity of itself. In indirect versions, the self-reference is effected by a closed chain of propositions that circles back on itself. Observe, however, that self-reference does not seem to be a sufficient condition for generating the Liar since the proposition

> What I am now saying is true

does not seem not paradoxical (but see the TRUTH-TELLER VARIATIONS OF THE LOGICAL PARADOXES). Nevertheless, logicians generally consider paradoxes that are generated by self-reference to be examples of the Liar, which thus becomes the archetype of this kind of paradox. It would be too tedious to list here all the paradoxes considered in this volume which are examples of the Liar, but special mention should be made of the EPIMENIDES and of RUSSELL'S PARADOX.

Resolution. Since our intuitions tell us that the source of the Liar Paradox is its self-reference — what Bertrand Russell has referred to as the "vicious circle principle" — most responses center on trying to block this self-reference. It is not sufficient, however, to just brand self-reference as meaningless since, as we have already seen, not all forms of self-reference are paradoxical. One way of blocking the self-reference is through the use of "hierarchy" theories such as those pioneered by Russell in set theory and Alfred Tarski in semantics. In this approach, "true," "false," and kindred predicates are not allowed to be applied indiscriminately to sentences containing these expressions. They are typically supplied with indexes to show their rank. "true_0" is only predicated of sentences containing no ranked expressions. If "true_0" appears in a statement, the truth or falsity of that statement can only be asserted by using the predicates "true_1" or "false_1." In general, if n is the highest rank that appears in a sentence, any statement about that sentence must be of rank $n+1$. This approach does seem to eliminate the paradox and it has some plausibility since, when we talk about a sentence, we seem to be doing so in a metalanguage; talk about a sentence in the metalanguage would be done in a meta-metalanguage, and so on. These series of metalanguages may serve as the basis of the rankings. Nevertheless, not all logicians accept such a solution because (1) it does not seem intuitively satisfying, (2) a metalanguage need not be distinct from the object language, and (3) most predicates can be used in similar contexts without generating paradoxical results. This last reason seems to indicate that the hierarchy approach is too radical and also that it does not explain the source of the paradox. Another suggestion, obviously related to the previous one, is to claim that the troublesome sentences are ill-formed or meaningless or vitiated by ambiguity. The basic problem with this approach is that, as soon as the relevant distinctions are made, a new version of the paradox, respecting those distinctions, is adduced (see M-VARIANTS OF THE LOGICAL PARADOXES). Another interesting approach is to use semantics with truth-value gaps and gluts to resolve the paradox, while still another suggestion is that we should just accept that the Liar is a contradiction. Don S. Levi, for example, claims that the Liar is just an example of a "strange loop," but that it does not interfere with any important project that we are interested in. Given the structural similarity of the Liar with other paradoxes, such as RUSSELL'S PARADOX in set theory, which do interfere with important projects, most thinkers will undoubtedly continue to hold that more has yet to be said. See PARADOXES OF SELF-REFERENCE.

READINGS

Barwise, John, and John Etchemendy. *The Liar: An Essay on Truth and Circularity.* New York: Oxford UP, 1987.

Buckner, Dean, and Peter Smith. "Quotation and the Liar Paradox." *Analysis*

46.2 (1986): 65-68.
Dumitriu, Anton. "The Antimony of the Liar." *International Logic Review* 11 (1980): 107-118.
Goldstein, Laurence. "The Paradox of the Liar: A Case of Mistaken Identity." *Analysis* 45.1 (1985): 9-13.
Gupta, Anil. "Truth and Paradox." *The Journal of Philosophy* 78 (1981): 735-736.
Huggett, W. J. "Paradox Lost." *Analysis* 19.2 (1958): 21-23.
Hugly, Philip, and Charles Sayward. "Paradox and Semantic Correctness." *Analysis* 39.4 (1979): 166-169.
Levi, Don S. "The Liar Parody." *Philosophy* 63 (1988): 43-62.
Martin, Robert L. "Toward a Solution to the Liar Paradox." *Philosophical Review* 76 (1967): 279-311.
——, ed. *The Paradox of the Liar.* New Haven: Yale UP, 1970.
——. "Reply to Hugly and Sayward." *Analysis* 39.4 (1979): 169-174.
——, ed. *Recent Essays on Truth and the Liar Paradox.* Oxford: Clarendon, 1984.
——, and P. W. Woodruff. "On Representing 'True in L' in L." *Philosophia* 5 (1975): 213-217.
Mates, Benson. *Sceptical Essays.* Chicago: U of Chicago P, 1981. 15-42.
Parsons, Terence. "Assertion, Denial, and the Liar Paradox." Journal of *Philosophical Logic* 13 (1984): 137-152.
Rozeboom, William W. "Is Epimenides Still Lying?" *Analysis* 18.1 (1957): 105-113.
Slater, B. H. "The Liar." *International Logic Review* 4 (1973): 86-89.
Slezak, Peter. "Descartes' Diagonal Deduction." *British Journal for the Philosophy of Science* 34 (1983): 13-36.
Ursic, Marko. "A Modest Proposal Concerning Paradoxes." *Syn Phil* 1 (1986): 193-203.
Visser, Albert. "Four Valued Semantics and the Liar." *Journal of Philosophical Logic* 13 (1984): 181-212.
Whitely, C. H. "Let Epimenides Lie!" *Analysis* 19.2 (1958): 23-24.

LIBERTARIANISM, PARADOX OF. Libertarianism is a political philosophy that prioritizes individual freedom and seeks to limit the role of the state to a minimum. Such a position, however, may fail to protect the rights of a significant portion of the citizenry. Harold J. Johnson identifies four aspects of libertarianism which contribute to its potential for becoming tyrannical:

> 1) In seeking the furtherance of his own interests, the individual's actions have consequences that may affect others; in particular, acquired advantages may lead to widespread bullying and violence.

(2)   There is a natural tendency in competitive markets towards monopolies.
(3)   Many of the institutions that operate in the free marketplace are themselves highly authoritarian in character.
(4)   Individuals can take on voluntary obligations, but have little opportunity to revise these in light of changing circumstances and consequently some persons may attain dominance over others by this means.

A parallel paradox is that of Socialism. Socialism seeks to guarantee not only the individual's rights, but also his well-being, through the active intervention of the state. But once the state is given the power to enforce its decision arbitrarily, the individual's rights become subject to the whim of collective decisions. The two paradoxes are similar in that, in each case, the social institutions may actually frustrate the realization of the social ends that they were instituted to secure. Johnson argues that the paradoxes are real in that the undesirable results do not come about by external circumstances, but are tendencies inherent in the systems themselves.

READING
Johnson, Harold J. "Extremism in the Defense of Liberty is a Vice."
University of Ottawa Quarterly 56 (1986): 19-27.

LITERARY PARADOXES. The word "paradox" has been understood variously as a logical contradiction, absurdity, enigma, or seeming contradiction. In *The Well Wrought Urn*, Cleanth Brooks sees paradox as a fundamental element of poetic language; the language of science depends essentially on the principle of noncontradiction, whereas poetry depends on the antithetical principle of contradiction, expressed as the literary trope of paradox. Thus, paradox both teases and challenges the mind by testing the limits of language. It is a unique way of bi-polar thinking; "more than a verbal artifice, the paradox bespeaks the dialectical tension intrinsic to everyday, personal existence" (Slaatte 33) and involves both the opposition and reciprocation of ideas. Since paradox in one sense is a phrase or statement that while seemingly contradictory or absurd may actually be well-founded or true, paradox may be used as a rhetorical and poetical device to attract attention or secure emphasis, to express insights that are not as fully stated in unequivocal language, and to challenge received opinions or values. Alternatively, paradox in the sense of real contradiction may be used to express the absurdity of life or the absurdity that man makes out of it. Howard P. Kainz understands literary paradox to differ from philosophical paradox in that "they depend on insight and imagination rather than argument," for though "literary paradoxes could be argued for . . . they would lose their aesthetic appeal and literary value if this happened" (40). Kainz admits, however, that certain literary paradoxes, such as those in the works of G. K. Chesterton (1874-1936), in Sir Thomas More's *Utopia*, Søren Kierkegaard's *Either/Or*, and Friedrich Nietzsche's *Thus Spake Zarathustra*, receive extended argument and are hence literary-philosophical hybrids. Writers celebrated for their use of paradox include Erasmus (1467-1536), John Donne (1572-1621), Joseph Hall (1574-1656), La Rouchefoucauld (1613-1680), George Bernard Shaw (1856-1950), Jorge Luis Borges (1899-1986), and Samuel Beckett (1906-1990). See also Catch 22, DONNE'S PARADOX OF THE HOLY GHOST, OSCAR WILDE'S PARADOXICAL EPIGRAMS, RENAISSANCE PARADOX, the SANCHO PANZA, and the SEEKER PARADOX.

READINGS

Brooks, Cleanth. *The Well Wrought Urn: Studies in the Structure of Poetry.* New York: Harcourt, 1947.

Slaatte, Howard A. *The Pertinence of the Paradox.* New York: Humanities P, 1968.

LOGICAL PARADOXES. Sometimes a logical paradox is taken to be the apparent or real contradiction between two statements, both of which seem to have good supporting evidence. Logical paradoxes may result from a misapprehension of the rules of logic (perhaps because they are not clearly expressed or recognized), a violation of those rules, or the inapplicability of the rules of a logic to the situation in question. There is also a more restricted sense of the term "logical paradox." Following F. P. Ramsey, it is customary to distinguish between logical paradoxes and semantic paradoxes. Logical paradoxes arise in the object language because they contain only the usual logical and set-theoretical symbols; they include the BURALI-FORTI PARADOX, CANTOR'S PARADOX and RUSSELL'S PARADOX. The semantic paradoxes arise in the metalanguage because they involve semantic concepts such as truth and meaning; they include BERRY'S PARADOX, the EPIMENIDES, the HETEROLOGICAL PARADOX, the LIAR, and RICHARD'S PARADOX. There is another school of thinking that refuses to make Ramsey's distinction and would call all of these paradoxes logical. See also M-VARIANTS OF THE LOGICAL PARADOXES and TRUTH-TELLER VARIANTS OF THE LOGICAL PARADOXES.

READINGS

Chihara, Charles S. "The Semantic Paradoxes: A Diagnostic Investigation." *Philosophical Review* 88 (1979): 590-618.

— —. "The Semantic Paradoxes: Some Second Thoughts." *Philosophical Studies* 45 (1984): 223-230.

Gardner, Martin. "Logical Paradoxes." *Antioch Review* 23 (1963): 172-178.

Grelling, Kurt. "The Logical Paradoxes." *Mind* ns 45 (1936): 481-486.

Hannson, Bregt. "Paradoxes in a Semantic Perspective." *Essays on Mathematical and Philosophical Logic: Proceedings of the Fourth Scandinavian Logic Symposium and of the First Soviet-Finnish Logic Conference, Jyvaskyla, Finland, June 29-July 6, 1976.* Ed. Jaakko Hintikka, Ilkka Niiniluoto, and Esa Saarinen. Dordrecht: Reidel, 1976. 371-385.

Heijenoort, John van. "Logical Paradoxes." *The Encyclopedia of Philosophy.* Ed. Paul Edwards. New York: Macmillan, 1967. Vol. 5; 45-51.

Mackie, J. L. *Truth, Probability and Paradox: Studies in Philosophical Logic.* Oxford: Clarendon, 1973. 237-301.

Perelman, M. Ch. "Les Paradoxes de la logique." *Mind* ns 45 (1936). 204-208.

Quine, W. V. O. "Paradox." *Scientific American* 217 (1962): 84-96.

— —. *The Ways of Paradox: And Other Essays.* Cambridge: Harvard UP, 1976.

LOGICAL PSYCHOLOGISM, THE PARADOX OF. This paradox arises on the view that logic is ultimately a department of psychology.

Formulation. The truths of logic are about certain mental activities of human subjects, but do not rely on these activities for justification.

Explanation. Logical psychologism affirms that logic is grounded in the particular thought processes of individual persons. While it is indeed true that a given individual's thought, and especially his activities of drawing inferences, are amenable to logical treatment, the evidence for the acceptance of logical principles does not depend on the examination of these activities. As Dallas Willard affirms, "this seems paradoxical. For how can claims about a certain sort of thing fail to draw their evidence from the examination of things of that sort" (43)? That is, how can logic be about our activities of drawing inferences and yet transcend those very activities for its justification?

Resolution. According to Willard, the only plausible way of avoiding the paradox is that formulated by Edmund Husserl. In particular, the notion of a "proposition" as the abstract, but objective referent of sentences and as the bearer of truth is rejected as being both mystical and superfluous. The basic relation of mind to the proposition is instantiation; that is, an act of speech or a thought is an instance of a complex of characteristics of such acts. These characteristics themselves have determinations, among which are truth and falsity. Thus, the principles of logic apply to individual acts of inference because the latter are instances of the former. Nevertheless, the validity of the inference is not derived from the particular acts themselves, but from the characteristics of the acts. These latter are universals.

READINGS

Husserl, Edmund. "A reply to a Critic of my Refutation of Logical Psychologism." In *Readings on Edmund Husserl's Logical Investigations.* Ed. J. N. Mohanty. The Hague: Martinus Nijhoff, 1977. 33-42.

Willard, Dallas. "The Paradox of Logical Psychologism: Husserl's Way Out." In *Readings on Edmund Husserl's Logical Investigations.* Ed. J. N. Mohanty. The Hague: Martinus Nijhoff, 1977. 43-54.

LOSCHMIDT'S PARADOX. This paradox purports to show that the second law of thermodynamics is invalid by considering the sudden reversal of the velocities of all the particles in a closed system. One consequence of this paradox is that physics would be unable to account for the irreversibility of certain macroscopic events. The present paradox is essentially similar to that engendered by MAXWELL'S DEMON.

LOTTERY PARADOX, THE. First adduced by Henry Kyburg, this paradox puts the confidence-threshold theory of acceptance in question. **Formulation.** Let us agree to accept any proposition whose degree of confirmation is greater than 0.9. We are given, *ex hypothese* (hence with degree of confidence = 1) that there is a fair lottery with 1000 tickets in which one, and only one, ticket will win. Let P_i, for i from one to 1000, be the proposition that the ith ticket will lose. Hence, the degree of confidence for each P_i is 0.999, which is greater than 0.9. Therefore, we accept each P_i and, in consequence, we accept that no ticket will win, which contradicts our acceptance of the proposition that one ticket will win. **Explanation.** The choice of 0.9 as our threshold of acceptance is immaterial. The paradox will follow for any threshold strictly less than 1, although should the threshold be very close to 1, the lottery would have to consist of a greater number of tickets. The 1000 ticket lottery will suffice, however, for most statistical studies, which require a 0.9, 0.95, or occasionally a 0.98 confidence level. The degree of confidence for each P_i is measured by the standard probability function. It is also assumed

that the subject is completely rational, which is taken to entail that he accepts all the logical consequences of any accepted propositions. Thus, the subject must accept that no ticket will win because this is a logical consequence of the 1000 propositions P_i that he accepts.
Resolution. R. P. Loui underlines the fact that the Lottery Paradox can be avoided by imposing a diachronic condition on acceptance, but that most theorists are unwilling to accept this counterintuitive solution. Another approach is suggested by Ellery Eells. Using Mark Kaplan's notion of arbitrariness for a chain of reasoning, Eells argues that the paradox could be avoided by relativizing the notion of rational acceptance to a given (formal) language. Eells nevertheless cautions that his is but a partial solution to the problem because (1) it leaves open the justification of the specific relativization to be adopted in any given case and (2) it does not give us a completely satisfactory account of why "arbitrariness" should be the source of the paradox.

READINGS

Eells, Ellery. "On a Recent Theory of Rational Acceptance." *Philosophical Studies* 44 (1983): 331-344.

Harman, Gilbert. *Change in View.* Cambridge: MIT P, 1986. 21-24 and 70-72.

Loui, R. P. "Nozick's Acceptance Rule and the Lottery Paradox." *Analysis* 47.4 (1987): 213-216.

Stalnaker, Robert. *Inquiry.* Cambridge: MIT P, 1985. 90-99.

LOYALTY, THE PARADOX OF. This metaethical paradox, concerned with the coherence of the notion of loyalty, was formulated by Philip Pettit.
Formulation. "Yet the ideal of loyalty generates a paradox, for it requires that the loyal agent satisfy two apparently conflicting assumptions. He must be sensitive to considerations of a sort that we can all find compelling; that is why it is an ideal. And he must be sensitive to considerations relating distinctively to the welfare of a particular person; that is why it is an ideal of loyalty. The first assumption casts the loyal agent as praiseworthy from an impartial point of view; the second presents him as the very exemplar of partial concern . . . To be loyal is to be dedicated to a particular individual's welfare and that seems to conflict with the idea that the loyal agent is idealistic or dutiful" (Pettit 163).
Explanation. Loyalty is a virtue that transcends any particular situation since, if it were bound to any given particulars, it would not be universalizable — that is, it would not be an ideal which everyone can

emulate. But, by way of contrast, anyone who is loyal to another must be concerned with the particulars of the person to whom he is loyal; but the particular situation of any individual is not universalizable. Pettit compares the paradox of loyalty to two closely related paradoxes in Christian belief and Kantian ethics: first, that no one is loved just for Christ's sake, because to be loved one must be loved for one's own sake; and second, that the friend who is loyal to another out of a sense of duty fails to display any sense of friendship.

Resolution. Identifying the source of the paradox in the difficulty of identifying motivating reasons that are at once particularized and universalizable, Pettit suggest that loyalty arises from context-bound agent-relative reasons that do not prevent universalization. We may observe, however, that the very formulation of the paradox seems to rest on an ambiguity. Loyalty, as such, is an abstract concept and is thus a universal. What we actually find in our world, however, are particular instances of loyalty (just as we perceive green things, but not "green" as such). These take the form "loyal to X," where X is a particular person, cause, *etc.* Thus, being loyal to X entails concern with the individual X, but it does not preclude our abstracting from the particular situation to the general concept.

READING

Pettit, Philip. "The Paradox of Loyalty." *American Philosophical Quarterly* 25 (1988): 163-171.

MATERIAL IMPLICATION, PARADOXES OF. These are paradoxes of propositional logic that involve conditional propositions.

Formulation. A false proposition implies anything; a true proposition is implied by anything.

Explanation. Conditional propositions in the logical formalism are supposed to represent "if-then" statements in English. But the conditional (also called material implication) is defined truth functionally in the following manner: The conditional is false if, and only if, both its antecedent (the if-clause) is true and its consequent (the then-clause) is false. Hence, if the antecedent is false the required combination for the falsity of the whole conditional cannot occur; hence, the conditional is true, regardless of the truth value of the consequent. Similarly, the conditional is true whenever its consequent is true, regardless of the truth value of the antecedent. Thus the conditional does not seem to adequately represent English if-then statements. The paradoxicality is even more pointed when we use if-then statements to express necessary or sufficient conditions. For example, the mere fact that the moon is not made of green cheese is not usually considered reason enough for us to call a green cheese moon a sufficient cause of Socrates' taking of the hemlock. Yet since "the moon is made of green cheese" is false, it materially implies "Socrates drank the hemlock."

Resolution. The present paradoxes were a major concern in the creation of modern modal and relevance logics. Many logicians, however, have defended material implication by claiming that the conditional does adequately represent the informational content of if-then statements as they are normally used since there is usually a presumption that the antecedent is true or because we are interested in what would be the case were it true. In any case, the source of the paradoxes is that, whereas (classical) propositional logic is truth functional, natural languages such as English are not. See also the Paradox OF ENTAILMENT.

READINGS

Brandom, Robert. "Semantic Paradox of Material Implication." *Notre Dame Journal of Formal Logic* 22 (1981): 129-132.

Bueno, Anibal A. "Aristotle; The Fallacy of Accident, and the Nature of Prediction: A Historical Enquiry." *Journal of the History of Philosophy* 26 (1988): 5-24.

MATHEMATICAL PARADOXES. As Edward Kasner and James R. Newman remark, "perhaps the greatest paradox of all is that there are paradoxes in mathematics" (1936). Indeed, those not actively engaged in mathematical thought — and some of those who are! — generally regard mathematics as an absolutely certain and rigorous science. Thus, it should not be the abode of paradox. Nevertheless, following Kasner and Newman, we may distinguish at least three types of paradox found in mathematics. The first type is really naught but fallacy. It usually results from some error or oversight, such as the illicit division by zero in a widely known purported proof that 1=2. Recall the proof that a live man equals a dead man, by arguing that a man who is half alive is half dead, so that 1/2 dead man = 1/2 live man, and then multiply through by 2. These "paradoxes," therefore, are not theoretically problematical, although they may be useful as a pedagogical tool if used skillfully. The second type of paradox encountered in mathematics is the counterintuitive result. Since mathematics often uses common terms in a narrow technical sense, some theorems may appear to violate common sense. A more interesting case, however, occurs when mathematics, as the science of the possible, goes beyond our limited experience and finds perfectly valid but highly counterintuitive theorems. This type of paradox is virtually ubiquitous in mathematics and almost invariably occurs, for example, when we leave our normal finite realm for the reign of the infinite, as in the BURALI-FORTI PARADOX. Finally, we sometimes find that antinomies are deduced in a mathematical theory. This, of course, means that the theory is inconsistent, which is generally disconcerting. Finding this type of paradox reveals that there is something in the formulation of the theory that was previously thought to be innocuous but which is in need of reformulation and which often leads to the development of whole new fields of mathematical research; see, for example, BERTRAND'S PARADOX. See PARADOXES OF SET THEORY. See also the BANACH-TARSKY PARADOX, DEMOCRITUS' DILEMMA, GOEDEL'S PARADOX OF UNDECIDABILITY, the PARADOX OF INTERESTING NUMBERS, the PARADOX OF IRRATIONAL NUMBERS, the PARADOX OF RULE FOLLOWING, WANG'S PARADOX, AND ZENO'S PARADOXES.

READINGS

Dumitriu, Anton. "The Logico-Mathematical Paradoxes." *History of Logic*. Vol. 4. Tunbridge Wells, Eng.: Abacus, 1977. 113-117.

Kneale, William, and Martha Kneale. The Philosophy of Mathematics After Frege." *The Development of Logic*. Oxford: Clarendon, 1962. Ch. 11.

Kasner, Edward, and James R. Newman. "Paradox Lost and Paradox Regained." *The World of Mathematics*. 4 vols. Ed. James R. Newman. New York: Simon, 1956. 1936-1955.

Northrop, Eugene P. *Riddles in Mathematics: A Book of Paradoxes*. New York: Van Nostrand, 1944.

MAXWELL'S DEMON. J. C. Maxwell conceived of the demon in 1871 as a being who could follow the movements of every molecule of a gas. **Formulation.** Suppose that a container is filled with a gas and partitioned into two chambers, A and B. A demon, who can see the movements of the molecules, opens and closes a small "door" in the partition in such a way as to allow only the swifter molecules to pass from A to B and only the slower ones to pass from B to A. The temperature of B will consequently be raised and that of A lowered without the expenditure of any work, which contradicts the second law of thermodynamics. **Explanation.** The second law of thermodynamics implies that work be expended in order to change the temperature of a closed system. The demon, however, is able to realize his unexpected results by a strategic

sorting of the molecules into the two chambers. In doing so, he merely makes use of the molecules's own velocities (he does not, for example, push any molecule from its course) and thus he purportedly does not disturb the system by introducing new sources of energy.
Resolution. According to one approach, L. Szilard found the key to this paradox by observing that the demon was changing the information that he obtained about the system into negative entropy. Thus, Leon Brillouin showed that it would be impossible for the demon even to see the individual atoms without disturbing the system. This result not only disarms the paradox but, according to Brillouin, presents us with the following important physical law: "every physical measurement requires a corresponding entropy increase, and there is a lower limit, below which the measurement becomes impossible" (168). According to another approach, however, Brillouin has completely misconceived the nature of the paradox. Joseph Wayne Smith contends that the demon is naught but a fanciful embodiment of the workings of chance. In this view, there is a certain, though perhaps small, probability that only (mostly) swift molecules would pass from A to B through a small hole in the partition, while only (mostly) slow molecules would go through in the other direction, and the paradox goes through as above.

READINGS
Brillouin, L. *Science and Information Theory.* 2nd ed. New York: Academic P, 1962. 162-182.
Smith, Joseph Wayne. *Reason, Science and Paradox: Against Received Opinion in Science and Philosophy.* London: Croom Helm, 1986. 13-16.

McTAGGART'S PARADOX. J. Ellis McTaggart was the author of an argument that seems to establish the paradoxical result that time is unreal.
Formulation. There are two separate temporal orders, the A-series that runs from the past through the present to the future and the B-series that runs from earlier to later. The A-series cannot be reduced to the B-series; and the B-series can exist only if the A-series exists. Yet since the A-series involves an inescapable contradiction, it cannot exist. Thus the B-series cannot exist either. And since neither order into which time is analyzable is real, time is unreal as well.
Explanation. The A-series cannot be reduced to the B-series because it implies a point of view with respect to which events are past, present or future while the B-series does not. The B-series can exist only if the A-series exists because it is definable in terms of the A-series. The A-series involves an unavoidable contradiction because the characteristics past,

present and future are incompatible, but every event has them all. McTaggart anticipates the immediate response that no object has all three characteristics simultaneously by rephrasing the tensed propositions as tenseless statements with an explicit temporal phrase and then adducing an infinite regress.

Resolution. Few are convinced by McTaggart's argument; its success lies in compelling so many philosophers to refute it. The dispute among the critics is chiefly over whether one can refute his argument by pointing out a few petty confusions or whether his errors at least touch upon the deepest aspects of reality. Nearly every part of McTaggart's analysis has been attacked by one critic or another, but the favorite target is the so-called "basic paradox" to the effect that the A-series involves an internal contradiction. C. D. Broad, for example, claims that the tensed structure of our language involves no contradiction at all and his claim is based on the very reason that McTaggart anticipated: no object is past, present, and future simultaneously. Furthermore, since there is no contradiction at this level of everyday speech, there is no reason to embark on McTaggart's infinite regress. In contrast to Broad, David Zeilicovici argues that the paradox does reveal deep philosophical problems in our conception of time. He rejects McTaggart's conclusion that time is unreal, however, contending that the paradox only shows that time is not a "flowing" or a becoming, but rather a static phenomenon.

READINGS

Broad, C. D. *An Examination of McTaggart's Philosophy*. 2 vols. Cambridge: Cambridge UP, 1938. Pt I.

Christensen, Ferrel. "McTaggart's Paradox and the Notion of Time." *Philosophical Quarterly* 24 (1974).

Dummett, Michael. "A Defense of McTaggert's Proof of the Unreality of Time." *Philosophical Review* 69 (1960): 417-504.

Gale, Richard M., ed. *The Philosophy of Time: A Collection of Essays*. London: Macmillan, 1968. 65-85.

Gotshalk, D. W. "McTaggart on Time." *Mind* ns 39 (1930): 26-42.

McTaggart, J. Ellis. "The Unreality of Time." *Mind* ns 17 (1908): 457-474.

— —. *The Nature of Existence*. 2 vols. Cambridge: Cambridge UP, 1927. 9-31.

Mink, Louis O. "Time, McTaggart, and Pickwickian Language." *Philosophical Quarterly* 10 (1960): 252-263.

Rankin, Kenneth. "McTaggart's Paradox: Two Parodies." *Philosophy* 56 (1981): 333-348. Roberts, Joy H. "Statements, Sentences and States of Affairs in McTaggart and in General." *Erkenntnis* 15 (1980): 73-89.

Sanford, David H. "McTaggart on Time." *Philosophy* 43 (1968): 371-378.

Schlesinger, George. *Aspects of Time*. Indianapolis: Hackett, 1980. Ch. 2.

Zeilicovici, David. "A (Dis)solution of McTaggart's Paradox." *Ratio* 28 (1986): 175-195.

MEEHL'S METHODOLOGICAL PARADOX. This is a puzzle involving statistics in the social sciences.

Formulation. "In the physical sciences, the usual result of an improvement in experimental design, instrumentation, or numerical mass of data, is to increase the difficulty of the 'observational hurdle' which the physical theory of interest must successfully surmount; whereas, in psychology and some of the allied behavior sciences, the usual effect of such improvement in experimental precision is to provide an easier hurdle for the theory to surmount" (Meehl 103).

Explanation. Statistical reasoning in science is based on the formulation of a null hypothesis which the investigation tries to refute. The results of a statistical study are subject to errors in measurement and errors of sampling and the statistician's job is to decide whether these errors are sufficiently small for accepting the results as significant. Rejection of the null hypothesis when it is true is called a Type I error; retention of the null hypothesis when it is false is called a Type II error. These two types of error are inversely related. Further, if p is the probability of a Type II error, $1-p$ is called the power of the test. By improving the experimental design, the power is increased. The social sciences tend to use directional hypotheses, as opposed to point hypotheses, with the implication that, if we obtain perfect power (false null hypotheses will always be detected), our hypothesis will be correct at least half the time. This is because even if there is no relation between the hypothesis and the sampling, it will be correct half the time just by chance — if there is a relation, it will be correct more often. Hence, by increasing the power to perfection, we have an a priori lower bound of 1/2 that the test will confirm our hypothesis (reject the null hypothesis). Therefore, by improving the experimental design, we make it as likely to confirm as it is to falsify an hypothesis, even if that hypothesis is completely without merit.

Resolution. According to Meehl, the paradox results from the fact that the social sciences are not precise enough to make point predictions. Although the paradox is inevitable, Meehl also claims that the situation is made even worse by certain social forces or intellectual habits among researchers, one of which is the inadequate appreciation of the present paradox.

READING
Meehl, Paul E. "Theory-Testing in Psychology and Physics: A Methodological Paradox." *Philosophy of Science* 34 (1967): 103-115.

MENO'S PARADOX. This epistemic paradox is generally used as an erudite allusion for those who want to expand on the topic of knowledge. See also PLATONIC PARADOX and SOCRATIC PARADOX.
Formulation. How can one inquire into what he does not know? What will be the topic of investigation? And if one did find what he wants, how might he know that this is the matter which he did not know?
Explanation. One cannot search for what he knows or for what he does not know. He cannot look for what he knows, because he already knows it; one who already possesses something cannot come into possession of it. And he cannot search for what he does not know, because he does not know what to look for (*Meno* 80e).
Resolution. This is originally a debater's puzzle that Socrates treats with scorn in the *Euthydemus*, (275d-278b). Yet in the *Meno* Plato treats it as a genuine quandary to be solved by his theory of knowledge as recollection. There seems to be no great difficulty, however, because an inquirer does know part of the topic he is investigating and something about the form of acceptable answers to the kinds of questions he has, so he knows something of where to start looking and in a general way what he needs to discover to satisfy his enquiry. That the inquirer can ask a meaningful question seems to testify to the correctness of this response. Nevertheless, some commentators have asserted that the present paradox expresses a genuine problem. Rosemary Desjardins, for example, assimilates it to the problem of the "hermeneutical circle": in order to know the whole one must first piece the parts together; but one cannot even recognize the parts as parts unless one already knows the whole.

READINGS
Bluck, R. S. *Plato's Meno.* Cambridge: Cambridge UP, 1961. 8-17.
Briskman, Larry. "Articulating Our Ignorance: Hopeful Skepticism and the Meno Paradox." *Et Cetera* 42 (1985): 201-227.
Desjardins, Rosemary. "Knowledge and Virtue: Paradox in Plato's *Meno*." *Review of Metaphysics* 39 (1985): 261-281.
Grene, Marjorie. "The Legacy of the *Meno*." *The Knower and the Known.* New York: Basic Books, 1966. Ch 1.
Polanyi, Michael. *The Tacit Dimension.* Garden City, NY: Doubleday, 1966. Ch. 1.
Popper, Karl. "On the Sources of Knowledge and of Ignorance." *Conjectures and Refutations.* New York: Basic Books, 1962. 3-30.

Sanford, David H. "McTaggart on Time." *Philosophy* 43 (1968): 371-378.
Thompson, E. Seymour. *The Meno of Plato.* 1901. Garland Press, NY:
    Garland P 1980.
Welbourne, Michael. "Meno's Paradox." *Philosophy* 61 (1986): 229-243.

MERE ADDITION PARADOX, THE. Related to the PARADOX OF
FUTURE INDIVIDUALS, this paradox was adduced by Derek Parfit.
Formulation. Let A be a population all of whose individuals have a very
high quality of life. Let B be A plus a group of individuals whose quality
of life is less than that in A, but still moderately high; further, suppose the
newcomers do not affect the quality of life of the original group. Finally,
let C result from B by the worse-off individuals gaining more than the
better-off individuals lose. Then, B is not worse than A and C is better
than A. Nevertheless, C is worse than A and our beliefs about the relative
values of these societies are inconsistent.
Explanation. Observe that B results from A by the mere addition of a
group of individuals with a moderately high quality of life. If B were
worse than A, then it would be better for this group not to have existed;
but this would be clearly counter to all our intuitions about the value of
this group. Hence, B must be no worse than A. Furthermore, C results
from B by a kind of leveling action; the final result, however, is not a
mere average of those who are better-off with those who are worse-off,
but rather the latter make substantial gains while the former suffer relatively
minor losses. Hence, we would conclude that C is better than B. But if C
is better than B, which is no worse than A, then C certainly cannot be
worse than A. The following argument, however, shows that C is worse
than A. In relation to A, C comes about by increasing the population and
lowering the quality of life (a little). The same process can be iterated
until we arrive at an enormous population living in abject misery — call
it M. If C is no worse than A, then the same can be said about each step
in the process. Thus, eventually we would conclude that M is no worse
than A, which is absurd. Therefore, C must be worse than A, which
contradicts our previous result.
Resolution. Larry S. Temkin denies the validity of the sub-argument
purporting to show that C is worse than A by denying the transitivity of
"is no worse than" for the concept in question of populations with different
levels of quality of life. This can happen because not all pairs of relevant
populations may be comparable. Even the inference

        C is better than B.

B is no worse than A.
Therefore, C is no worse than A.

may be invalid, if we cannot compare C and A. Nevertheless, even though we may have trouble deciding which society is better, it is hard to see why any two of them would be in principle incomparable. Rather, the plausibility of the paradox depends on the assumption that quality of life can be quantified in a straightforward manner; once this assumption is disallowed, however, it is not clear whether the paradox can be generated.

READINGS

Parfit, Derek. "Future Generations: Further Problems." *Philosophy and Public Affairs* 11 (1982): 113-172.
Temkin, Larry S. "Intransitivity and the Mere Addition Paradox." *Philosophy and Public Affairs* 16 (1987): 138-187.

METAPHYSICAL PARADOXES. Metaphysics attempts to comprehend being as a whole and in its essence through the systematic deployment of concepts, and thereby generates a rich vein of paradox.. Metaphysical paradoxes include BRADLEY'S PARADOX OF RELATIONS, GEACH'S PARADOX OF 1,001 CATS, PARADOXES OF OMNIPOTENCE, PARADOXES OF OMNISCIENCE, HUME'S PROBLEM OF INDUCTION, KANT'S ANTINOMIES, MCTAGGART'S PARADOX, the PARADOX OF PRIME MATTER, RECENT AND TRADITIONAL SORITES, the SHIP OF THESEUS, the SOLIPSISTIC PARADOX, ZENO'S PARADOXES and many others.

MILLET SEED, THE. One of Zeno's paradoxes, mentioned by Aristotle at *Physics* 250a19-21 and by Simplicius at *In Physica* 1108, 18-28, the Millet Seed is a falsidical paradox or even a pseudo-paradox.

Formulation. If a gross of millet seeds makes a noise when it falls, a single millet seed will make a proportionately smaller sound when it falls.

Explanation. Motivated by an Eleatic prejudice against perception, Zeno is apparently suggesting that if our senses fail us in the case of the fainter sound, we should think twice about believing what our senses register in the case of the louder sound.

Resolution. Zeno's argument presumes that we should hear disturbances in the air as sounds no matter how slight they are, but there is no special difficulty in the circumstance that our auditory powers are limited in this particular manner. See ZENO'S PARADOXES.

MIND-BODY PROBLEM, THE. Daniel Cohen suggests presenting Keith Campbell's treatment of the mind-body problem as a paradox.

Formulation. There are four propositions that express common beliefs or intuitions, but which are not mutually consistent. First, the mind is immaterial. Second, the body is material. Third, the material and the immaterial cannot interact causally. And fourth, the mind and the body do interact causally.

Explanation. This is just the classic mind-body problem set out as a paradox. The mind, as Descartes has it, is not spatially extended, but the body is. It appears that an extended substance cannot interact causally with a unextended substance, but thoughts and physical objects do seem to influence each other in perception and the will. Therefore, one of the four propositions has to go.

Resolution. The four straightforward responses each reject one of the four propositions. Spinoza, for example, denies the first proposition by claiming that the mind is ultimately immaterial. Berkeley rejects that the body is material, while Descartes denies that the material and the immaterial cannot interact causally. Finally, Malbranche claims that the mind and the body do not interact causally. An entirely different approach is to deny that the mind-body distinction can be drawn in the first place.

READINGS

Campbell, Keith. *Body and Mind.* New York: Doubleday, 1970.
Cohen, Daniel. "Putting Paradoxes into Pedagogical Use in Philosophy."
    Teaching Philosophy 8 (1985): 309-317.

MINIAC. This paradox, modelled on PRIOR'S FAMILY OF PARADOXES, was presented by Thomas Storer.

Formulation. To build the world's smallest electronic brain, MINIAC, write the words 'YES' and 'NO' on two pieces of paper and glue one to each side of a penny. To operate the machine, ask MINIAC a question, flip the coin, and record the answer; then ask MINIAC if its answer to the present question will have the same truth value as its previous answer and flip the coin again. The answer to the second question will determine the correct answer to the first question. Storer adds that the electronic nature of MINIAC is assured by the fact that the copper atom has two free electrons in the outer shell.

Explanation. MINIAC'S logical gearwork can be exhibited in the following table:

Answer to First Question	YES				NO			
Answer to Second Question	YES		NO		YES		NO	
Truth Value of Second Question	t	f	t	f	t	f	t	f
Truth Value of First Question	t	t	f	f	t	t	f	f
Final Answer to First Question	YES		NO		NO		YES	

The first three lines of the table merely exhibit the various possible combinations. The fourth line is calculated from lines two and three in the following manner: if MINIAC answered that the truth values are the same (YES) and it "spoke" truly, then both answers have the same truth value; but if MINIAC answered YES and it spoke falsely, then the answers have opposite truth values; if MINIAC answered that the truth values are not the same (NO) and it spoke truly, then the answers have opposite truth values; finally, if MINIAC answered NO and it spoke falsely, the answers have the same truth value. Comparing lines two and four of the table, we see that MINIAC answers YES to the second question when, and only when, the truth value of the first question is true (be that answer either YES or NO); further, MINIAC answers NO to the second question when, and only when, the truth value of the first question (again, be that answer either YES or NO) is false. The last line gives the final answer by comparing lines one and four. J.L. Mackie concludes that "what is puzzling about this is that we appear to get logically guaranteed answers to all yes-no questions by a method which common sense tells us has no reliability at all" (280-281).

Resolution. Perhaps the easiest way to see the fallacy involved is for the reader, if he be willing, to play the part of the world's smallest electronic brain. We now ask you if Meei-Ling — a person unknown to you— is nine years old. Playing the odds, perhaps, you answer NO. Now we ask you if the truth value of the present question is the same as that of the previous question. Just to be contrary, you answer YES. Thus, from the table given above, your final answer is that Meei-Ling is not nine years old. As it turns out, however, she is indeed nine years old. What went wrong? Observe that your final answer was false. Was your second answer true or false? If it were true, it would have to have the same truth value as your first answer; that is, it would be false. But, if it were false, it would have to have the opposite truth value as your first answer; that is it would be true. Thus, your second answer is true if, and only if, it is false. Thus, it is a LIAR-type sentence. (See Mackie for an analysis of all the possible combinations of answers.) Indeed, if we recall how the table was constructed, we see that the fourth line was calculated from the previous two lines, both of which have to do with the second question. This process imputes a truth value to the first question independently of the state of affairs in the external world through the self-reference present in the second question. The process is thus typical of Liar-type paradoxes.

READINGS

Mackie, J. L. *Truth, Probability and Paradox: Studies in Philosophical Logic*. Oxford: Clarendon, 1973. 281-283.
Storer, Thomas. "Miniac." *Analysis* 22.6 (1962): 151-152.

MODAL LIAR, THE. For this formulation of the LIAR in modal logic, see the POSSIBLE LIAR.

MOORE'S PARADOX. This paradox about knowledge and belief was discussed extensively by G. E. Moore.

Formulation. "I went to the pictures last Tuesday, but I don't believe that I did" (Moore, *Reply* 543).

Explanation. The paradox does not involve a contradiction since it is possible to imagine circumstances in which someone might naturally utter sentences like the one above. Thus, someone might sheepishly admit to his friend: "I know that this rabbit's foot isn't magical, but I really don't believe it's not." Nevertheless, sentences of this sort seem to involve us in a puzzle because the speaker purports to disbelieve what he knows to be true.

Resolution. Moore himself responds that when the aforementioned kind of statements are asserted, there is a strong presumption that the speaker does know the facts of the matter and is telling the truth. If either of these assumptions should not hold, however, the paradox vanishes. Another approach to the paradox is to claim that the assertion is not completely expressed in the statement itself, but that context, background knowledge, or shared presuppositions must also be taken into account. John Searle's theory of speech acts, for example, holds that speaking is governed by a set of implicit rules, some of which are broken by Moore's troublesome statement. Approaches of this type tend to find a real contradiction in the larger context posited. The rabbit's foot example, however, does not seem to be fully addressed by either of these approaches; rather, it seems more akin to the PARADOX OF SELF-DECEPTION. Charles E. Caton argues that there may be epistemic quantifiers of different strengths. In this way, the epistemic strength of an assertion would be greater than that of a belief statement; thus, the assertion of a statement and the belief of its negation would not be countenanced as a well-formed proposition.

READINGS

Armstrong, D. M. "Does Knowledge Entail Belief?" *Proceedings of the Aristotelian Society* 70 (1969-70). 21-36.

Black, Max. "Saying and Disbelieving." *Analysis* 13.2 (1952). 25-33.

Caton, Charles E. "Moore's Paradox, Sincerity Conditions, and Epistemic Qualification." *On Being and Saying: Essays for Richard Cartwright.* Ed. Judith Jarvis Thompson. Cambridge: MIT P, 1987. 133-150.

Deutcher, M. "A Note on Saying and Disbelieving." *Analysis* 25.3 (1965). 53-57.

——. "Bonney on Saying and Disbelieving." *Analysis* 27.6 (1967). 184-186.

Gombay, Andre. "Some Paradoxes of Counterprivacy." *Philosophy* 63 (1988): 191-210.

Harnish, Robert M. "Searle and the Logic of Moore's Paradox." *International Logic Review* 11 (1980): 72-76.

Hintikka, J. *Knowledge and Belief.* Ithaca: Cornell UP, 1962. 64.

Linsky, Bernard. "Factives, Blindspots and Some Paradoxes." *Analysis* 46.1 (1986): 10-15.

Martinich, A. P. "Conversational Maxims and Some Philosophical Problems." *Philosophical Quarterly* 30 (1980): 215-228.

Moore, G. E. "A Reply to My Critics." *The Philosophy of G. E. Moore.* Ed. P. A. Schilpp. Evanston: Northwestern UP, 1942. 540-543, 660-677.

——. "Russell's 'Theory of Descriptions'." *The Philosophy of Bertrand Russell*. Ed. P. A Schilpp. Evanston: Northwestern UP. 1944. 205-206.
White, A. R. *Modal Thinking*. Ithaca: Cornell UP, 1975. 172.
Williams, J. N. "Moore's Paradox: One or Two." *Analysis* 39.3 (1979): 141-142.

MORNING STAR PARADOX, THE. W. V. O. Quine adduced this paradox in quantified modal logic (with identity).
Formulation. The Morning Star and the Evening Star are naught but the planet Venus, but they are not necessarily identical for if our solar system had evolved differently Mercury, for example, could have always appeared in the morning and Venus always at night. Thus, "the claim can be made that the Morning Star has a property or attribute not possessed by the Evening Star, namely the property of being necessarily identical with the Morning Star. This result leads to the conclusion that the Morning Star is a different individual from the Evening Star, since otherwise it would have exactly the same properties. But of course there is good empirical evidence that the Evening Star and the Morning Star are one and the same individual, known as the planet Venus. Hence, the paradox" (Fitch 273-274).
Explanation. As indicated above, it is not logically necessary that the Morning Star be identical to the Evening Star. The Morning Star is, however, necessarily identical to the Morning Star. Hence, the Morning Star has a property that the Evening Star does not have; the two can thus be distinguished by using this property, so that the Morning Star is not the same object as the Evening Star.
Resolution. Quine contends that this paradoxical result reveals that quantification over modal contexts is an inherently irrational procedure when identity is involved. Hence, he proposes to replace identity in modal contexts by a weaker "congruence" relation. Frederic B. Fitch (following Raymond Smullyan) argues that there are at least two ways of avoiding the paradox. First, 'Morning Star' and 'Evening Star' may be regarded as proper names of the same individual; hence, it would indeed be necessarily true that the Evening Star is identical with the Morning Star. Second, 'the Morning Star' and 'the Evening Star' may be regarded as definite descriptions according to Bertrand Russell's definition; in this case, it is not necessary that the Morning Star be identical with the Morning Star (since that would imply that the Morning Star exists necessarily). Thus, in either case, Quine's argument would fail. One of the pioneers of

quantified modal logic, Ruth Barcan Marcus, opts for the first alternative in her response to Quine. Note that the present paradox was historically important in that it seemed to become a paradigm case of the kind of problems that arose elsewhere in quantified intensional logics, such as deontic and epistemic logic.

READINGS

Copi, Irving M., and James A. Gould, ed. *Contemporary Readings in Logical Theory.* New York: Macmillan, 1967.

Fitch, Frederic B. "The Problem of the Morning Star and the Evening Star." In Irving M. Copi and James A. Gould, ed., *Contemporary Readings in Logical Theory.* 273-278.

Kanger, Stig. "The Morning Star Paradox." *Theoria* 23 (1957): 1-11.

Marcus, Ruth Barcan. "Modalities and Intensional Languages." In Irving M. Copi and James A. Gould, ed., *Contemporary Readings in Logical Theory.* 278-293.

Quine, W. V. O. "The Problem of Interpreting Modal Logic." In Irving M. Copi and James A. Gould, ed., *Contemporary Readings in Logical Theory.* 267-273.

— —. "Reply to Professor Marcus." In Irving M. Copi and James A. Gould, eds. *Contemporary Readings in Logical Theory.* 293-299.

MOVING BLOCKS, THE. The fourth and last of Zeno's arguments against motion, this paradox is also called the Stadium.

Formulation. Our source for this paradox is Aristotle's *Physics*, 239b33-240a17. "The fourth argument is that concerning the two rows of bodies, each set being composed of an equal number of bodies of equal size, passing each other on a race-course as they proceed with equal velocity in opposite directions, the one row originally occupying the space between the goal and the middle point of the course and the other that between the middle point and the starting-post. This, he [Zeno] thinks, involves the conclusion that half a given time is equal to double that time."

Explanation. Aristotle's telegraphic style makes the paradox difficult to decipher. Nevertheless, the basic structure of the action in the paradox is easily seen. Body A moves its own length (say, a unit) to the right, while Body B , equal in length and vertically aligned with Body A, moves its own length to the left (see figure).

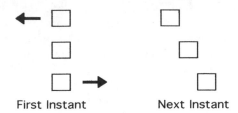

First Instant   Next Instant

Relative to the stationary ground, Body B has moved a unit in a given amount of time t. Relative to Body A, however, Body B has moved a distance of two units in the same time t and, therefore, it has moved a single unit in time $t/2$. Since both t and $t/2$ are the times that Body B took to move a single unit of distance, we have that $t = t/2$; that is, "half a given time is equal to double that time."

Resolution. The fallacy involved in this paradox is, at first sight, all too obvious. As Aristotle explains, "The fallacy of the reasoning lies in the assumption that a body occupies an equal time in passing with equal velocity a body that is in motion and a body of equal size that is at rest." There is, however, an alternative interpretation first proposed by Paul Tannery, according whom, the time t is an atomic quantum of time. The argument then proves that Body B, relative to Body A, would traverse the unit length (perhaps itself an atomic quantum) in one-half the atomic quantum of time, thereby dividing a supposed indivisible. Although Tannery's interpretation makes the paradox veridical instead of ridiculous, Gregory Vlastos rejects it on the grounds that it has not been documented in historical sources. See ZENO'S PARADOXES.

READINGS

Aristotle, *Physics* VI, IX.

Tannery, Paul. "Le Concept Scientifique de Continu: Zénon d'Élée et George Cantor." Revue *Philosophique de la France et de l'Éstranger* 20 (1885): 385-410.

Vlastos, Gregory. "Zeno of Elea." *The Encyclopedia of Philosophy*. Ed. Paul Edwards. New York: Macmillan,1967. Vol. 8, 375.

M-VARIANTS OF THE LOGICAL PARADOXES. One of the most common strategies for disarming the logical paradoxes is to try to show that the paradoxical sentence is somehow meaningless. This is especially true of Liar-like and other semantical paradoxes. Take the straightforward version of the LIAR, for example,

(1)   This sentence is false.

The claim is that sentence (1) fails to express a proposition and, thus, is meaningless. The M-variant (the term is due to J. L. Mackie) of the paradox, however, accepts the challenge of the charge of meaninglessness and turns it to account in adducing a new paradox:

(2)   This sentence is false or meaningless.

If (2) is true, then what it says is the case. Hence, (2) is either false or meaningless (in either case it is not true). In contrast, if (2) is false, then what it asserts is not the case and, consequently, it is true. Similarly, if (2) is meaningless, then what it asserts is again the case (*i.e.*, that it is meaningless) and thus it is again true. Therefore, (2) is true if, and only if, it is either false or meaningless. This result, although a bit more cumbersome than the original version, is just as paradoxical as the original. "Hierarchy' approaches (see the LIAR and RUSSELL'S PARADOX) to the resolution of the paradoxes, however, seem to be immune to M-variants because "meaningless" is a semantical concept and would thus receive a rank, just as "true" and "false" do. See the PARADOX OF THE NON-COMMUNICATOR.

READINGS
Mackie, J. L. *Truth, Probability and Paradox: Studies in Philosophical Logic.* Oxford: Clarendon, 1973. 242-247, 290-295.
— —, and J. J. C. Smart. "A Variant of the 'Heterological' Paradox." *Analysis* 13.3 (1953):   61-66.

NAMING, THE PARADOX OF. Proposed by Saul Kripke, this paradox is also called Kripke's Pierre.
Formulation. Pierre, a monolinguistical French speaker who has never left France, has heard enough about London to agree that *Londres est jolie.* On this basis, we are inclined to say:

(1)   Pierre believes that London is pretty.

Pierre's circumstances change and he ends up living in a city, inhabited by people speaking a foreign language, which he learns through day-to-day interaction with those people. Pierre has no opportunity to travel from the neighborhood in which he finds himself, but finds that in the native language the city is called "London." The part of the city where

Pierre lives is dirty and run down, and he forms the opinion that London is not pretty. We are inclined to say:

(2)   Pierre believes that London is not pretty.

Pierre never associates London with the city he knows as Londres, and is still prepared to agree with the statement, *Londres est jolie.* Thus, not only does Pierre hold inconsistent beliefs but, in trying to describe Pierre's beliefs, we are forced into a contradiction.

Explanation. Given Pierre's behavior as a French speaker, we are forced to conclude that he believes that the city of London is pretty. Nevertheless, given his behavior as an English speaker, we are forced to conclude the exact opposite. Thus, Pierre's beliefs seem to be inconsistent. Yet it seems unfair to Pierre to brand his beliefs as inconsistent since he lacks the knowledge that 'London' and 'Londres' refer to the same object. The challenge is to give a rational account of Pierre's beliefs which respects our intuitions about the facts involved in the story.

Resolution. We should observe that the part of the problem that ascribes an inconsistency to Pierre's beliefs is similar to many paradoxes in modal, deontic, and epistemic logic, in which the substitution of identity fails in contexts governed by an intensional operator. An interesting aspect of the wider part of the problem is that it involves a translation from one language to another. Philosophical reflection on the nature of meaning and truth has led to the concept of a proposition as the meaning of a sentence partially in response to the question of how two sentences in different languages can have the same meaning: they are supposed to express the same proposition. Kripke's Pierre, however, seems to show that, at least in intensional contexts, this propositional analysis of meaning is inadequate.

READINGS

Biro, John. "What's In a Belief?" *Logique et Analyse* 107 (1984): 267-282.

Elugardo, Reinaldo. "Lewis's Puzzle about Singular Belief-Attribution." *Philosophia* 17 (1987): 461-476.

Kripke, Saul. "A Puzzle About Belief." *Meaning and Use.* Ed. Abvishai Margalit. Dordrecht: Reidel, 1979. 239-283.

Kvart, Igal. Kripke's Belief Puzzle." *Philosophy Research Archives* 9 (1984): 369-412.   Lewis, David. What Puzzling Pierre Doesn't Believe." *Australasian Journal of Philosophy* 59 (1981): 283-289.

Lycan, William G. "The Paradox of Naming." *Analytic Philosophy in Comparative Perspective.* Ed. B. K. Matilal and J. L. Shaw. Dordrecht: Reidel, 1985. 81-102.

NATURAL RIGHTS, PARADOX OF. This is a paradox in John Locke's Theory of Natural rights.
Formulation. In Jeffrie G. Murphy's formulation, ". . . the prelegal infliction of harm for felt wrongs is morally wrong. Thus we need the rule of law in order to *acquire* the right to punish" (270).
Explanation. According to Locke's political theory, the individual abrogates his natural right to punish those who wrong him and establishes a civil government that will, among other things, fulfill this function. Murphy, however, argues that the notion of a natural right to punish is paradoxical because it involves inflicting harm on another. But deliberately inflicting harm on another, even in response to harm received, is morally wrong and one cannot have a natural right to do what is morally wrong. Hence, it is only after civil government has been created and the rule of law established that the individual acquires the right of punishment (which is then exercised through the agency of the civil government).
Resolution. According to Murphy, the paradox is resolved by Kant's political theory, for whom the individual has no prelegal natural right to punish wrongdoers, but has a natural need to do so. By establishing a civil government and acquiring the legal right of extracting punishment through the agency of the government, the individual's need is fulfilled and his freedom is expanded, because he can now do what would not have been permissible in the state of nature.

READING
Murphy, Jeffrie G. "A Paradox in Locke's Theory of Natural Rights." *Dialogue* 8 (1969): 257-271.

NATURAL SCIENCE, PARADOXES IN. The physical sciences have always been a source of paradox because the rational, detailed study of physical nature has often resulted in conceptions that not only seem truly marvelous to the layman but also conflict sharply with our pre-scientific or non-scientific or extra-scientific conceptions of the world about us. COPERNICUS' PARADOX is of this sort. Recent advances in science, however, have given rise to a plethora of paradoxes that, in the aggregate, seem to challenge the presupposition of the rationality of physical nature (that is, that it can be comprehended by rational means). This is especially true of the paradoxes arising from relativity theory and quantum theory. See the BOOTS PARADOX, the CLOCK PARADOX, COPERNICUS' PARADOX, the EINSTEIN-PODOLSKY-ROSEN PARADOX, GIBBS' PARADOX, THE HYDROSTATIC PARADOX, LOSCHMIDT'S PARADOX, MAXWELL'S DEMON, OLBER'S PARADOX, PHILOTAS'

PARADOX, the POTENTIAL ENERGY BARRIER PARADOX, the PRECESSION OF THE EQUINOXES PARADOX, SCHRÖEDINGER'S CAT, the SHADOW PARADOX, the PARADOXES OF TIME TRAVEL, the TWIN PARADOX, ZENO'S PARADOXES and ZERMELO'S PARADOX.

READINGS

Kak, Subash. *The Nature of Physical Reality.* New York: Lang, 1986.

Kuhn, Thomas S. *The Structure of Scientific Revolutions.* 2nd ed. rev. Chicago: 1970.

Nathan, Amos. "False Expectations." *Philosophy of Science* 51 (1984): 128-136.

Rorlich, Fritz. *From Paradox to Reality: Our New Concepts of the Physical World.* Cambridge: Cambridge UP, 1987.

Smith, Joseph Wayne. *Reason, Science and Paradox: Against Received Opinion in Science and Philosophy.* London: Croom Helm, 1986.

Whitehead, Alfred North. *Science and the Modern World.* New York: Macmillan, 1925.

Wohlmuth, Paul C. "Nested Realities and Human Consciousness: The Paradoxical Expression of Evolutionary Processes." *World Futures* 25.3-4 (1988): 199-235.

NEGATION, PARADOX OF. A generalization of the Paradox of Nonexistent Objects, this paradox is termed "scandalous" by Eric Toms. **Formulation.** The proposition

Unicorns do not exist.

predicates nonexistence of unicorns and, thus, is contradictory.

Explanation. The result is paradoxical because it would seem that one cannot predicate anything of that which does not exist. In fact, all talk about nonexistent objects seems paradoxical. Toms maintains that all theories of negation are based on one or other of the following four conceptions:

(1)   the negation of a proposition (or possibility)
(2)   opposition
(3)   difference
(4)   nonexistence.

He then goes on to argue that the first three of these conceptions do not provide an adequate theory of negation and, hence, it is necessary to resort to nonexistence in order to explain negation. In consequence, "every negative proposition and every negative fact is self-contradictory" (96). **Resolution.** There have been many attempts to give an intuitively satisfactory characterization of negation, including Bertrand Russell's theory of descriptions and Terence Parson's resurrection of Meinongian nonexistent objects. If Toms is correct, however, in affirming that only nonexistence truly explains negation, the paradox would be inevitable. Thus the adherent of one of the other conceptions of negation would have to show that it does not involve the circularity or infinite regress that Toms argues that it exhibits. Alternatively, one could argue that negation is a fundamental mode of thought that is intuitively clear and, therefore, not in need of further explanation. Nonexistence could then be explicated in terms of negation.

READINGS

Toms, Eric. *Being, Negation and Logic.* Oxford: Blackwell, 1962
Parsons, Terence. *Nonexistent Objects.* New Haven: Yale UP, 1980.

NEWCOMB'S PARADOX. This is a PARADOX OF GAME THEORY related to the PRISONER'S DILEMMA.

Formulation. An agent is to make a choice between receiving the contents of an opaque box and the contents of both the opaque box and a transparent box. He can see that there is $1,000 in the transparent box. The content of the opaque box is determined by an extraordinarily able predictor (he has yet to err in similar situations!) in the following manner: if he predicts that the agent will take just the opaque box, he puts $1,000,000 in it; if, however, he predicts that the agent will opt for both boxes, he leaves the opaque box empty. How should the agent choose?

Explanation. On the one hand, it seems evident that the agent's choice has been accurately predicted by the predictor and, hence, he should choose the opaque box, thereby receiving the $1,000,000. On the other hand, the agent's choice cannot determine the predictor's prior action (as it seems to do on the previous account) and, hence, the agent should choose both boxes, thereby guaranteeing at least the $1,000 and possibly resulting in $1,001.000.

Resolution. G. Schlesinger, for example, argues that there are only two possibilities: the predictor predicts correctly that the agent will choose the opaque box or he predicts correctly that the agent will choose both boxes. Thus, choosing the opaque box will be the rational choice. Don Locke, however, contends that this analysis depends on the infallibility of the predictor. Since this infallibility has not been established, the argument fails. Locke suggests that if a third party had peeked into the opaque box and could advise the agent, his advice — regardless of the contents of the opaque box — would be to take both: if the opaque box contained $1,000,000 the agent would gain the maximum payoff (and the predictor would get his first setback); if the box were empty, the agent would get $1,000 (rather than nothing). André Gallois, however, argues that the invalidity of Locke's argument can be shown by modifying the situation so that the predictor places the money (or not) in the opaque box only after the agent makes his choice; this also removes the suggestion that the agent's choice causes the prior action of the predictor. We may observe here that Newcomb's Paradox is a rich philosophical puzzle, linked as it is to such perennial problems as those of counterfactuals and divine omniscience.

READINGS

Ben-Menahem, Yemina. "Newcomb's Paradox and Compatibilism." *Erkenntnis* 25 (1986): 197-220.

Bar-Hillel, M., and A. Margalit. "Newcomb's Paradox Revisited." *British Journal for the Philosophy of Science* 23 (1972): 295-304.

Cargile, J. "Newcomb's Paradox." *British Journal for the Philosophy of Science* 26 (1975): 234-239.

Craig, William Lane. "Divine Foreknowledge and Newcomb's Paradox." *Philosophia* [Israel] 17 (1987): 331-50.

Eells, Ellery. "Newcomb's Many Solutions." *Theory and Decision* 16 (1984): 59-106.

Gallois, André. "How Not to Make a Newcomb Choice." *Analysis* 39.1 (1979): 49-53.

Horgan, Terence. "Counterfactuals and Newcomb's Problem." *The Journal of Philosophy* 78 (1981): 331-356.

Horne, James R. "Newcomb's Problem as a Theistic Problem." *International Journal for Philosophy of Religion* 14 (1983): 217-223.

Kavka, Gregory S. "What Is Newcomb's Problem About?" *American Philosophical Quarterly* 17 (1980): 272.

Levi, I. "Newcomb's Many Problems." *Theory and Decision* 6 (1975): 161-175.

Locke, Don. "How to Make a Newcomb Choice." *Analysis* 38.1 (1978): 17-23.

Mackie, J. L. "Newcomb's Paradox and the Direction of Causation." *Canadian Journal of Philosophy* 7 (1977): 213-224.

Nozick, R. "Newcomb's Problem and Two Principles of Choice." *Essays in Honor of Carl G. Hempel.* Ed. N. Rescher. Dordrecht: Reidel, 1969. 114-146.

Schlesinger, G. "The Unpredictability of Free Choices." *British Journal for the Philosophy of Science* 25 (1974): 209-221.

Sasieni, Maurice. "Newcomb's Paradox." *Theory and Decision* 16 (1984): 217-223.

Smith, Joseph Wayne. *Reason, Science and Paradox: Against Received Opinion in Science and Philosophy.* London: Croom Helm, 1986. Ch. 8.

Sorensen, Roy A. "Newcomb's Problem: Recalculations for the One-Boxer." *Theory and Decision* 15 (1983): 399-404.

NEW MEMBERS, THE PARADOX OF. Political wisdom has it that an effective way of reducing the voting power of a dominant member in a weighted body of voters is to increase the size of the body. It turns out, however, that the addition of one or several new members may actually increase the voting power of some of the old members. Amnon Rapoport and Ariel Cohen analyze computational results that show that, although the paradox is indeed inevitable in certain situations, it has little practical significance for groups that have five or more members. The details, involving indices of voting power in game theory, are too excessively technical to be recounted here.

READINGS

Raanan, J. "The Inevitability of the Paradox of New Members." *Technical Report No. 311.* School of Operations Research and Industrial Engineering, Cornell U, 1976.

Rapoport, Amnon, and Ariel Cohen. "Expected Frequency and Mean Size of the Paradox of New Members." *Theory and Decision* 17 (1984): 29-46.

NEW RIDDLE OF INDUCTION, THE. See GOODMAN'S PARADOXES OF CONFIRMATION.

NICHOLAS OF CUZA'S COINCIDENCE OF OPPOSITES. In *De Docta Ignorantia*, Nicholas of Cuza (1401-1464) applies to God the paradoxical logic of the coincidence of opposites (*coincidentia oppositorum*). Since HERACITUS' PARADOXICAL APHORISMS, thinkers have attributed antithetical attributes to God in an attempt to wrap the human mind around divine ineffability: He is X and not X at one and the same time and in one and the same respect, at once Y and not Y, both Z and not Z. The paradox, however, is not always so boldly stated. For example, God is often supposed to be both infinitely just and infinitely merciful. The joint assumption of these predicates is nevertheless paradoxical because the former implies that He will punish wrongdoers, while the latter implies that He will forgive them. Although this result is not, strictly speaking, a logical contradiction, it does highlight man's inability to comprehend God. In fact, paradoxical discourse about God is frequently designed to drive home the lesson of the Voice from the Whirlwind in Job, namely, that the Lord moves in mysterious ways, that God is inscrutable to humankind. Compare VIA NEGATIVA.

NIRVANA, THE PARADOX OF. There are at least two separate paradoxes in Buddhist thought about nirvana. The first asserts that the very concept of nirvana is paradoxical because it entails both the ultimate annihilation of the individual and individual fulfillment in eternal life. Robert Slater adduces two other related paradoxes and affirms that nirvana "is a paradox set within a context of paradox" (4). The second Paradox of Nirvana, which will be discussed here, is related to the HEDONISTIC PARADOX.

Formulation. "Those who pursue or desire nirvana, or desirelessness, will never (logically), or are least likely to (practically), get it" (Herman, 5).

Explanation. Nirvana is not the kind of thing that one just happens upon or which just happens to one, but rather a state that requires quite a bit of effort on the part of anyone who is to achieve it and, thus, we must want to achieve it in order to do those things necessary for its acquisition. Hence, we can never achieve nirvana, a state of complete desirelessness, because in order to obtain it we must desire to do so. Stated differently, we cannot make nirvana the end of our actions because that would defeat the very purpose of our undertaking; but without making nirvana the end of our actions, we cannot do what is necessary to achieve it.

Resolution. The Buddhist solution to the paradox is to recognize that there is nothing that one can do in order to escape the paradox and thus the devotee "lets go" of the desired goal. Upon doing so, nirvana is obtained. Observe, however, that nirvana is not just a "laid back" attitude in the face of a practical conundrum: it is founded in some sense on the insight gained from the struggle to come to terms with the paradox. As Arthur L. Herman expresses it, "the philosophic argument was necessary before the rational insight was possible, and that rational insight, namely, that there is no way out, was necessary before "letting go" could occur, and "letting go" was necessary before nirvana was possible" (7). Western responses generally emphasize an indirect approach, although at least one fictional character — Nicholas in John Fowles's *The Magus* — reasons to a "letting go" reminiscent of this description of attaining nirvana.

READINGS

Fossa, John A. "Through Seeking to Mystery: A Reappraisal of John Fowles' *The Magus.*" *Orbis Litterarum* 44 (1989): 161-180.

Herman, Arthur L. "Hedonism and Nirvana: Paradoxes, Dilemmas and Solutions." *Philosophica* [India] 10 (1981): 1-10.

Slater, Robert. *Paradox and Nirvana.* Chicago: U of Chigago P, 1951. 3-4.

NON-COMMUNICATOR, THE PARADOX OF THE. Adduced by Theodore Drange and related to the M-VARIANTS OF THE LOGICAL PARADOXES, this paradox purports to show that all hierarchical theories are contradictory.

Formulation. Consider the sentence

(1)   (1) is meaningless.

According to hierarchical theories, (1) is true. Thus, it is both meaningless and not meaningless, which is a contradiction.

Explanation. Hierarchical theories (see RUSSELL'S PARADOX) brand a statement as meaningless whenever the hierarchy conditions are violated. In particular, the theory is used to deal with sentences such as (1) which refer to themselves. Hence, (1) is meaningless. Yet (1) asserts that it itself is meaningless and, thus, is in accord with what is the case. Therefore, (1) is true. But a true sentence cannot be meaningless. Therefore, (1) is not meaningless and the contradiction is established.

Resolution. Robert W. Beard formulates two basic objections to the purported paradox. First, Drange admits (1) as a premise and thus either assumes the truth of (1) in order to prove the truth of (1), making the argument circular, or presupposes that truth and meaninglessness are not exclusive, vitiating the validity of the argument (by falsifying the principle that true sentences cannot be meaningless). Presumably, Drange would reply that (1) is not a premise at all, but rather a consequence of hierarchical theory; nevertheless, no hierarchical theorist would be willing to accept (1). Beard's second objection is that Tarski's definition of truth is relativized to the language being used, but Drange employs it in an unrestricted manner.

READINGS

Beard, Robert W. "Semantic Theory and the Paradox of the Non-Communicator." *Philosophical Studies* 17 (1966): 44-45.

Drange, Theodore. "The Paradox of the Non-Communicator." *Philosophical Studies* 15 (1964): 92-96.

NONEXISTENT OBJECTS, PARADOX OF. See the PARADOX OF NEGATION.

OLBER'S PARADOX. Formulated by H. W. M. Olbers in 1826 independently of earlier formulations (most notably one by J. P. L. de Cheseaux in 1744), this is a problem for various cosmologies, including Newton's.

Formulation. "An infinite number of stars distributed evenly in infinite space would logically create a sky blazing all over with extraordinary brilliance in obvious contradiction to the factual darkness of the night sky" (Jali, 10).

Explanation. According to Newtonian cosmology space is Euclidean and basically static. There are supposed to be an infinite number of stars, essentially similar to the sun, evenly distributed throughout this space. Since the area of the sky is finite, the evenly distributed, infinite number of stars should fill up the whole sky, thereby completely illuminating it.

Resolution. Early attempts to avoid the paradox centered on tinkering with the inverse square law of the propagation of light and on the possibility of light energy being absorbed by the medium through which it passes. The latter hypothesis would not seem to eliminate the paradox, however, because, according to then acknowledged principles, the continual adsorption of energy would cause the medium itself to glow. Eventually, however, most of the Newtonian hypotheses were abandoned. For example, although space is still thought of as being homogeneous on the large scale, stars are not completely evenly distributed on a smaller scale: they form clusters (galaxies) and clusters of clusters. Nevertheless, an infinite number of stars is not actually needed to generate the paradox; in fact, a universe of very modest dimensions will do so as well, depending on the density of matter in, say, the observable part of the universe. The observed density in fact seems compatible with the Olbers Paradox. Once the universe was seen to be expanding, however, rather than static, the consequent shift of light towards the red end of the spectrum (akin to the Doppler effect for sound waves produced by a moving source) reduces the energy of light from distant stars so that the Olbers Paradox does not arise. The paradox nevertheless is still troublesome for some forms of finite models of the universe.

READINGS

Dickson, F. P. *The Bowl of Night: The Physical Universe and Scientific Thought.* Cambridge: MIT P, 1968.

Jali, Stanley L. The *Paradox of Olber's Paradox: A Case of Scientific Thought.* New York: Herder, 1969.

OMNIPOTENCE, PARADOXES OF. This is a class of RELIGIOUS PARADOX. By God's omnipotence is meant that He is all powerful, in the sense that nothing is as powerful as or more powerful than God, and/or that He is infinitely powerful, in the sense that His power is indefinitely great. Sometimes God's omnipotence is taken to mean that God can do anything. This interpretation of His omnipotence inspires a whole set of traditional paradoxes. If God can do anything, can He square a circle? Can He make a stone so heavy that He cannot lift it (see the PARADOX OF THE STONE)? In general, can He invent problems that He cannot solve. In order to avoid these difficulties, God's omnipotence is often taken as a more modest attainment to the effect that He can do anything that is logically possible. It is sometimes asked, moreover, if God can do such things as annihilate Himself and never return to being, or deny His own essence. These quandaries — and more importantly the PROBLEM OF EVIL — lead in turn to further restrictions of His powers, such as: God can do anything that is worthwhile doing or (what is nearly the same) He can do anything that expresses His necessary essence as God. Since logical consistency is typically taken to be part of God's essence, this formulation usually implies that He cannot do anything logically impossible.

READING

Flint, Thomas P. and Alfred J. Freddoso. "Maximal Power." *The Existence and Nature of God.* Ed. Alfred J. Freddoso. Notre Dame: Notre Dame UP, 1983. 81-113.

OMNIPRESENCE AND TIMELESSNESS, THE PARADOX OF. Richard La Croix identifies this paradox in the theology of St. Thomas Aquinas. Aquinas holds that God is necessarily omnipresent and eternal; that is, both of these properties belong to God's very essence and are indeed part of what it means to be God. Eternity, however, can be understood either as temporal infinity or as timelessness. Temporal infinity is the claim that God somehow stretches throughout all times past, present, and future, whereas timelessness asserts that God is somehow outside of time and not bound by temporal considerations. Aquinas argues for the view that God is timeless. But, then, argues La Croix,

> if God is indeed omnipresent then it would appear that he must have been in the United Nations Building *yesterday* as well as the day *before* yesterday. And if God was in the United Nations building *both* yesterday *and* the day before, then it would appear that he is in time and that temporal predicates do apply to him. So, it would appear that God

is *not* a timeless being if he is omnipresent and that two
doctrines crucial to the theology of Thomas Aquinas are
logically incompatible (391).

La Croix admits that a more sophisticated understanding of omnipresence
would resolve the paradox, but he also argues that the conception used in
his argument is true to that of Aquinas.

READING

La Croix, Richard R. "Aquinas on God's Omnipresence and Timelessness."
Philosophy and Phenomenological Research 42 (1982): 391-399.

OMNISCIENCE, PARADOXES OF. These are RELIGIOUS PARADOXES
deriving from the view that God is omniscient. God has been said to be
omniscient in three inter-related senses. First, God perceives all things as
they happen and hence knows of their occurrence. Second, God knows
everything in the past, present and future. Third, God knows everything
that it is possible to know. It follows from these powers of God that all
truth is eternal, that all truths are known by God, and that nothing can
occur unless it accords with these eternal truths. Yet if this is true, in what
sense can either man or God have free will? Man cannot have it because
there is nothing that he might do that is not already known by God. God
too cannot be said to have willed to do things in one way rather than
another when He already knew what He would will to be done.

READING

Stenner, Alfred J. "A Paradox of Omniscience and Some Attempts at a
Solution." *Faith and Philosophy* 6 (1989): 303-319.

OSCAR WILDE'S EPIGRAMMATIC PARADOXES. Here is a brief
selection of paradoxical *bons mots* from Oscar [Fingal O'Flahertie Wills]
Wilde (1854-1900):

> (1)   There is only one thing in the world worse than being
> talked about, and that is not being talked about (*The Picture
> of Dorian Grey*, Ch.1).
> (2)   In this world there are only two tragedies. One is not
> getting what he wants, and the other is getting it (*Lady Wind-
> ermere's Fan*, Act 3).
> (3)   I suppose society is wonderfully delightful. To be in it
> is merely a bore. But to be out of it simply a tragedy (*A Woman
> of No Importance*, Act III).
> (4)   Anybody can make history. Only a great man can write
> it (*Aphorisms*).

(5) Yet each man kills the thing he loves,
     By each let this be heard,
     Some do it with a bitter look,
     Some with a flattering word.
     The coward does it with a kiss,
     The brave man with a sword.
     (The B*allad of Reading Gaol I*, st. 7).

OSTROGORSKI'S PARADOX. This is one of the PARADOXES OF VOTING, involving competition of two parties in a majority rule context. **Formulation.** A party can win an election even though its opponent's positions are preferred by a majority of voters on every issue in question. **Explanation.** Consider an election disputed by party X and party Y, whose positions on the issues are x and y, respectively. The following chart tabulates the results, where V_1-V_5 are the five voters of the constituency and I_1-I_3 are the three issues involved:

		Issues			
		I_1	I_2	I_3	Ballot
Voters	V_1	x	x	y	X
	V_2	x	y	x	X
	V_3	y	x	x	X
	V_4	y	y	y	Y
	V_5	y	y	y	Y
Preferred Position		y	y	y	

Each row of the chart records a voter's preference on each issue and the ballot cast by that voter. V_1, for example, prefers position x on issues I_1 and I_2 and position y on I_3; he consequently votes for party X. The chart shows that a majority of voters prefers position y on each of the three issues. Nevertheless, party X wins the election by a vote of 3 to 2. Clearly, V_1-V_5 may be five (equinumerous, or nearly so) groups of voters instead of five individuals.
Resolution. That configurations like the one considered above are possible is often taken to imply that democratic processes are deeply flawed.

READINGS

Rae, D. W. and H. Daudt. "The Ostrogorski Paradox: A Peculiarity of
Compound Majority Decision." *European Journal of Political Research*
4 (1976): 391-398.

Shelley, Fred M. "Notes on Ostrogorski's Paradox." *Theory and Decision*
17 (1984): 267-273.

OXYMORON. Paradoxical expressions, such as "square circle" or
"honest thief," are not called paradoxes but rather oxymorons, or
antisyzygies. Although appearing contradictory, such phrases are, strictly
speaking, neither true nor false. Paradoxes, by contrast, admit of truth
and falsity. A paradox usually results when someone tries, either directly
or indirectly, to predicate one of these phrases of something, as in "A
point is a square circle" or "He's an honest thief." Observe that in at least
one sense "honest thief" is not a contradiction because someone might
make a profession of stealing and yet always tell the truth; even if stealing
does not imply lying, however, the conjunction of the two terms may still
be considered an oxymoron in that it is, based on our expectations, an
apparent contradiction. These expectations result not only from our
experience with thieves, but also from the sense of "dishonest" which
includes thievery.

PAIN, THE PARADOX OF. Bernard E. Rollin adduces ten "apparent
paradoxes" in the medical sciences. The following is perhaps the most
interesting of these.

Formulation. "Although a good deal of pain research has traditionally
been done on animals, the scientific community has been loath to affirm
that one can know that animals feel pain, rather than simply exhibit pain
responses and mechanisms" (Rollin 211).

Explanation. The result is not strictly contradictory since the feeling of
pain may be associated with pain mechanisms in humans, but not in
animals even if the mechanisms themselves were identical. Nevertheless,
this logical possibility is clearly not a satisfactory response since, were it
true, it would itself be paradoxical to most people.

Resolution. The scientist is supposed to limit himself to physical
principles and thus must remain agnostic about the subjective pain of
animals. Yet, as Rollin points out, the same would apply to subjective
human pain (despite the fact that humans have language). Moreover,
science is supposed to be value-free and thus ignores these subjective

considerations unless forced to do so by societal pressures (which non-human animals are not in a position to apply). Therefore, argues Rollin, science tends to invoke methodological fiats in order to avoid moral questions that might hinder business as usual. In particular, "the ideology and value system of scientists contribute to their very perception of pain (or lack of such perception); and thus, such ideology and its attendant moral system (or lack thereof) has profound moral consequences" (Rollin, 217).

READING

Rollin, Bernard E. "Pain, Paradox, and Value." *Bioethics* 3 (1989): 211-225.

PARADOX, DEFINITION OF. According to the Oxford English Dictionary, the word "paradox" is used in several closely related senses. For our purposes, only the two or three most important of these are relevant. As first sense, the OED gives:

> A statement or tenet contrary to received opinion or expecta-
> tion; often with the implication that it is marvellous or in-
> credible; sometimes with unfavorable connotation, as being
> discordant with what is held to be established truth, and hence
> absurd or fantastic; sometimes with favorable connotation,
> as a correction of vulgar error.

The OED goes on to say that this sense is rare since the seventeenth century, but that later writers often insist that this sense is the proper one. Indeed, this is the etymological sense of the word, which comes through French and Latin from the Greek para-, "against," plus *doxa*, "the taken," hence "received opinion," which derives from an Indo-European root meaning "to take." In Greek and Latin the adjective was more common than the substantive, but in French and English the substantive is attested earlier and is more important. With regard to the definition from the OED, we would like to say that the question of whether the connotation is favorable or unfavorable is pretty much irrelevant, the point being rather that paradoxes are all somewhat incredible. All paradox partakes of the character of the absurd, that is to say that paradoxical utterances are those that tend to strike the hearers as ridiculous, incongruous or unreasonable. Paradoxes are incongruous statements in that they are inconsistent with what is correct, proper or logical. In this first sense of paradox, the paradox strikes the hearer as absurd because it flies in the face of what is commonly accepted to be true. We would not generally classify a statement as paradoxical, however, on the basis of its absurdity alone. There should also be some putatively cogent reason for accepting the assertion. Thus were we to claim, despite the fact that everyone believes the matter to be otherwise, that the moon is indeed made of green cheese, we would be more likely to be accused of uttering a falsehood than a paradox. If we were able to argue to this conclusion from, say, the discovery of millions of mice on the moon's surface, or should some space probe discover that the moon actually is made of green cheese after all, then we would have a paradox. Of course, if everyday people have no opinion at all about something, there can be no question of contradicting their beliefs, and it suffices to make something a paradox that it stand in opposition to learned opinion. Thus in A *Budget of Paradoxes*, the paradoxes that Augustus De Morgan chronicles are claims to have achieved the quadrature of the circle or to have invented a perpetual motion machine, technical advances about whose impossibility scientific gentlemen are convinced, but which other people are prepared to accept if and when they are forthcoming. One of the most remarked paradoxes since the fall of Byzantium is COPERNICUS' PARADOX. Calling Copernicus' opinion a paradox in this first sense illustrates that, when they are corrections of vulgar error, such paradoxes may indeed be true despite their incongruous character. In a second sense of paradox, the OED has:

> A statement or proposition which on the face of it seems self-contradictory, absurd, or at variance with common sense, though, on investigation or when explained it may prove to be well-founded (or, according to some, though it is essentially true).

It adds the following sub-sense:

> Often applied to a statement or proposition that is actually contradictory, or contradictory to reason or ascertained truth, and so, essentially absurd and false,

explaining that

> some have denied statements to be paradoxes when they can be proved after all to be true, or have called them 'apparent paradoxes' when they are real paradoxes in sense 2.

The differences between this second sense and the first are twofold. First, in the the first sense the inconsistency is between the paradox and accepted opinion, whereas in the second the paradox may be contrary to known truths or simply self-contradictory. The class of paradoxes whose appearance of absurdity lies in the possibility of their contradicting themselves, which class is recognized in the second sense of paradox but not the first, is called "logical paradox." Second, while in the first sense a paradox could be either true or false, in this second sense writers tend to differ about whether paradoxes are always true or always false or not always either one or the other. It seems to be a clumsy use of the term "paradox," however, to insist that paradoxes are always true or always false. If always true, paradoxes are "crypto-truths"; and if always false, "pseudo-truths." So once again, it would seem rather that the paradoxicality of the paradox lies essentially in the questionable character of its appearance, quite apart from the reality of its truth value. We say this because if a statement is too clearly false, it would not be a paradox. Consider the classical example of an antilogism, a triad of statements whereby if two are true the third can be seen as inconsistent, false or contradictory, as in the case of a syllogism in which the stated conclusion is the opposite of the valid conclusion. In the textbook antilogism, "All men are mortal; Socrates is a man; Socrates is immortal," there is nothing paradoxical because the fallacy is too straightforward. The statement is self-contradictory but without anything that would lead us to believe otherwise. Again, when we use paradox only in the case of true statements that seem false on the surface, we place the paradoxicality in the wrong place, in its success in being true, and not where it would appear to belong, namely, in its success in making itself questionable. Let us leave aside paradoxes that fly in the face of accepted opinion, and consider only logical paradoxes, whose putative falsity is a matter of their appearing to contradict themselves. Such paradoxes would seem to be objects of the science of logic, which determines questions of consistency, and the term "paradox" would seem to be a term of logic. In truth, logic does treat of paradoxes up to a point and "paradox," like Antinomy, "paralogism," and so on, is sometimes treated as a technical term in logic. Yet logic is not the only science that treats of logical paradoxes. Prosody does as well, and rhetoric too. In both these "literary studies," paradox is treated as a trope of thought rather than of speech, even though the trope inevitably associates itself with certain figures of speech. That is why logic always has something to say about paradoxes. But even when logic has said its piece, the poet or the writer still must determine the use to which he might put the paradox. Again, even if the statement is contradictory, there are circumstances in which such statements are appropriate: to evoke a sense of mystery, or pathos, in sophism, in irony or humor. That the OED identifies no sense in which paradoxes are always a matter of self-consistency indicates that logic is only one of the special studies relevant to the comprehension of paradox. Also relevant are the studies of nature and of human society.

More important than any of these for the treatment of paradox would be rhetoric in a robust (or medieval) interpretation. Rhetoric in this sense does not restrict itself to the polite forms of speechifying, but takes in the whole question of what we say when, and in so doing becomes the master science of language. See also BRIDGE PARADOX, DILEMMA, OXYMORON, SOPHISM, and VERIDICAL AND FALSIDICAL PARADOX.

READINGS

Colie, Littell. *Paradoxia Epidemica*. Princeton: Princeton UP,1966.
De Morgan, Augustus. *A Budget of Paradoxes*. 2 vols. 2nd ed. Ed. David Eugene Smith. Chicago: Open Court, 1915.
Fallatta, Nicholas. *The Paradoxicon*. Garden City, NY: Doubleday, 1983.
Minton, Arthur J., and Thomas J. Shipka, eds. *Philosophy: Paradox and Discovery*. 2nd ed. New York: McGraw, 1982.
Saintsbury. *Paradoxes*. Cambridge: Cambridge UP, (1988).

PARADOXICAL COLD. See PERCEPTUAL PARADOXES.

PARADOXICAL HEAT. See PERCEPTUAL PARADOXES.

PARADOXICAL SLEEP. This term refers to the REM (rapid eye movement) sleep in which we dream. Dream sleep is paradoxical because, whereas in normal sleep patterns of brain waves are rhythmic and subdued, in dream sleep brain fibers fire rapidly and at random. Thus, dream sleep seems more akin to wakeful activity than to sleep.

PASCAL'S WAGER. Invented by the eighteenth-century mathematician Blaise Pascal, this argument takes the form of a dilemma for non-believers. **Formulation.** If God exists and one believes in Him, He will reward one's faith with eternal happiness, and if He exists and one does not believe in Him, He will consign one's soul to eternal damnation. If God does not exist and one believes in Him, one loses limited means invested in an erroneous belief, and if He does not exist and one does not believe, one has not lost these limited means. In other words, the risk of finite means allows one to win an infinite reward and the failure to invest these finite means makes one liable to an infinite loss. Therefore, it is rational to believe in God even if the chances of His existence are very, very small; and only if it is absolutely certain that He does not exist is it rational not to believe in Him. Yet since there is no such absolute certainty, one ought to believe in God.

Explanation. Pascal constructs a simple decision matrix. One can believe or not. If God exists, believers win an infinite reward and nonbelievers receive an infinite punishment. These payoffs are such that reason obliges one to risk the finite investment of belief, even if there is no evidence for God's existence, so long as there is at least a minimal (finite) chance for God to exist.

Resolution. Three main objections are raised to the Wager. First, even if God exists He might believe that rational disbelief is more to be rewarded than blind faith, on the grounds that the principled atheist better employed the divine gift of reason. Second, even if God exists He might reward the person whose life was more virtuous and benevolent than the person who merely believed. Third, and this is the central objection from a spiritual point of view, if one believes in God on the basis of the logic of Pascal's Wager, one has diminished the value of one's belief so much that it is unlikely that it is worth anything. For to believe in God in order to be rewarded is to treat God in a calculating, even mercenary manner; the rewards of belief derive from loving and respecting God, not from treating Him as a mere instrument for one's own advantage. According to Moses A. Makinde, for example, Pascal himself did not intend the Wager to be an argument for mercenary belief, but an incentive for the nonbeliever to begin to seek for God.

READINGS

Duff, Antony. "Pascal's Wager and Infinite Utilities." *Analysis* 46.2 (1986): 107-109.

Goldman, Lucien. *The Hidden God: A Study of the Tragic Vision in the Pensées of Pascal and the Tragedies of Racine.* Trans. Philip Thody. London: Routledge, 1964. 283- 309.

Makinde, Moses A. "Pascal's Wager and the Atheist's Dilemma." *International Journal for Philosophy of Religion* 17 (1985): 115-129.

Pascal, Blaise. *Thoughts.* Trans. W. F. Trotter. Harvard Classics ser. 48. New York:Collier, 1910. Sec. 3.

PERCEPTUAL PARADOXES. There are a very large number of perceptual illusions and most of them have been termed "paradoxical" at one time or another. The nature of the paradox is not always the same, however. Such illusions seem to divide themselves into two main kinds. One kind of illusory experience is a result of distortions in the stimulus rather than in the perceiver. Some visual illusions, for example, are the result of the refraction of light. Thus mirages, such as the "pools" of water that appear on asphalt on a hot day, are considered illusions, but these effects would be paradoxical only if one were taken in by the illusion. In the same sense, rainbows are thought to be illusions, though how we are taken in by them is hard to say (unless, of course, one expects to find a pot of gold at its end). A better example of a paradoxical illusion of this kind is the stick that appears bent when it is partly immersed in a pool of water, because in that case there is a contradiction between what our eyes tell us (that the stick is bent) and what our hands tell us (that it is not bent). There are various auditive illusions of this kind. The best known is the Doppler effect, as seen in the fact that the pitch of an automobile horn seems to drop after it has passed us and is heading away from us. The wind also affects the pitch that we perceive. The paradox here is the contrast between the true and the apparent pitch. Again, two nearby sounds of nearly the same frequency can arrive at the ear in phase, producing a combined louder sound. Other stimulus-distortion illusions are the result of a physical apparatus, such as the eyeglasses that flip images from top to bottom, or the earphones that switch the sounds arriving at the left and right ears. Such devices for reversing stimuli may be disorienting, but there is little reason to call them paradoxical. There is, however, a nice paradox of a bathroom cabinet apparatus:

> Why does a mirror reverse images from left to right but not from top to bottom?

The other main kind of experiential illusion is not already contained in the incoming perceptual array, but arises from the perceiver's perceptual apparatus.

Optical illusions, such as the figure-and-ground illusion, are good examples. In the famous Duck-Rabbit illusion, the figure appears first as a duck and then as a rabbit, depending how one looks at it, but one cannot make the duck and the rabbit appear together. Other ambiguous figures include the one that appears to be either two black faces in profile or a white vase, and the Necker cube that switches orientation as one observes it. Ambiguous figures of this sort are so striking that it is hard not to appreciate their "paradoxical" character. Stimuli also affect the senses differently depending upon the immediately preceding experiences. Thus if one stares long enough at an American flag in which the red, white and blue have been changed to green, black and yellow, and then looks at a white wall, the true colors of the flag will appear as after images on the surface. Again, perception varies depending upon what is being experienced through the other senses (in synesthesia, intersensory rivalry, and intersensory facilitation), or upon the perceptual context (a gray paper appears lighter against a black background than a white one). In these cases the paradox lies in the contrast between what is experienced and what would have been experienced under normal conditions or circumstances. (Note that Wittgenstein discusses most of the illusions mentioned in this paragraph at one place or another.)

More clearly paradoxical is the result of the experiment in which one leaves one hand in cold water and the other in warm water until they have become accustomed to the temperature, and then puts them both in a bowl of lukewarm water. Here the paradox is that the same stimulus produces conflicting sensations of warmth and coldness in one's hands. It is in conjunction with certain tactile illusions, however, that the term "paradoxical" is standardly applied. The skin contains numerous areas that are sensitive to either hot or cold. Sometimes a warm stimulus will produce the sensation of cold when placed on an area sensitive to cold. This occurrence is termed the illusion of "paradoxical cold." The illusion of "paradoxical heat" occurs when a warm stimulus affects warm and cold areas at the same time; the mixture of warmth and "paradoxical cold" causes an uneasy even painful feeling of heat. One of the most intriguing illusions, both as perceived and in thinking it over, is that moon appears larger on the horizon than it does high in the sky. Innumerable theories have been adduced to explain this phenomenon, and theorists are divided about which kinds of illusory experience it is — that which arises from the stimulus or that which arises from the perceiver.

READINGS

Gombrich, Ernst H. *Art and Illusion.* New York: Pantheon, 1960
Robinson, Helier J. "The Two Head Hypothesis and the Paradoxes of Perception." *International Logic Review* 3 (1972): 99-123.
Wittgenstein, Ludwig. *Philosophical Investigations.* Trans. G. Anscombe. Oxford: Blackwell, 1953.

PHILOTAS' PARADOX. Plutarch relates the following tale, in which Philotas uses a paradox to silence a blowhard! "Philotas the physician told my grandfather this tale, and said moreover that it was his chance shortly after to serve the eldest son of the said Antonius, whom he had by his wife Fulvia, and that he sat commonly at his table with his other friends, when he did not dine nor sup with his father. It chanced one day there came a physician that was so full of words that he made every man weary of him at the board, but Philotas to stop his mouth put out a subtle proposition to him. 'It is good in some sort to let a man drink cold water that hath an ague: every man that hath an ague hath it in some sort, ergo it is good for a man that hath an ague to drink cold water.' The physician was so gravelled and amated withal that he had not a word more to say. Young Antonius burst out in such a-laughing at him, and was so glad of it that he said unto him, 'Philotas, take all that, I give it thee,' showing him his cupboard full of plate with great pots of gold and silver."

READINGS

Plutarch of Chaeronea. *The Lives of the Noble Grecians and Romans.* 2 vols. Trans. Thomas North. New York: Heritage, 1941; 1692-1693.

PLATONIC PARADOXES. "If a person shows that such things as wood, stone, and the like, being many are also one, we admit that he shows the coexistence of the one and the many, but he does not show that the many are one or the one many; he is uttering not a paradox but a truism" (Plato, *Parmenides*, 129).—There are many paradoxes in Plato (BC c. 428-c. 248); for a few of the better known, see MENO'S PARADOX, PLATO'S PARADOX, SOCRATIC PARADOXES, and the THIRD MAN.

READINGS

Griswold, Charles. "Philosophy, Education, and Courage in Plato's *Laches*." *Interpretation* 14 (1986): 177-193.

Lentz, Tony M. "The Third Place from Truth: Plato's Paradoxical Attack on Writing." *Communication Quarterly* 31 (Fall 1983): 290-301.

Mackenzie, Mary Margaret. "Putting the *Cratylus* in Its Place." *Classical Quarterly* ns 36 (1986): 124-50.

——. "The Virtues of Socratic Ignorance." *Classical Quarterly* ns 38 (1988): 331-50.

Rankin, Kenneth. "The Duplicity of Plato's Third Man." *Mind* ns (1969).

Vlastos, Gregory. *Platonic Studies.* Princeton: Princeton UP, n.d. Ch 2, 12.

PLATO'S PARADOX. E. J. Lemmon attributes this paradox, also called the CONFLICT-OF-DUTY PARADOX, to Plato. In Lemmon's version, a neighbor entrusts his friend with a gun after extracting his promise to return it that evening. At the appointed time, the neighbor demands the gun's return so that he can kill his unfaithful wife. The conflict of duties occurring in this paradox can be resolved by supposing a hierarchy of moral values so that, in the case at issue, the saving of human life takes precedence over keeping a promise. See, however, SARTRE'S PARADOX for another Conflict-of-Duty Paradox which is not amenable to this kind of resolution.

POLITICAL PARADOXES. Political paradoxes occur when our institutions of social regulation give rise to conflicting duties or impossible situations for the citizen or when those institutions inhibit the very ends that they were established to facilitate. See the PARADOX OF FUTURE GENERATIONS, the PARADOX OF INDOCTRINATION, the PARDOX OF LIBERTANIANISM, THE PARADOX OF NATURAL RIGHTS, and SEN'S PARADOX. Many political paradoxes may also be categorized as ETHICAL PARADOXES, LEGAL PARADOXES or PARADOXES OF VOTING.

POSSIBLE LIAR, THE. This paradox is one of the many modal variants of the LIAR. The sentence

This sentence is possibly false.

entails considerations essentially similar to the PARADOX OF THE PREFACE.
READINGS
Post, John F. "Presupposition, Bivalence and the Possible Liar." *Philosophia* 8 (1979): 645-650.
— —, "The Possible Liar." *Nous* 4 (1970): 405-409.

POTENTIAL ENERGY BARRIER PARADOX, THE. First described by the Hillary Putnam, this veridical paradox is related to SCHRÖEDINGER'S CAT.
Formulation. "In quantum physics, if we use the (original) Born interpretation, then. . .we get (the figure 10 per cent has been inserted at random in the example):

Every atom in the population P has the energy level e.
10 percent of the atoms in the population P have values of D (the proton-electron separation which exceeds d).
Those statements are of course in logical contradiction"
(Putnam 144).

Explanation. In classical physics, the total energy of a system is equal to the sum of the potential energy of the system and the kinetic energy of the system. In the example given by Putnam, every atom is assumed to have total energy e. The potential energy is a function of the distance between the proton and the electron; the potential energy increases as the distance increases. Now, for ten per cent of the atoms, the distance between the proton and the electron is sufficiently large so as to make the potential energy greater than e. But, since the kinetic energy must be greater than or equal to zero, the total energy of these atoms is also greater than e. Thus, the total energy of these atoms is both equal to e and greater than e, which is contradictory.

Resolution. One resolution is to abandon quantum mechanics altogether, not a likely move in the absence of a legitimate competing theory. Putnam suggests that a more plausible resolution would result by dropping what he calls "the principle of no disturbance." This principle affirms that "measurement does not disturb the observable measured — that is, the observable has almost the same value an instant before the measurement as it does at the moment the measurement is taken" (138). By dropping the principle of no disturbance, the original conditions of the problem become

> If an energy measurement is made on any atom in P, then the value e is obtained.
> If a D-measurement is made on any atom in P, in ten percent of the cases a value greater than d will be obtained (114).

Since, according to quantum mechanics, measurements of the total energy and the distance cannot be made simultaneously, this formulation is consistent. The principle of no disturbance is integral to the Born interpretation of quantum mechanics, but not to the subsequent Copenhagen interpretation. On the latter interpretation, the fact that some of the atoms have a proton-electron separation greater than d does not mean that they had approximately the same separation before the measurement was made and, hence, no contradiction results. Another approach to the paradox attempts to preserve the Born interpretation by introducing the assumption of hidden-variables. Arthur Fine, for example, suggests that energy measurements on atoms are possible only for atoms where the separation of proton and electron is less than d (perhaps due to a limitation of energy measuring devices). If this be so, even granting that distance can be accurately measured, in measuring the energy none of those atoms with separation greater than d will register on the device and no contradiction arises.

READING

Putnam, Hillary. "A Philosopher Looks at Quantum Mechanics." In Robert G. Colodny, ed., *Beyond the Edge of Certainty.* Englewood Cliffs, NJ: Prentice-Hall, 1965. 75- 101.

PRAGMATIC PARADOXES. As Roy Sorensen points out, there are various pragmatic paradoxes. We shall examine only two varieties:

paradoxical questions and paradoxical imperatives.

Formulation. Pairs of paradoxical questions and answers include the following:

"Are you there?"	"No, I am not here."
"Are you asleep?"	"Yes, I am asleep."
"Are you alive?"	"No, I am dead."
"Are you mute?"	"Yes, I am mute."
"Are you deaf?"	"Yes, I am deaf."
"Can you hear me?"	"No, I cannot hear you."
"Do you speak any English?"	"No, I do not speak any English."

Paradoxical imperatives are of this sort:

A sign that reads: "Ignore this sign."
A note that says only: "Do not read this note."
"Don't listen to this utterance."
A posted bill that reads: "Post no bills."

Explanation. In the first case, the questions seem to ask for either a negative or an affirmative answer, but in fact only one of these answers would make sense, because one cannot consistently answer the question in the standard manner if one is not there, asleep, dead, deaf, dumb, cannot hear, or not an anglophone. Answering in the paradoxical manner is often a witty, snappy or sarcastic manner of saying the opposite. Unlike the questions, which can elicit useful information, the first three examples of imperatives not only have the scent of paradox but tend to be pragmatically useless, unless they are meant as some kind of joke. The last example of an imperative paradox does function to inform people of a policy of not posting bills in a certain place, but it does so by violating the policy in question, and might strike people as a somewhat absurd manner of implementing the policy in question.

Resolution. We sometimes avoid paradoxical responses by restating the questions in such a form that only one response is expected: "Tell me if you are there," or "Raise you hand if you can hear me." Sometimes we use a special form of diction that assumes the person cannot understand if he were to hear the more conventional form of the question: "Do you savvy my lingo?" Such measures do not guarantee success, however: does the other really not hear our statement, or does he just not raise his hand out of a perverse refusal to comply with our request?

READINGS

Sorensen, Roy A. "Pragmatic Paradox Liable Questions." *Philosophical Studies* 39 (1981): 155-162.

Campbell, C. A. "Common-Sense Propositions and Philosophical Paradoxes." *Proceedings of the Aristotelian Society* 45 (1945): 1-26.

PRECESSION OF THE EQUINOXES, THE PARADOX OF. The configuration of the night sky was of considerable importance to many peoples as a time-keeping device. The regularity of astronomical movements was used in order to determine the onset of spring and the consequent sowing of the fields. Naturally, not only most agricultural rhythms, but also most major ritual occurrences were determined by celestial signposts. The regularity of the yearly cycles was also considered evidence for the stability and well-being of the universe. Nevertheless, the yearly cycle, say as measured by the spring equinox, is not completely regular. That is, the once yearly occurrence of the spring equinox does not occur at exactly the same spot in the sky each year. This phenomenon is known as the precession of the equinoxes. The difference from year to year is too small to be noticed, but over time the familiar celestial signposts began to lose their significance. The Pleiades, for example, once marked the spring equinox, but due to the precession they seemed to slip ever lower into the horizon like someone who was falling into the sea or into the sun's glow. This was indeed a wondrously paradoxical occurrence, full of foreboding for the stability of the universe. Early astronomers such as Hipparchus (who reputedly discovered the phenomenon of the precession) resolved this paradoxical situation by positing a "great year," the period in which the precession would make a full cycle in the sky. Earlier resolutions, however, are found in mythology as changes in epochs. The slaying of the Mithraic bull, for example, corresponded to the constellation Taurus losing its place as regent of the spring equinox. Again, at about the beginning of the Christian era Pisces became the new regent of this equinox and thus the fish symbolizes a new Christian era which many expect to culminate in an apocalyptical new age of Aquarius.

READING

Worthen, Thomas D. *The Myth of Replacement.* Tucson: U of Arizona P, 1991.

PREDICTION PARADOX, THE. The prediction paradox arises when the very ability to predict the occurrence or non-occurrence of an event makes the realization of that event impossible. Some of the most well known versions of the paradox are Hollis's Paradox, the Unexpected Hanging, the Surprise Air Raid Drill, and the Surprise Quiz. In the Surprise Quiz, for example, a teacher announces that he will give a surprise quiz next week. The students know that it cannot be on Friday, the last day of the week, because then it would not be a surprise. Thus, Thursday becomes the last day that it could be given and, thus, if the teacher waits until

Thursday, it will again be no surprise. Similarly, each day of the week can be eliminated and the quiz can never be given. See the BOTTLE IMP, the CHAIN STORE PARADOX, and the PRISONER'S DILEMMA.

READING

Alexander, Peter. "Pragmatic Paradoxes." *Mind* ns 59 (1950): 536-538.

Austin, A. K. "The Unexpected Examination." *Analysis* 39.1 (1979): 63-64.

Blinkley, R. "The Surprise Examination in Modal Logic." *Journal of Philosophy* 65 (1968): 127-136.

Burge, Tyler. "Buridan and Epistemic Paradox." *Philosophical Studies* 34 (1978): 21-35.

Cohen, L. J. "Mr. O'Connor's 'Pragmatic Paradoxes.'" *Mind* ns 59 (1950): 85-87.

Ferguson, Kenneth. "Equivocation in the Surprise Exam Paradox." *The Southern Journal of Philosophy* 29 (1991): 291-302.

Holtzman, Jack M. "An Undecidable Aspect of the Unexpected Hanging Problem." *Philosophia* 17 (1987): 195-198.

— —. "Schöedinger's Cat and the Unexpected Hanging Paradox." *British Journal for the Philosophy of Science* 39 (1988): 397-401.

Janaway, Christopher. "Knowing about Surprises: A Supposed Antinomy Revisited." *Mind* ns 98 (1989): 391-409.

Kaplan, David, and Richard Montague. "A Paradox Regained." *Notre Dame Journal of Formal Logic* 1 (1980): 79-90.

Kirkham, Richard. "The Two Paradoxes of the Unexpected Examination." *Philosophical Studies* 49 (1986): 19-26.

Loesser, J. G. "Three Perspectives on Schöedinger's Cat." *American Journal of Physics* 52.12 (1984): 1089-93.

Margalit, A., and M. Bar-Hillel. "Expecting the Unexpected." *Philosophia* 13 (1983): 263-289.

O'Connor, D. J. "Pragmatic Paradoxes." *Mind* ns 57 (1948): 358-359.

Olin, Doris. "The Prediction Paradox Resolved." *Philosophical Studies* 44 (1983): 225-234.

— —. "The Prediction Paradox: Resolving Recalcitrant Variations." *Australasian Journal of Philosophy* 64 (1986): 181-189.

Quine, W. V. "On a So-Called Paradox." *Mind* ns 62 (1953): 65-67.

Scriven, Michael. "Paradoxical Announcements." *Mind* ns 60 (1951): 403-407.

Sorensen, Roy A. "Conditional Blindspots and the Knowledge Squeeze." *Australasian Journal of Philosophy* 62 (1984): 126-135.

— —. "A Strengthened Predication Paradox." *Philosophical Quarterly* 36 (1986): 504-513. Discussion: 38: 111-15.

— —. "Blindspotting and Choice Variations of the Prediction Paradox." *AmericanPhilosophical Quarterly* 23 (1986): 337-52.

Weiss, Paul. "The Prediction Paradox." *Mind* ns 61 (1952): 265-269.

PREFACE, THE PARADOX OF THE. This logical paradox was first adduced by D. C. Makinson in 1965. **Formulation**. "It is customary for authors of academic books to include in their prefaces statements such as this: 'I am indebted to . . . for their invaluable help; however, any errors which remain are my sole responsibility.' Occasionally an author will go further. Rather than say that *if* there are any mistakes *then* he is responsible for them, he will say that *there will* inevitably be some mistakes and he is responsible for them... If he has already written other books, and received corrections from readers and reviewers, he may also believe that not everything he has written in his latest book is true. His approach is eminently rational; he has learnt from experience... Yet [since he believes of each of the assertions in his book that it is true] he is holding logically incompatible beliefs... The man is being rational though inconsistent" (Makinson 205).

Explanation. The author believes that each assertion in his book is true; nevertheless, he also believes that at least one of these assertions is false. Hence, he holds contradictory beliefs. Even worse, we judge the author to be acting rationally, not in spite of, but because of his inconsistency!

Resolution. Makinson suggests that the author's beliefs about each statement (that it is true) as well as his belief that at least one statement is false are all individually rational beliefs, but that the set of all those beliefs is not rational. Such a position seems to give up too much, however, because the author presumably does not intend his book to be a mere collection of independent assertions, but a coherent "position" on the question addressed. Bernard Linsky suggests that the belief that at least one of the assertions is false is a meta-belief, so that a type theory would resolve the paradox. Linsky's suggestion is perhaps strengthened by the observation that there is no one assertion which the author believes to be both true and false. Indeed, he seems ready to abandon his belief in any one of the statements should future events warrant it. Alternatively, we might accept the paradox and claim that the author spoke too rashly: perhaps he should only affirm the possibility of error. A. M. MacIver, however, has adduced similar paradoxes involving modalities. Other versions of the paradox are formulated in terms of rational acceptance using probability theory.

READINGS

Laraudogoitia, Jose Perez. "A Doxastic Paradox." *Analysis* 50.1 (1990): 47-48.

Linsky, Bernard. "Factives, Blindspots and Some Paradoxes." *Analysis* 46.1 (1986): 10-15.

MacIver, A. M. "'How Can I Think it Possible that I Might be Mistaken?'" *Analysis* 17.2 (1956): 25-30.

Makinson, D. C. "The Paradox of the Preface." *Analysis* 25.6 (1965): 205-207.

Moser, Paul K., and Jeffrey Tlumak. "Two Paradoxes of Rational Acceptance." *Erkenntnis* 23 (1985): 127-142.

Pollock, John L. "The Paradox of the Preface." *Philosophy of Science* 53 (1986): 246-258.

PRIME MATTER, THE PARADOX OF. This paradox purports to show the incoherence of Aristotle's doctrine of prime matter.

Formulation. Prime matter is real because it is the substratum for elemental change. Nevertheless, prime matter has no characteristics of its own and, hence, is not real.

Explanation. All change, for Aristotle, requires a substance that persists throughout the process, which is understood as an alteration of some of its accidental qualities. Thus, a statue of Euclid can be melted down and recast into a statue of Archimedes. In this example, it is the bronze that is the substratum to which the change occurs. In elemental change, however, there is a problem since the elements (fire, air, water, and earth), which are transformed into one another, are not composed of anything more basic than themselves. Thus, there seems to be no substance that supports, for example, the evaporation of water into air. Aristotle, therefore, posits the existence of an amorphous stuff without any characteristics of its own to support elemental change. This is prime matter. If it is to serve as the substrate of elemental change, prime matter must be a substance and, hence, a real thing. But all substance, for Aristotle, is determinate. Since prime matter, however has absolutely no determinations, it cannot be a substance, nor can it be a real thing.

Resolution. Aristotle's response was that, since the elements have pairs of characteristics, one of these must remain the same during the change. Thus, when the cold, wet element is transformed into the warm wet element, a lump of wet prime matter is the substratum for the change. Daniel W. Graham, however, argues that the persistence of the wetness is not relevant and thus Aristotle's solution fails. Sheldon Cohen suggests that prime matter could be essentially extended.

This would indeed resolve the paradox. Graham, however, points out that Aristotle explicitly argues against this possibility and locates the source of the paradox in Aristotle's conflicting criteria of reality: On the one hand reality is a function of determinacy and concreteness: to be a 'this,' a particular thing. On the other hand reality consists in being a subject for predication, but never a predicate. As one approaches the limits of being in descending through the chain of being to simple substance, the substances become more real or at least no less real as subjects; at the same time they become less real as determinate particulars. At the point where one meets prime matter the divergence has become complete. Prime matter is both an ultimately real substratum and an ultimately unreal particular (489).

READINGS

Cohen, Sheldon. "Aristotle's Doctrine of Material Substrate." *Philosophical Review* 93 (1984): 171-194.

Graham, Daniel W. "The Paradox of Prime Matter." *Journal of the History of Philosophy* 25 (1987): 475-490.

Sokolowski, Robert. "Matter, Elements and Substance in Aristotle." *Journal of the History of Philosophy* 8 (1970): 263-277.

PRIOR'S FAMILY OF PARADOXES. Building on certain observations made by Alonzo Church, A. N. Prior adduced this set of paradoxes related to the LIAR.

Formulation. "If it is said by a Cretan that whatever is said by a Cretan is not the case, then at least two things are said-by-a-Cretan" (Prior, 17).

Explanation. If the Cretan spoke the truth, his statement — which is a statement made by a Cretan — must be false. If the Cretan spoke falsely, no contradiction arises, but we must conclude that something else is said by a Cretan and that something else must be true. Such a result is decidedly odd, however, because the Cretan's (false!) affirmation does not seem to be sufficient evidence to conclude a substantive fact (that another Cretan affirmation must have been made). The latter would seem rather an empirical result than a matter of logic. We certainly seem to be able to imagine other scenarios. Suppose that only one Cretan ever learned to talk and that he was very reticent, making only one assertion during his life. The paradox seems to imply that it would be logically impossible for him to affirm "whatever is said by a Cretan is not the case." (In fact, given the circumstances as described, his statement would reduce to the LIAR).

Resolution. Prior observes that the paradox is a corollary of the obvious truism that "If no fact is asserted by a Cretan, then that very fact is also not asserted by a Cretan." It is hard to see how this observation ameliorates the paradoxicality of the original statement. Nevertheless, Prior adduces further related examples that "appear as odd and unpleasant gaps" (20) in our logical methods. In discussing one of these examples, Tyler Burge contends that the paradox is actually rooted in an ambiguity. J. L. Mackie, however, argues that the source of the paradox is to be found in the fact that logic assumes that the Liar Paradox cannot occur. This is because if the Cretan were to affirm the utterance that logic says is impossible (in the described circumstances), a formal contradiction would result. See also MINIAC.

READINGS
Burge, Tyler. "Epistemic Paradox." *Journal of Philosophy* 81 (1984): 5-29.
Mackie, J. L. *Truth, Probability and Paradox: Studies in Philosophical Logic.* Oxford: Clarendon, 1973. 276-285.
Prior, A. N. "On a Family of Paradoxes." *Notre Dame Journal of Formal Logic* 2 (1961): 16-32.

PRIOR'S PARADOXES OF DERIVED OBLIGATION. These PARADOXES OF DEONTIC LOGIC parallel the PARADOXES OF MATERIAL IMPLICATION.

Formulation. The following paradoxes were adduced by A. N. Prior:

(1) A forbidden action makes all actions obligatory.
(2) Any action commits us to what is already obligatory.

Explanation. Just as a false proposition (materially) implies all propositions, (1) states that a forbidden action makes any action obligatory; one wrong makes everything right, so to speak. Again, just as a true proposition is (materially) implied by any proposition, (2) states that if something is obligatory we are committed to it by any action at all even though it may seem irrelevant to the obligatory action. Prior derived the formal analogues of (1) and (2) in an early form of deontic logic.

Resolution. The second paradox seems less pernicious; of the two it is also the more easily resolved. Georg Henrik von Wright suggests that we disallow simple commitments. Thus no simple action would be obligatory of itself and the paradox cannot be formulated. Von Wright resolves the first paradox by reformulating commitments as dyadic obligation predicates in deontic logic.

READINGS
Prior, A. N. "The Paradoxes of Derived Obligation." *Mind* ns 63 (1954): 64-65.
von Wright, Georg Henrik. *An Essay in Deontic Logic and the General Theory of Action.* Amsterdam: North-Holland, 1968. 76-78.

PRISONER'S DILEMMA, THE. In this classic example of the
PARADOXES OF GAME THEORY, two prisoners must choose whether to confess
or not with variable payoffs.
Formulation. "If both prisoners confess, they will both be convicted of
their crime but will receive some leniency in light of their confessions
and receive 5 years in prison. If neither confesses, there will only be
enough evidence to send each to prison for one year. However, if one
confesses while the other does not, the confessor will be set free while the
'sucker' receives twenty years in prison" (Sorensen 157). Given that
neither prisoner knows what the other will decide, the most rational choice
is to confess.
Explanation. Game theorists tend to argue that confessing is the rational
strategy because it maximizes one's payoff. The first prisoner reasons as
follows:

> If the second prisoner confesses, I will get twenty years by
> not confessing, but only five years by confessing. Hence,
> confessing is better in this case.

Similarly, if the second prisoner does not confess,

> I will get one year by not confessing, but I will go free by
> confessing. Once again, confessing is the better choice.

The second prisoner obviously reasons in a parallel fashion. Consequently,
both prisoners confess. As Anatole Rapoport puts it, "the paradox is that
if both players make the rational choice, . . . both lose" (51). That is, by
acting rationally and confessing, both get five years; if they had both
acted irrationally and refused to confess, they would both receive but a
single year in jail. Yet, that is not the end of the paradoxicality of the
present dilemma, for Roy A. Sorensen presents an argument for the
rationality of not confessing. Since each prisoner knows that the other is
rational, each knows that the other will come to the same decision as he
himself does. Thus, they will either both confess or both not confess.
Given that these are the only two choices, it is obviously better for both
not to confess. Therefore, there are strong arguments for both the
rationality of confessing and the rationality of not confessing.
Resolution. Perhaps the most promising response to the present dilemma
is to use conditional strategies to construct metagames. Nigel Howard
shows that two metagames are sufficient to determine joint nonconfession
as the rational choice; he also shows that no further metagames will alter
this result. We should observe that the metagames should not be confused

with the Iterated Prisoner's Dilemma. In the latter, the two players play the game various times in a row (the payoffs may be regarded as monetary rewards instead of years in jail). In the iterated version each player must take into account the other player's previous moves, but the underlying reasoning is otherwise the same as in the simple version. See also NEWCOMB'S PARADOX.

READINGS

Davies, Lawrence. "Prisoners, Paradox, and Rationality." *American Philosophical Quarterly* 14 (1877): 319-327.

Gordon, David. "Is the Prisoner's Dilemma an Insoluble Problem?" *Mind* ns 93 (1984): 98-100.

Guiasu, Silviu. "Prediction Paradox Revisited." *Logical Analysis* 30 (1987): 147-154.

Howard, Nigel. "The Theory of Meta-Games." *General Systems* 11 (1966): 167-186.

— —. "The Mathematics of Meta-Games." *General Systems* 11 (1966): 187-200.

Lewis, D. "Prisoner's Dilemma Is a Newcomb Problem." *Philosophy and Public Affairs* 8 (1979): 235-240.

Olin, Doris. "Predictions, Intentions and the Prisoner's Dilemma." *Philosophical Quarterly* 38 (1988): 111-116.

Porter, Joseph Paul. "Relevant Interest and the Prisoner's Dilemma." *Mind* 93 (1984): 101-102.

Rapoport, Anatol. "Escape from Paradox." *Scientific American* 217 (1967): 50-56.

Snow, Paul. "The Value of Information in Newcomb's Problem and the Prisoner's Dilemma." *Theory and Decision* 18 (1985): 129-133.

Sorensen, Roy A. "The Iterated Versions of Newcomb's Problem and the Prisoner's Dilemma." *Synthese* 63 (1985): 157-166.

Steiner, Hillel. "Prisoner's Dilemma an Insoluble Problem." *Mind* ns 91 (1982): 285-286.

PROBABILITY THEORY, PARADOXES OF. See especially the BEAKER PARADOX, BERTRAND'S PARADOX, the PARDOX OF INFORMATION, the PARADOX OF INDUCTIVE PROBABILITY, the INFINITE SERIES PARADOX, the PROBABLE LIAR, SIMPSON'S PARADOX and the ST. PETERSBURG PARADOX.

PROBABLE LIAR, THE. A variation of the LIAR introduced by William G. Lycan.

Formulation. "The probability of the title of this paper, given itself (and the fact of its being a generalization), is less than 1/2. Yet the probability of any contingent statement given itself is 1. So 1 is less than 1/2" (Lycan, 202). **Explanation.** The title of Lycan's paper is "Most Generalizations are False." Given that most generalizations are false, the probability that any given generalization is true is less than 1/2. The probability is here calculated by the frequency distribution of the favorable cases: since less than half of all generalizations are true (given the truth of the title of Lycan's paper), the probability of any one of them being true is less than 1/2. But the title of Lycan's paper is itself a generalization and hence, given itself, must have probability less than 1/2. Yet, if something is true, it is true. Hence, the probability of a statement, given itself, is 1. Therefore, 1 is the probability of the title of Lycan's paper, given itself. And since this probability was already found to be less than 1/2, 1 is less than 1/2. **Resolution.** R. D. Boyd and S. K. Wertz argue that the paradox depends on an equivocation. The first premise — most generalizations are false — is, according to Boyd and Wertz, an estimate and not the initial probability that it purports to be. This is because initial probabilities range over single events and not generalizations. In contrast, the second premise — the probability of a statement, given itself, is 1 — is a total probability, describing a general situation. The two probabilities, therefore, cannot be directly compared.

READINGS

Lycan, William G. "Most Generalizations are False." *Pacific Philosophical Quarterly* 65 (1984): 202.

Boyd, R. D. and S. K. Wertz. "Probability and Lycan's Paradox." *Southwest Philosophy Review* 4 (1988): 85.

PROBLEM OF EVIL, THE. Traditionally, this paradox has played the devil with Christian theology.
Formulation. If God is omnipotent, omniscient and perfectly good, why is there evil in the world?
Explanation. If God knows all, can do all, and still lets evil exist, then in what sense may he be characterized as having good will toward men?
Resolution. There are several traditional responses to this question. That which enters into the mind of those who take the unnecessary suffering of the world to heart is often that there is no God. Another answer is that evil is the result of man's fall from grace. He could have withstood temptation and maintained himself in an Edenic state, but he exercised his free will and is reaping the consequences. If it is asked further why

God gave man free will, thus allowing his fall, the answer is that God made the world as perfect, that is, complete, as possible, and the world is more complete for having a being with free will such as man in it. This answer is inadequate because it only explains the kinds of evil that are a direct result of man's fall. Yet, if all evil is explained in this manner, that is to say if the world's evil comes to us by way of punishment or test, then God does not seem particularly good after all, because either way, the torment is excessive. Besides it is the good rather than the deserving wicked who seem to suffer most in this life. A more mystical answer to the question is to deny that evil exists. It is mere privation, or distance from the fullness of God's being, and we suffer it because we are, or became, distant from the divine wholeness. The problem with this response is that it is wholly counterintuitive that the pain and anguish we suffer is, from the divine standpoint, nothing at all. Either He is constitutionally blind to our dolorous reality and hence not omniscient or else His point of view is so detached that there is little of what we might recognize as "goodness" in it. More satisfactory, perhaps, is the Manichean, and ultimately Zoroastrian, solution to the effect that God is not all-powerful after all, but competes with another God, one of darkness, whose presence explains the world's evil. This view, banished in the West more by the sword than by argument, plays a significant but surreptitious role in those forms of vulgar Christianity in which the Devil is a powerful rival to God. The weight of occidental theological opinion, however, seems to be that a dualism of Jehovah and Satan is too high a price to pay for resolving the problem of evil.

READINGS

Andre, Shane. "The Problem of Evil and the Paradox of Friendly Atheism."
  International Journal for Philosophy of Religion 17 (1985): 208-216.
Anglin, Bill, and Stewart Goetz. "Evil Is Privation." *International Journal
  for Philosophy of Religion* 13 (1982): 3-12.
Clark, Kelly James. "Evil and Christian Belief." *International Philosophical
  Quarterly* 29 (1989): 175-189.
Mackie, J. L. "Evil and Omnipotence." *Mind* ns 64 (1955): 200-212.
Wachterhauser, Brice R. "The Problem of Evil and Moral Scepticism."
  International Journal for Philosophy of Religion 17 (1985): 167-174.
Yandell, Keith E. "The Problem of Evil and the Content of Morality."
  International Journal for Philosophy of Religion 17 (1985): 139-165.

PROBLEM OF GOODNESS. Steven M. Cahn poses the following problem: "could a world containing goodness have been created by an omnipotent, omniscient, omnimalevolent being?" (69). The problem, exactly paralleling the PROBLEM OF EVIL, purports to show that The Demon does not exist. Cahn, like Edward Madden and Peter Hare before him, concludes that the conjunction of these two problems makes both demonism and theism highly improbable. One of the basic elements in Cahn's argument is that there is a strict isomorphism between theodicy and cacodaemony (the demonic analogue to theodicy). John King-Farlow, however, contends that Cahn has merely demonstrated the isomorphism for one theodicy and one cacodaemony; since there are many variations of theodicies, however, Cahn's case is not complete. King-Farlow also appeals to PASCAL'S WAGER and to the fact that there has been a long history of profound numinous experiences, whereas there has not been a similarly strong history of diabolical experiences.

READINGS

Cahn, Steven M. "Cacodaemony." *Analysis* 37.2 (1977): 69-73.

King-Farlow, John. "Cacodaemony and Devilish Isomorphism." *Analysis* 38.1 (1978): 59-61.

Madden, Edward and Peter Hare. *Evil and the Concept of God.* Springfield, IL: Thomas, 1968.

PRODUCTIVITY PARADOX, THE. Despite strenuous efforts to increase productivity, many manufacturing concerns have experienced little return on this effort and some have even experienced negative results. Wickham Skinner argues that "the very way managers define productivity improvement and the tools they use to achieve it push their goal further out of reach" (56), thereby engendering the paradox. According to Skinner, the focus on cost reductions, which is the essence of most productivity programs, is harmful in that it hinders innovation and creates a need to insure efficiency in the workplace that both alienates the workers and is excessively time consuming for the managers. Avoiding the paradox, according to Skinner, requires the development and implementation of long-range manufacturing strategies.

READING

Skinner, Wickham. "The Productivity Paradox." *Harvard Business Review* 64 (1986): 55-59.

PROMISING, THE PARADOX OF. This paradox of ethical theory
was introduced by Julia Driver.
Formulation. The following three statements are individually true yet
jointly inconsistent:

> (1)   When someone makes a promise to do something, he
> thereby puts himself under an obligation to do it.
> (2)   If someone is obligated to do something, he can do it.
> In the philosophical rubric: "Ought implies can."
> (3)   People sometimes make promises they cannot keep.

Explanation. The first statement is unassailable because it just explains
part of what is involved in the concept of promising: if one has promised
to do something, one is obliged to do it. The second statement is intuitively
correct and has been argued for by a variety of philosophers, including
Kant, Hare and Von Fraasen. And the third statement is in line with
common sense; politicians, for example, are always being charged with
making promises they cannot keep. Nevertheless, if promising puts one
under an obligation and one cannot be under an obligation unless one can
do what one is obliged to do, then one cannot in principle make a promise
one cannot keep.
Resolution. Since the first statement must stand, the paradox must be
met by denying either the second or the third statement and by explaining
why people might have found them compelling despite their falsehood.
E. J. Lemmon rejects the second statement. One difficulty with (2) seems
to be that if 'ought implies can', then, by the contrapositive, 'cannot implies
ought not.' But just because, say, someone in a wheelchair cannot save a
drowning man, it seems counterintuitive to insist that he ought not save
him. A more careful formulation of the contrapositive, however, alleviates
the difficulty: 'cannot implies not obliged to' (instead of 'obliged not
to'). Certainly, we would not want to hold that the person in the wheelchair
was obliged to refrain from saving the drowning man. Rather we would
only claim that he is not obliged to save him. A. P. Martinich rejects the
third statement, partly on the view that "politician's promises" are not to
be taken as real promises until investigation determines whether they can
be kept in the first place. Using Grice's theory about conversation,
Martinich argues that (3) is intuitively plausible because it centers attention
on the promiser's intentions rather than his inabilities and one's intentions
are thought to be central to the activity of promising.
READINGS
Driver, Julia. "Promises, Obligations, and Abilities." *Philosophical Studies*
44 (1983): 221-223.

Martinich, A. P. "A Solution of a Paradox of Promising." *Philosophia* 15
    (1985): 117-122.
— —. "Obligations, Ability and *Prima Facie* Promising." *Philosophia* 17
    (1987): 323-330.
Sinnott-Armstrong, Walter. "A Resolution of a Paradox of Promising."
    Philosophia 17 (1987): 77-83.

PROTAGORAS, THE. See the EUALTHUS.

PYGMALION EFFECT, THE. See the EXPERIMENTER EXPECTANCY
PARADOX.

RACE COURSE, THE. See the DICHOTOMY.

RAVEN(S) PARADOX, THE. See HEMPEL'S PARADOXES OF
CONFIRMATION.

RELATIVISM, THE PARADOX OF. See the PARADOXES OF COGNITIVE
RELATIVISM.

RELIGIOUS PARADOXES. Religious paradoxes differ from
philosophical paradoxes insofar as religious paradoxes depend on mystical
experience, scripture or orthodox systems of belief. One main class are
those that arise from the attributes of God. There are hence paradoxes of
OMNIPOTENCE (such as the paradox of the STONE), of OMNISCIENCE, of
OMNIPRESENCE AND TIMELESSNESS, of divine existence (such as ROSS'S
ANTIMONY), and of divine perfecton (such as the PROBLEMS OF EVIL AND OF
GOODNESS). The main class of paradoxes specific to Christianity are, of
course, the Christological paradoxes, such as the paradoxes of the TRINITY,
the Immaculate Conception, the INCARNATION, the Virgin Birth, and of the
Resurrection. La Croix's PARADOX OF EDEN concerns the fall of man and
the paraclete appears in DONNE'S PARADOX OF THE HOLY GHOST. Paul
pronounces many paradoxes, particularly in 2 Corinthians, as when he
says, "For when I am weak, then I am strong." Again, Christianity and

Judaism are founded on the paradox that the world will be saved by failure—see the PARADOX OF THE FORTUNATE FALL. See also: ANTINOMIANISM, BODHISATTVA PARADOX, BUDDHIST PARADOXES, the DEVIL'S OFFER, NICHOLAS OF CUZA'S COINCIDENCE OF OPPOSITES, PASCAL'S WAGER, ROSS'S ANTIMONY, TERTULLIAN'S PARADOX and the VIA NEGATIVA.

READINGS

Calhoun, Robert L. "The Language of Religion." *The Unity of Knowledge.* Ed. LouisLeary. Garden City, NY: Doubleday, 1955. 248-262.

Ramsey, I. T. "Paradox in Religion." In *New Essays on Religious Language.* Dallas M. High, ed. New York: Oxford UP, 1969. 138-161.

Stenger, Mary Ann. "The Significance of Paradox for Theological Verification: Difficulties and Possibilities." *International Journal for Philosophy of Religion* 14.3 (1983): 171-182.

Yusa, Michiko. "Paradoxes and Riddles." *Encyclopedia of Religion.* Mircea Eliade, ed. New York: Macmillan, 1987. Vol. 11, 189-195.

RENAISSANCE PARADOXES. Rosalie Colie sees Shakespeare's *King Lear* as expressing the range of stock Renaissance paradoxes. Following Lando, she gives these as follows:

(1) It is better to have no servants than to have them.
(2) It is better to weep than to laugh.
(3) It is better to be ignorant than learned.
(4) It is better to be mad than wise.
(5) It is not a bad thing for a prince to lose his state.
(6) It is better to live in a cottage than a great palace.
(7) It is better to be poor than rich.
(8) It is neither shameful nor odious to be a bastard.
(9) A frugal life is better than a splendid and sumptuous one.
(10) It is better to be blind than have sight.
(11) It is better to have an ugly wife than a beautiful one.
(12) It is better to be in prison than at liberty.
(13) It is better to live in exile than to languish in one's native land.

READING

Colie, Rosalie. *Paradoxia Epidemica: The Renaissance Tradition of Paradox.* Princeton: Princeton UP, 1966.

RHETORICAL PARADOXES. In rhetoric, paradox sometimes means "a conclusion or apodosis contrary to what the audience has been led up to expect" (OED). See also PARADOX, DEFINITION OF and LITERARY PARADOX.

RICHARD'S PARADOX. Adduced by Jules Richard in 1905, this paradox is concerned with finite definability.

Formulation. Let D be the set of all functions of one variable from the set of natural numbers into itself that can be defined in a finite number of words. Given an enumeration of D, let f be defined as "the function from the set of natural numbers into itself whose value for any given argument is one more than the value, for that same argument, of the function that corresponds to the argument in the enumeration of D." By the definition of f, it must differ from every element of D and, therefore, f does not belong to D. Nevertheless, f is defined in a finite number of words and thus belongs to D.

Explanation. Let E be the set of all expressions of the form

$$a_1 a_2 \ldots a_n$$

where n is a natural number (called the length of the expression) and each of the a_i is a letter of the Latin alphabet, a semi-colon (used to separate words), or a comma. The set D is clearly a subset of E. We can order these symbols by using an augmented form of the natural alphabetical order, as follows:

$$a{<}b{<}c \ldots {<}z{<};{<},$$

We can then use this symbol order to define an order on E and, hence, on D (this is known as the lexicographical order):

$$a_1 a_2 \ldots a_n < b_1 b_2 \ldots b_m$$

if (1) $n{<}m$ or (2) $n{=}m$ and there is some $i{\leq}n$ such that for all $j{<}i$

$$a_j = b_j \text{ and } a_i < b_i.$$

The order on D determines an enumeration of D. Let f_1 be the first element of the enumeration, f_2 the second element, and so on. Then, the function f, as defined above, is $f(k) = f_k(k) + 1$, for each natural number k. Since f was defined using only a finite number of words, f is an element of D. Thus,

$$f = f_n \text{ for some } n. \text{ But } f(n) = f_n(n) + 1,$$

so f differs from f_n for the argument n. Therefore, $f \neq f_n$, which is a contradiction. Thus, the notion of finite definability seems paradoxical.

Resolution. As in most SEMANTICAL PARADOXES, it seems that the root of the trouble is the element of self-reference that issues in a vicious circle. In particular, the definition of f is impredicative. That is, f is a member of the set D, but the very definition of f refers to D in an essential way. The responses to this paradox, as for the other semantical paradoxes, have centered on ways to block the formation of the circular definition.

READINGS

Hazen, Allen. "Predicative Logics." *Handbook of Philosophical Logic. Volume One: Elements of Classical Logic.* Ed. D. Gabbray and F. Guenthner. Dordrecht: Reidel, 1983. 331-407.

Kleene, Stephen C. *Introduction to Metamathematics.* Amsterdam: North-Holland, 1952. 38-39.

ROBBER'S PARADOX, THE. This is a version of the Victim's PARADOX in which the paradoxical conclusion is that it is forbidden for the thief to repent his deeds.

ROSS'S ANTIMONY. This paradox results from James Ross's modal argument for God's existence.

Formulation Ross deduces a contradiction from the supposition that God does not exist and the following premises:

(1) It is possible that there is an explanation for the non-existence of God.
(2) The existence of God is not inconsistent.
(3) It is impossible that anything could prevent God from existing.

He thus concludes that God's existence is necessary. Yet a similar proof of the necessity of God's non-existence follows from the supposition that He does exist and the premises:

(4) It is possible that there is an explanation for the existence of God.
(5) The non-existence of God is not inconsistent.
(6) It is impossible that anything could cause God to exist.

Explanation. Ross's original argument is an indirect proof: starting from the supposition that God does not exist, he deduces a contradiction, thereby proving God's non-existence is impossible. The premises that he uses in the deduction seem innocuous. Premise (1) is a weakened form of the Principle of Sufficient Reason; premise (2) merely states that the affirmation of God's existence is not self-contradictory; and premise (3) seems to follow from the very notion of God. If, however, we grant (1), it would seem that we should also grant (4). Similarly, (2) and (5) seem to stand or fall together, while (6) follows from the very notion of God. But, once we have (4)-(6), we can construct an argument for the impossibility of God's existence. Hence, we have proved that God's existence is both necessary and impossible, which is a contradiction.

Resolution. John Zeis points out that the antinomy depends on premises (2) and (5) either standing or falling together. This will be the case if the statement "God exists" is contingent. If, however, "God exists" is either necessarily true or contradictory, (2) and (5) will have opposite truth values and the antinomy fails. Interestingly, then, the antinomy reveals that "God exists" is not a contingent statement. Thus, either God necessarily exists or His existence is impossible. Thus, a demonstration of either (2) or (5) would entail respectively either Ross's proof of God's existence or the parallel proof of His non-existence. But Zeis argues further that a proof of (2) or (5) would already have to be a proof of God's existence or non-existence, thereby obviating the need for the purported demonstrations. All modal proofs (or disproofs) of God's existence, according to Zeis, share this flaw.

READING
Zeis, John. "Ross's Antimony and Modal Arguments for God's Existence." *International Journal for Philosophy of Religion* 20 (1986): 159-164.

RULE FOLLOWING, THE PARADOX OF. This paradox was supposedly advanced by Ludwig Wittgenstein as an argument for scepticism.
Formulation. "When I respond in one way rather than another to such a problem as '68+57,' I can have no justification for one response rather than another. Since the sceptic, who supposes that I meant quus [instead of plus], cannot be answered, there is no fact about me that distinguishes between my meaning plus and my meaning quus" (Kripke, 21).
Explanation. Consider the function "quus," defined as follows:

$$x \text{ quus } y =_{def} x \text{ plus } y \text{ if } x \text{ and } y \text{ are both less than } 57$$
$$=_{def} 5 \text{ otherwise.}$$

Now suppose that Jones has never had occasion to add numbers greater than 56. The sceptic then argues that there is no evidence in any of Jones's past actions that would count against the hypothesis that he actually meant "x quus y" when he said "x plus y." This is because Jones has never reached the point at which the two functions diverge and, thus, any action that supports the hypothesis that Jones means plus also supports the hypothesis that he really means quus. Even Jones himself, according to Wittgenstein, is in the same quandary, for it is precisely the notion of intentional meaning that the sceptic is attacking, due to the lack of independent evidence for it.

Resolution. According to Saul Kripke's interpretation, Wittgenstein is committed to an anti-realist solution to the paradox, in which our practice of communication enables us to establish conditions for legitimate assertability of such statements as "Jones is following this or that rule." Roger Scruton, however, contends that both Kripke's interpretation of Wittgenstein and his (Kripke's) response to the paradox are flawed. For Scruton, the paradox does imply that meaning is socially generated, but rules may nevertheless "be understood by the participants as defining modes of 'correspondence' with an independent reality" (598) and, thus, we are not forced to adopt an anti-realist position. In contrast, Barry Allen argues that the paradox reveals the inconsistency of the notion of such a thing as a proposition as that which grounds meaning.

READINGS

Allen, Barry. "Gruesome Arithmetic: Kripke's Sceptic Replies." *Dialogue* 28 (1989): 257-264.

Anscombe, G. E. M. "Review of *Wittgenstein on Rules and Private Language,* by Saul Kripke." *Canadian Journal of Philosophy* 15 (1985): 103-109.

Baker, J., and P. Hacker. *Scepticism, Rues, and Meaning.* Oxford: Blackwell, 1984.

Goldfarb, W. "Kripke on Wittgenstein on Rules." *Journal of Philosophy* 82 (1985): 471-488.

Kripke, Saul. *Wittgenstein on Rules and Private Language.* Cambridge; Harvard UP, 1982.

McDowell, J. "Wittgenstein on Following a Rule." *Synthese* 58 (1984): 325-363.

Rudebusch, George. "Hoffman on Kripke's Wittgenstein." *Philosophy Research Archives* 12 (1986-87): 177-182.

Scruton, Roger. "Wittgenstein on Rule and Private Language." *Mind* ns 93 (1984): 592-602.

Stock, Guy. "Liebniz and Kripke's Sceptical Paradox." *Philosophical Quarterly* 38 (1988): 326-329.

Tait, W. W. "Wittgenstein and the Sceptical Paradoxes." *Journal of Philosophy* 83 (1986): 475-88.

Wittgenstein, Ludwig. *The Philosophical Investigations.* Trans. G. E. M. Anscombe. New York: Macmillan, 1953.

RUSSELL'S PARADOX. Called Russell's Class Paradox and named by Bertrand Russell himself "the Contradiction," this paradox in set theory was historically important because it put Frege's attempt to reduce mathematics to logic in check.

Formulation. Consider the set of all sets that do not contain themselves as a member; this set contains itself as a member if, and only if, it does not contain itself.

Explanation. Some sets are not members of themselves, while other sets do contain themselves. The set of small sets, for example, is not small. The set of large sets, however, is itself large and thus the set of large sets is itself an element of the set of large sets. Define the set ¬ to be the set of all sets that are not members of themselves:

(1)   ¬ = {X / X œ X}.

There are many elements of ¬ most of which are not problematical. Like the set of small sets given above, the set of tea kettles, for example, is not itself a tea kettle and thus belongs to ¬. From the definition of ¬, the criterion for membership in ¬ is that a set not be an element of itself; that is

(2)   X e ¬ if, and only if, X œ X.

We may then ask if ¬ itself is a member of ¬; this amounts to instantiating the variable X in (2) to ¬, whereupon we obtain the following contradiction:

(3)   ¬ e ¬ if, and only if, ¬ œ ¬.

This is Russell's Paradox. It is a formal contradiction in Fregian logic: if ¬ is an element of itself, then, by definition, it is not an element of itself; but if ¬ is not an element of itself, it satisfies the definition of ¬ and thus is an element of itself.

Resolution. Russell himself argued that the paradox was due to the element of self-reference that introduces a vicious circle into logic. He thus proposed his Theory of Types to eliminate the problem. According to the Theory of Types, $type_0$ is assigned to individuals, $type_1$ to sets of individuals, $type_2$ to sets of sets of individuals, and so on. Each type was also divided into orders (Ramified Theory of Types), but a Simple Theory of Types was presented by F. P. Ramsey that seems to be sufficient for avoiding the paradox. The theory would block the paradox by making it impossible to affirm "¬ e ¬" since the second occurrence of ¬ would have to be of a higher type than the first occurrence. W. V. O. Quine simplified the theory considerably by eliminating the types in favor of building the hierarchy into the definition of well-formed formula. Russell was of the opinion that the solution to the LOGICAL PARADOXES should also give us the key to the solution of the SEMANTICAL PARADOXES and, indeed, a hierarchical semantical theory was developed by Alfred Tarski. Even the

Simple Theory of Types, however, has undesirable consequences, such as the apparent reproduction of the whole of logic for each type. Some logicians also object that it is too radical in that it disallows all self-reference, even though not all self-reference is paradoxical. Since it became evident that one of the roots of the paradox was an axiom of unrestricted abstraction — that for any property, there is a set of all and only those things having that property — another response to the paradox was to develop a consistent axiomatization of set theory. In the standard Zermelo-Fraenkel axiomatization, the strategy is to limit the size of sets so that such troublesome sets as the Russell set ¬ above cannot be formed. This is done by replacing unrestricted abstraction with an axiom that allows us to affirm the existence of a set corresponding to a given property only if that set can be separated off from an already given set. Although sets having a transfinite number of elements are countenanced in Zermelo-Fraenkel set theory, one counterintuitive result is that there is no universal set (that is, a set of all sets). Another approach to the paradox was developed by Stanislaw Lesniewski, who argued that Russell's Paradox arises because of an ambiguity in the terms used to talk about sets. According to Lesniewski the relation between part and whole — hence also the terms "an element of" and "the set of" — can be thought of either distributively or collectively. When Russell's Paradox is formulated consistently either in distributive terms or in collective terms, certain presuppositions turn out to be false, thereby invalidating the paradox. See RUSSELL'S PARADOX IN MANY VALUED LOGIC.

READINGS

Castañeda, Hector-Neri. "Ontology and Grammar: I Russell's Paradox and the General Theory of Properties in Natural Languages." *Theoria* 42 (1976): 44-92.

Champlin, T. S. *Reflexive Paradoxes*. London: Routledge, 1988

Hart, W. D. "Russell and Hart." *Pacific Philosophical Quarterly* 64 (1983): 193-210.

Jackson, Joseph E. "Shaving Russell's Paradox with Occam's Razor." ETC 22 (1965): 114-116.

Rodrigues Consuergra, Francisco A. "Russell's Theory of Types, 1901-1910: Its Complex Origins in the Unpublished Manuscripts." *History of Philosophical Logic* 10 (1989): 131-164.

RUSSELL'S PARADOX IN MANY VALUED LOGICS. Many-valued logic has often been seen as a promising way of escaping from the logical paradoxes. If, beside truth and falsity, we have a third truth value — say, "indeterminate"— then the set of all sets that are not members of themselves, for example, can be assigned this third truth value and RUSSELL's PARADOX will be avoided. In various many-valued logics, however, the paradox can be resurrected by modifying the definition of the troublesome "Russell set." In set theory based on three mutually exclusive truth values, the third of which corresponds to "the possibility that a set has a fuzzy penumbra, so that a given element lying in this penumbra can be regarded neither as inside the set nor as outside it" (Rescher, 208), the troublesome set becomes

> the set of all sets that are not members of themselves nor in the fuzzy penumbra of themselves.

In order to avoid the paradox in a finitely-valued logic, very strong indeterminacy conditions must be imposed. Alternatively, one may have recourse to infinitely-valued logic.

READING

Rescher, Nicholas. *Many-Valued Logic.* New York: McGraw Hill, 1969. 207-209.

SANCHO PANZA, THE. Also called the Gallows, this logical paradox poses an existential dilemma. In the Middle Ages, this paradox in various versions was rightly considered as a form of the Liar (Jones).

Formulation. "A certain manor was divided by a river upon which was a bridge. The lord of the manor had erected a gallows at one end of the bridge and had enacted a law that whoever would cross the bridge must first swear whither he were going and on what business; if he swore truly, he should be allowed to pass freely; but if he swore falsely and did then cross the bridge he should be hanged forthwith upon the gallows. One man...swore 'I go to be hanged on yonder gallows', and thereupon crossed the bridge. The vexed question whether the man should be hanged is brought to Sancho Panza as governor of Barataria" (Cervantes, *Don Quixote*, Pt. 2 Ch. 51, quoted by A. Church, Intr*oduction to Mathematical Logic* 105).

Explanation. If the man were hanged, he would have sworn his business truly, and therefore would not have merited hanging. If the man were not hanged, he would have sworn his business falsely and must, according to the policy in force, be hanged.

Resolution. One could, of course, have the paradoxer hanged on general principles. Sancho Panza's first solution is just as decisive: to have the fellow cut in twain, hanging half and letting the other go free. In the end, Sancho Panza applies a Quixotic principle — that when there is equal justice on both sides of a case, the judge should favor mercy — and lets the fellow go.

READING

Jones, Joseph R. "The Liar Paradox in *Don Quixote* II, 51." *Hispanic Review* 54 (1986): 183-193.

SARTRE'S PARADOX. Construed by Jean-Paul Sartre and often called the Conflict-of-Duty Paradox, this problem involves conflicting obligations. Compare PLATO'S PARADOX.

Formulation. One of Sartre's pupils wanted to join the Free French Forces in order to avenge his brother, who was killed by the German army of occupation. But he also wanted to stay by his mother, who was deeply wounded by the loss of her eldest son. What should he do?

Explanation. Sartre's student has two options; both are compelling, but neither absolutely binding. They are incompatible, however, in that the student cannot do both and this is reflected in the formalization of them in deontic logic.

Resolution. Azizah al-Hibri suggests that while the very similar Plato's Paradox may be resolved by resorting to ethical hierarchies, the present paradox resists this kind of solution because neither option seems to have precedence over the other, thereby making the configuration of the attendant circumstances crucial to the argument. Thus, according to al-Hibri, the paradox cannot be used to undermine the principle of standard deontic logic which asserts that obligations should not conflict. This is because the global context does not decide the issue so that the student's duty would not be expressed as conflicting obligations, but as a disjunctive obligation: the student should either join the fight or stay by his mother. Thus the erstwhile moral quandary is reduced to the student's personal choice. Al-Hibri's contention, from a logical point of view, is that a decision on whether to allow conflicts of duty is prior to the present paradox since the latter does not force the issue.

READINGS

Al-Hibri, Azizah. *Deontic Logic*. Washington: UP of America. 1978. 25, 69-72.

Forrester, James W. *Why You Should, The Pragmatics of Deontic Speech*. Hanover, NH: Brown UP, 1989. 15-17.

SCHRÖEDINGER'S CAT. Described by Erwin Schröedinger in 1935, this veridical paradox concerns the difficulty of understanding the 'wave function' collapse and the role of the registration or measuring system or of a conscious observer. It is related to the EINSTEIN-PODOLSKY-ROSEN PARADOX and the POTENTIAL ENERGY BARRIER PARADOX.

Formulation. "A cat is penned up in a steel chamber, along with the following diabolical device (which must be secured against direct interference by the cat): in a Geiger counter there is a tiny bit of radioactive substance, *so* small, that *perhaps* in the course of one hour one of the atoms decays, but also, with equal probability, perhaps none; if it happens, the counter tube discharges and through a relay shatters a small flask of hydrocyanic acid. If one has left this entire system to itself for one hour, one would say that the cat still lives *if* meanwhile no atom has decayed. The first atomic decay would have poisoned it. The [wave-] function of the entire system would express this by having in it the living and the dead cat (pardon the expression) mixed or smeared out in equal parts" (Schröedinger 328).

Explanation. The wave function description of quantum mechanics does not allow for precise specification of all variables simultaneously (see the EINSTEIN-PODOLSKY-ROSEN PARADOX). According to Schröedinger, this circumstance reflects either a limitation on knowledge or an indeterminate blurring of the variables in reality. Schröedinger argues that quantum mechanics is incompatible with the first of these options, but that his Cat Paradox shows that it is "ridiculous" to accept the second. Thus, the counterintuitive consequences of quantum mechanics are not limited to systems involving only very small particles.

Resolution. As with the EPR Paradox, an instrumentalist attitude toward 'quantum mechanical wave functions is capable of resolving the paradox. The instrumentalist approach is to resist the temptation to interpret wave functions realistically by insisting that they are merely devices allowing the calculation of probabilities of certain observations. Schröedinger makes this suggestion himself: "Reality resists imitation through a model. So one lets go of naive realism and leans directly on the indubitable proposition that *actually* (for the physicist) after all is said and done there is only observation, measurement" (328). Nevertheless, such instrumentalism remains controversial, and various "hidden variable" theories have been developed to restore a realist model of quantum interactions (see the POTENTIAL ENERGY BARRIER PARADOX). So far, however, physicists have found no direct evidence of hidden variables.

READINGS

D'Espagnat, B. *Conceptual Foundations of Quantum Mechanics.* 2nd ed. Reading, MA: Benjamin, 1976. Ch. 8.

Holtzman, Jack M. "A Note on Schröedinger's Cat and the Unexpected Hanging Paradox." *British Journal for the Philosophy of Science* 39(1988): 397-401.

Loesser, J. G. "Three Perspectives on Schöedinger's Cat." *American Journal of Physics* 52.12 (1984): 1089-1093.

Primas, H. *Chemistry, Quantum Mechanics, and Reductionism.* 2nd. ed. Berlin: Springer, 1983.

Schröedinger, Erwin. "The Present Situation in Quantum Mechanics: A Translation of Schröedinger's 'Cat Paradox' Paper." Trans. John Trimmer. *Proceedings of the American Philosophical Society* 124 (1980): 323-338.

SEEKER PARADOX, THE. This is a paradox in the fiction of Patrick White, winner of the 1973 Nobel Prize in Literature, which is analyzed by Carolyn Bliss.

Formulation. "One of White's most baffling and important paradoxes [is] that the self must be sought and found only to be relinquished, that the individuality so powerfully expressed by his major characters paradoxically enables them to seek a state of understanding in which selfhood is finally subsumed. In a further permutation of the paradox, the surrender of the self which this understanding demands somehow functions to permit the the character's fullest realization of the essential self; that is, he becomes most himself when he least seeks to be. In terms of the related Christian paradox, he finds his life by losing it, or as Emerson put it, 'The man who renounces himself comes to himself'" (Bliss, 8).

Explanation. White has been greatly influenced by the Judeo-Christian concept of the religious quest and its inevitable failure due to man's inability to comprehend the infinite. In particular, man's search for an understanding of his own nature cannot be successful by an investigation of himself.

Resolution. True understanding of human nature cannot be obtained from self-examination because it entails man's relation to the Absolute. This observation does not, perhaps, resolve the paradox; rather, the paradox reveals the ineffable nature of the Judeo-Christian belief that "the center of gravity of existence is outside existence" (Adin Steinsaltz, cited in Bliss, 206).

READING

Bliss, Carolyn. *Patrick White's Fiction: The Paradox of the Fortunate Failure.* New York: St. Martin's, 1986.

SELF-AMENDMENT, THE PARADOX OF. This is a Legal Paradox, first adduced by Alf Ross.

Formulation. Suppose that we have a constitution that specifies a method for making amendments. Should we try to change the method of amendment to one that is incompatible with the original method, we find that we are involved in a contradiction. Hence, the original method of making amendments is immutable.

Explanation. Any true change in the method of making amendments will result in a method inconsistent with the original method "in the sense that each permits something that the other forbids and forbids something that the other permits" (Suber 39). Further, if the new method is to be legally valid, it must be the conclusion of a valid deductive argument that models the act of self-amendment. Since one of the premises of this argument must be the original method of making amendments and since the two methods are by hypothesis inconsistent, the conclusion (the new method) and the premise (the original method) are contradictory; therefore, the argument is invalid. Hence, it is impossible to make valid changes in the original method of making amendments (except, of course, for merely cosmetic changes). This purported immutability, as Suber observes, makes the present paradox resemble that of divine OMNIPOTENCE.

Resolution. One response to the paradox is to observe that the original method and the new method do not hold at the same time and, hence, a temporal logic might validate the modeling argument. Suber, following Ross, rejects this solution because it is the original method that must validate the new method yet the two methods, considered abstractly without regard to time, are contradictory. Since the whole point of appealing to a temporal logic, however, was to eliminate the logical contradiction in the modeling argument, Suber's objection does not seem pertinent. Another response to the paradox would be to deny that deductive inference is an adequate model for legal amendment. To do so would be to countenance the inconsistency of self-amendment which would necessitate a compelling explanation. Suber, however, argues that it would in fact shift the foundations of the legal system to one based on authority.

READING

Suber, Peter. *The Paradox of Self-Amendment: A Study of Logic, Law Omnipotence, and Change.* New York: Lang, 1990.

SELF-DECEPTION, THE PARADOX OF. "A man can love a paradox without either losing his wit or his honesty" (Ralph Waldo Emerson, *Walter Savage Landor* XII). This psychological paradox arose from the difficulties of the concept of self-deception.
Formulation. Deception is convincing someone of something one knows to be false, but if one knows something to be false, how can one deceive oneself about it?
Explanation. There are two closely related problems of self-deception, both generated by applying the logic of interpersonal deception to cases in which one deceives oneself. In order for someone to deceive another person into believing some proposition P, it is necessary for the deceiver to believe that P is false and to intend to make the other person believe that P is true. One contradiction seems to be that in order to deceive myself I must intend to fool myself into believing that P is true when I already believe that P is false. The other apparent contradiction is that after I have deceived myself I must believe both that P is true and that P is false.
Resolution. M. R. Haight argues that the paradox reveals that self-deception is impossible since it would require not only that the self-deceiver simultaneously holds contradictory beliefs but also that he both knows and does not know the same proposition. Roy A. Sorensen argues that self-deception is possible because it occurs over a period of time, not instantaneously, and thus the perpetrator of the self-deception need not hold contradictory beliefs simultaneously. Raphael Demos claims that there are two levels of awareness, one being just a simple awareness and the other an awareness with attention. Thus, one can simultaneously entertain contradictory beliefs by having one's attention distracted from certain aspects of the question entertained. Demos's approach is typical of those responses that argue that self-deception is possible because one or another type of mental fragmentation allows intrapersonal deception to parallel interpersonal deception. Still another response is to argue that self-deception does not parallel interpersonal deception at all, but rather operates in some other manner. H. Fingarette, for example, claims that the paradox arises from an undue emphasis on the cognitive aspects of our self-deceptive activities. An analysis of the interaction of volition and action would reveal, according to Fingarette, that the basic feature of self-deception is disavowal — the refusal to identify oneself as a certain kind of person or with a certain project.

READINGS

Canfield, John, and Patrick McNally. "Paradoxes of Self-Deception." *Analysis* 21.6 (1961): 140-144.

Champlin, T. S. "Self-Deception: A Reflexive Dilemma." *Philosophy* 52 (1977). 281-299.

Demos, Raphael. "Lying to Oneself." *Journal of Philosophy* 57 (1960): 588-595.

Fingarette, H. *Self-Deception.* London: Routledge, 1969.

Foss, Jeffrey. "Rethinking Self-Deception." American Philosophical *Quarterly* 17 (1980). 237-243.

Haight, M. R. *A Study of Self Deception.* New Jersey: Humanities P, 1980.

Martin, M., ed. Self-*Deception and Self-Understanding.* Lawrence: U of Kansas P, 1985.

Mele, Alfred. "Self-Deception." Philosophical *Quarterly* 33 (1983): 365-377.

— —. "Incontinent Believing." *Philosophical Quarterly* 36 (1986): 212-222.

— —. "Recent Work on Self-Deception." *American Philosophical Quarterly* 24 (1987): 1-17.

Sorensen, Roy A. "Self-Deception and Scattered Events." *Mind* ns 94 (1985): 64-69.

— —. "Dogmaticism, Junk Knowledge, and Conditionals. *Philosophical Quarterly* 38 (1988): 433-454.

SELF-REFERENCE AND CIRCULARITY, PARADOXES OF. Two main cycles of paradox, those related to the LIAR and to RUSSELL'S PARADOX, involve problems of self-reference and circularity. Among entries that relate to this feature of discourse and thought are: the BARBER PARADOX, the PARADOX OF COGNITIVE RELATIVISM, the CROCODILE'S DILEMMA, the EUALTHUS, EUBILIDES'S PARADOXES, the EPIMENIDES, GEACH'S PARADOX, the HETEROLOGICAL PARADOX, INSOLUBILIA, the PARADOX OF THE KNOWER, MENO'S PARADOX, the POSSIBLE LIAR, PRAGMATIC PARADOXES, the PROBABLE LIAR, PRIOR'S FAMILY OF PARADOXES, RUSSELL'S PARADOX IN MANY VALUED LOGIC, the SANCHO PANZA, the PARADOX OF SELF-AMENDMENT, the PARADOX OF SELF-REFERENCE IN SCEPTICISM, AND ZALCMAN'S PARADOX.

SELF-REFERENCE IN SCEPTICISM, THE PARADOX OF. This is a classical version of the paradox of relativism.
Formulation. "Just as, for example, fire after consuming the fuel destroys also itself, and like as purgatives after drinking the fluids out of the bodies expel themselves as well, so too the argument against proof, after abolishing every proof, can cancel itself also. And again, just as it is not impossible for the man who has ascended to a high place on a ladder to

overturn the ladder with his foot after his ascent, so also it is not unlikely that the Sceptic after he has arrived at the demonstration of his thesis by means of argument proving the non-existence of proof, as it were by a step-ladder, should then abolish this very argument" (Sextus Empiricus, *Against the Logicians*, 480-481).

Explanation. If the sceptic denies that philosophical knowledge is possible, then his own views must not count as philosophical knowledge either.

Resolution. Avner Cohen argues that the noble skeptic must, for the sake of consistency, abandon philosophy altogether, but finds that sceptics such as Sextus Empiricus and Ludwig Wittgenstein are of two minds about quitting philosophy. Once one accepts the position that philosophical knowledge is unattainable, however, perhaps consistency ceases to be an overriding concern!

READING

Cohen, Avner. "Sextus Empiricus: Scepticism as Therapy." *Philosophical Forum* 15 (1984): 405-424.

SEMANTICAL PARADOXES. These paradoxes involve such semantical concepts as meaning and truth, and include the PARADOX OF ANALYSIS and DAVIDSON'S PARADOX OF IRRATIONALITY. For a technical distinction with logical paradoxes, see LOGICAL PARADOXES.

SENIOR SNEAK WEEK. This is a version of the PREDICTION PARADOX.

SEN'S PARADOX. Adduced by Amartya K. Sen, this political paradox purports to show that the "Paretian liberal" concept of society is inconsistent.

Formulation. Any society that incorporates the Pareto Principle and a minimal degree of personal freedom cannot have a reasonable decision procedure.

Explanation. The Paretian liberal view of society affirms that any society will be tolerable only in so far as it employs reasonable (rational) decision procedures and allows its members a large degree of personal freedom. The requirement that decision procedures be rational implies that the society have a means of consistently ranking policy options. It also implies the Pareto Principle: whatever is preferred by all the members of the society should be selected by the society's decision procedure. The requirement of personal freedom implies that some options are completely determined by the individual's preference. As a minimal condition, the society should respect A's choice between the pair (x,y) and B's choice between the pair (t,u). Jonathan Barnes gives an example of a society (club) in which the only two members are A and B. A's preferences are ranked in the following decreasing order:

$$t, y, x, u,$$

whereas B's ranking is

$$x, u, t, y.$$

Thus, the society must make the following rankings:

(1)	y is preferred to x	decisiveness of A
(2)	x is preferred to u	Pareto Principle
(3)	u is preferred to t	decisiveness of B
(4)	t is preferred to y	Pareto Principle.

Hence, the society cannot establish a linear order among the options and thus its decision procedure is not reasonable. The foregoing is, of course, only an example, but it displays the spirit of Sen's proof.

Resolution. The model assumes that all the choices must be ranked. Should A and B in the above example abstain from making some pairwise rankings, the cycle might be broken. Ultimately, however, this is perhaps a minor matter (although Barnes gives it as the solution to the paradox). The decision procedure is not rational because it cannot handle all the possible configurations of personal preferences. In any particular society, it may be that the troublesome configurations just never arise. Thus Sen observes,

> The ultimate guarantee for individual liberty may rest not on rules for social choice but on developing individual values that respect each other's personal choices. The conflict posed here is concerned with societies where such a condition does not hold and where pairwise choice based on liberal values may conflict with those based on the Pareto Principle. (155-156)

Indeed, the delineation of the spheres of individual liberty and collective responsibility has been and continues to be a major concern of political theory. Nevertheless, other responses to the present paradox include attempts to invalidate one or other of the premises, for example, by only attributing rights to individuals conditionally.

READINGS

Barnes, Jonathan. "Freedom, Rationality, and Paradox." *Canadian Journal of Philosophy* 10 (1980): 545-565.

Krüger, Lorenz, and Wulf Gaertner. "Alternative Libertarian Claims and Sen's Paradox." *Theory and Decision* 15 (1983): 211-229.

Sen, Amartya K. "The Impossibility of a Paretian Liberal." *Journal of Political Economy* 78 (1970): 152-157.

— —. *Collective Choice and Social Welfare*. San Francisco: Holden Day, 1970. Ch. 7.

— —. "Liberty, Unanimity and Rights." *Economica* 43 (1976): 217-245.

SET THEORY, PARADOXES OF. Various LOGICAL PARADOXES have emerged involving Set Theory, of which RUSSELL'S PARADOX is perhaps the paradigmatical example. Others include BARRY'S PARADOX, the BURALI-FORTI PARADOX, CANTOR'S PARADOX, the CURRY PARADOX, DUMITRIU'S ANTINOMY OF THE THEORY OF TYPES, the HETEROLOGICAL PARADOX, the PARADOX OF THE NON-COMMUNICATOR, RICHARD'S PARADOX, the SKOLEM PARADOX, and the ZERMELO-KÖNIG PARADOX.

SHADOW PARADOX, THE. Daniel Cohen attributes this didactic paradox to J. Tienson. It is what might be called a "toy" paradox.

Formulation. There are four principles in which we might summarize what we know about shadows:

(1) Shadows are dark spots on the surfaces of opaque objects caused by the interruption of a beam of light.
(2) All shadows are the shadows of something.
(3) A shadow cannot be cast through an opaque object.
(4) An object must be illuminated to cast a shadow.

Now consider the following case. There is a dark spot on a wall caused by the interruption of a beam of light — hence, by the first principle, there is a shadow on the wall. Between the shadow and the light source are two disks either of which by itself would cast the exact shadow on the wall. Yet the disk closer to the light source cannot be that of which the shadow is the shadow because, if it were, the shadow on the wall would have to be cast through the second disk; but this is disallowed by the third principle. Moreover, the disk closer to the wall cannot be that of which the shadow is the shadow because it is not illuminated, as is required by the fourth principle. So what is the something of which the shadow is the shadow, as demanded by the second principle?

Explanation. The paradox assumes that the light source has no dimensions in order to rule out the question of a penumbra. The problem is that, on the principles enumerated, neither disk can cast the shadow in question. The following diagram, adapted from Cohen, explicates the paradox:

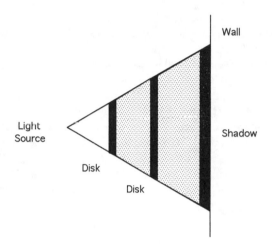

Resolution. Since Cohen cites the present paradox as an instance of how paradoxes may be used to stimulate thought, the reader is left to work out his own response.

READING

Cohen, Daniel. "Putting Paradoxes into Pedagogical Use in Philosophy."
Teaching Philosophy 8 (1985): 309-317.

SHIP OF THESEUS, THE. This paradox concerns the criteria for the identity of artifacts.

Formulation. Plutarch is the sole ancient source for this paradox (*Life of Theseus*; taken from Dillon, 411): "The ship [the *Theoris*] on which Theseus sailed with the youths and returned safely, the thirty-oared galley, was preserved by the Athenians down to the time of Demetrius of Phaleron [regent of Athens, 317-307 B.C.]. They took away the old timbers from time to time, and put new and sound ones in their places, so that the vessel became a standing illustration for the philosophers in the much-

debated 'Augmentation Argument' [*auxomenos logos*], some declaring that it remained the same, others that it was not the same vessel."
Explanation. There is a ship A that is entirely overhauled by gradually replacing all of its old parts with new ones. Call the ship at the end of this process ship B. At the same time, the old parts have been scavenged and used to build another ship, C, with the same configuration as A. The question is which of the later ships, B or C, is identical with ship A? Both B and C have good claims to being identical with A. On the one hand, there is a spatio-temporal continuity of A and B. The transition from A to B is achieved in a series of substitutions of one old part for one new part, and there is no reason to say that A ceases to be A when a single part is replaced. On the other hand, ship C is materially and formally identical with ship A. If one left ship A and came back to find ship C, there would be no question that C was the same as A, and even if one were told (without mentioning ship B) that A had been taken apart and reassembled as C, one would still say that they were the same ship.
Resolution. There are various arguments for both B and C as identical with A, with the intuitions of various philosophers differing. Perhaps the Wittgensteinian line that the some philosophical questions have the status of a civil dispute is right: what we should say in these cases depends upon what is finally at stake in the dispute, because there are no identity conditions abstractly considered. See GEACH'S PARADOX OF THE 1,001 CATS.

READINGS

Davies, Laurence. "Smart on Conditions of Identity." *Analysis* 33.3 (1973): 109-110.

Dauer, Francis. "How Not to Reidentify the Parthenon." *Analysis* 33.2 (1973): 63-64.

Dillon, John. *The Middle Platonists: 80 B.C. to A.D. 220*. Ithaca: Cornell UP, 1977. 411-412.

Garrett, B. J. "Noonan, 'Best Candidate' Theories and the Ship of Theseus." *Analysis* 45.4 (1985): 212-224.

Heller, Mark. "The Best Candidate Approach to Diachronic Identity." *Australasian Journal of Philosophy* 65 (1987): 434-451.

Noonan, Harold. "Wiggins, Artifact Identity and "Best Candidate' Theories." *Analysis* 45.1 (1987): 4-8.

Scaltsas, Theodore. "The Ship of Theseus." *Analysis* 40.3 (1980): 152-157.

Smart, Brian. "How to Reidentify the Ship of Theseus." *Analysis* 32.5 (1972): 145-148.

— —. "The Ship of Theseus, the Parthenon, and Disassembled Objects." *Analysis* 34.1 (1973): 24-27.

SIMPSON'S PARADOX. This paradox in probability theory has been used to undermine the probabilistic theory of causality.

Formulation. "The fact is this: any association — $P(A|B) = P(A)$; $P(A|B) > P(A)$; $P(A|B) < P(A)$ — between two variables which holds in a given population can be reversed in the subpopulations by finding a third variable which is correlated with both" (Cartwright, 422).

Explanation. Let a given population be partitioned into two subpopulations. In each of these subpopulations A and B might be highly correlated and yet not be correlated on the entire population. Cartwright gives the following example. It may be that smoking and heart disease are not correlated very highly in a given society because a large number of smokers exercise regularly, thereby offsetting some of the harm done by smoking. Nevertheless, the society can be split into two distinct groups: those who exercise and those who do not. Those who exercise and smoke may have a significantly higher rate of heart disease than those who exercise but forgo smoking. Similarly, heart disease may be higher among those who do not exercise and smoke than those who do not exercise but abstain from smoking. Hence, smoking and heart disease are highly correlated in both subpopulations, but not in the entire population. There is also a connection with causality: if we are to give a probabilistic account of causality, the probability of the effect, given the cause, should be higher than the probability of the effect in the absence of the cause. The present paradox, however, suggests that this expected increase of the probability of the cause in the presence of the effect does not always occur.

Resolution. Observe that Simpson's Paradox is not in itself contradictory (though it may become so in conjunction with certain kinds of rules for combining probabilities). Hence, the paradoxicality of the result is its unexpectedness. Once a clear example of how the paradox arises is understood, however, it seems to lose its bite. Nevertheless, it remains a problem for those who hold a probabilistic theory of causality. These latter argue that the paradox arises when the population is partitioned according to a variable that has a causal relation with the effect being studied. For example, in the situation described above exercising was used to partition the population, but it also has a causal relation to heart disease, the effect in question. This fact is then used to devise appropriate restrictions on the definition of causality.

READINGS

Cartwright, Nancy. "Causal Laws and Effective Strategies." *Nous* 13 (1979): 419-437.

Eells, Ellery. "Cartwright and Otte on Simpson's Paradox." *Philosophy of Science* 54 (1987): 233-243.

Otte, Richard. "Probabilistic Causality and Simpson's Paradox." *Philosophy of Science* 52 (1985): 110-125.
Suppes, P. *A Probabilistic Theory of Causality*. Amsterdam: North Holland, 1970.

SINCERITY, PARADOX OF. People, such as salesmen, whose jobs depend on convincing others of their sincerity, face the following practical paradox: by deliberately acting in such a way as to appear sincere, sincerity itself is lost. In so far as it is the agent's intentional actions that are self-defeating, this paradox is similar to that of the BODHISATTVA. Observe that the paradox arises because the salesman cannot afford to just be sincere and hope that his prospective clients will perceive his sincerity. In order to maximize his chances to close the sale, he must rather take steps to appear sincere. As stated above, this results in a lack of sincerity which may be perceived by the client. In any case, most clients are aware of the fact that the salesman must "sell himself" and are thus reticent about crediting the salesman as sincere. For another, similar problem in the art of salesmanship, see the PARADOX OF TRUST.

READING

Oakes, Guy. "The Sales Process and the Paradoxes of Trust." *Journal of Business Ethics* 9(1990): 671-679.

SKOLEM PARADOX, THE. This purported paradox arises from certain results in model theory when they are applied to set theory.
Formulation. The Löwenheim-Skolem theorem states that, if an enumerable set of first order formulas has a model, it has an enumerable model. The theorem can be applied to set theory even though certain set theoretic theorems assert the existence of non-enumerablly many sets. Consequently, set theoretic notions like cardinality are relative.
Explanation. An enumerable set is one that is finite or that can be put into a one-one correspondence with the natural numbers. The Löwenheim-Skolem theorem shows that if a certain set of first order formulas has a model, then it has a model with an enumerable domain. Set theory, however, can be formulated as a first order theory using an enumerable number of axioms. Hence, set theory (since it has non-enumerable models) has an enumerable model despite the fact that the theory affirms that there are a non-enumerable number of sets. This result is called Skolem's Paradox, although Skolem himself did not believe it paradoxical.

Nevertheless, he did believe that it entailed certain noteworthy results such as the relativity of concepts like cardinality. According to this result, the cardinality of a set is not an inherent property of the set, but rather depends on other parameters. **Resolution.** Skolem's Paradox is only paradoxical in the sense that it is a surprising result. There is no contradiction involved. The relativity of set theoretic notions, often called the "Skolemite position," is more controversial. On the one hand, concepts such as cardinality (in particular, non-enumerability) may be thought of as having an objective content; in that case, no enumerable set of axioms can adequately characterize this content. On the other hand, the concepts themselves may be thought of as being relative to the axiom systems in which they are defined. The latter view seems more consistent with the modern view of set theory as a formal system, susceptible of various interpretations.

READINGS

McIntosh, Clifton. "Skolem's Criticisms of Set Theory." *Nous* 13 (1979): 313-334.

Moore, A. W. "Set Theory, Skolem's Paradox and the *Tractatus*." *Analysis* 45.1 (1985): 13-20.

Resnick, M. D. "On Skolem's Paradox." *Journal of Philosophy* 63 (1966): 425-437.

Skolem, Thoralf. "Some Remark's on Axiomized Set Theory." In *From Frege to Gödel: A Source Book in Mathematical Logic.* Ed. Jean van Heijenoort. Cambridge: Harvard UP, 1967. 290-301.

Thomas, William J. "Platonism and the Skolem Paradox." *Analysis* 28.6 (1968): 193-196.

— —. "On Behalf of the Skolemite." *Analysis* 31.6 (1971): 177-186.

SLIPPERY SLOPE PARADOX, THE. Also called Chisholm's Paradox, this paradox of modal logic was adduced by Roderick Chisholm. The term "slippery slope" is often applied to any Sorites-like argument in which, once the first step is granted, a series of similar steps must also be granted because they rely on the same principle.
Formulation. Consider, say, the Empire State Building. It is composed of a number of parts, girders, stones, pieces of glass, and so forth. Presumably it could have been made of a slightly different set of parts and have still been the Empire State Building; imagine, for instance, that a stone had been cracked before it was placed and was replaced by another. Suppose that saying that the Empire State Building could have been composed of a slightly different set of parts means that in some other possible world the Empire State Building is made of slightly different

parts, differing by one stone only. We can now imagine another possible world which differs from this first possible world just by having another stone different in the construction of the Empire State Building. Indeed, there is a sequence of possible worlds in which the Empire State Building differs in each one by just part from the one before; at the end of the sequence the Empire State Building is made of none of the parts of the actual one!

Explanation. In the formulation given above, the modal nature of the paradox is only reflected in the use of possible world semantics. Chisholm's argument, however, is directed against the unrestricted acceptance of the following axiom of (S4) modal logic: if a proposition is necessarily true, then it is necessary that it is necessarily true. The result is paradoxical because it is usually assumed that if two physical objects are made of different parts, then they are not the same physical object. Yet Chisholm's paradox seems to force us to the conclusion that the identity of a physical object does not depend upon its parts.

Resolution. One way of responding to the paradox is to insist that the identity of a physical object is determined by its parts, thereby denying that the two "Empire State Buildings," only differing by a stone, are the same. A second approach would be to claim that while the first Empire State Building is identical to the second and that the second is identical to the third, the first is nevertheless different from the third. In other words, one could deny the transitivity of identity across possible worlds. As in most Sorites, however, it is difficult to justify this step in an intuitively satisfying manner. Still another approach would be to eschew talk of trans-world identity altogether. The puzzle, however, can be reformulated in such a manner as to avoid the use of possible world semantics. In fact, the paradox has occasioned some debate over whether there is a temporal analogue where changes occur to a physical object over time instead of across worlds.

READINGS

Chisholm, R. "Identity Through Possible Worlds: Some Questions." *Nous* 1 (1967): 1-8.

Lowe, E. J. "On a Supposed Temporal/Modal Parallel." *Analysis* 46.4 (1986): 195-197.

— —. "Reply to Over." *Analysis* 46.4 (1986): 200.

Over, D. E. "On a Temporal Slippery Slope Paradox." *Analysis* 46.1 (1986): 15-18.

— —. "Is There a Temporal Slippery Slope Paradox?" *Analysis* 46.4 (1986): 197-200.

— —. "Reply to Lowe." *Analysis* 46.4 (1986): 201.

Salmon, Nathan. "Impossible Worlds." *Analysis* 44.3 (1984): 114-117.

SMULLYAN'S PARADOX. A legal paradox adduced by Raymond Smullyan in 1978.

Formulation. "Three men, conveniently named A, B and C, converge for a night at an oasis in the desert, parting company the next day. For whatever reasons, A decides to murder C and sneaks some poison into his canteen late that night. Shortly afterwards, B, acting quite independently, also decides to murder C and punches a small hole in C's canteen. The next day, C dies of thirst. It all comes out in the trial. The question is: who killed C?" (Cohen 311).

Explanation. Defendant A argues that he is not responsible for C's death because C never drank any of the poison. Defendant B also claims that he is not responsible for C's death because he did not deprive C of potable water, but only of poisoned water. Nevertheless, someone must be responsible for C's demise.

Resolution. Cohen suggests unless it is decided that the case is not one of murder, the paradox might be resolved by revising our concepts of legal and moral guilt or of causality. Defendant B, however, seems to have the weaker case because his action was intended to cause C to die of thirst in the desert and, in fact, C's intention was realized. Defendant A performed an act that was intended to lead to C's death by poison; his intentions, through no fault of his own, were not realized. It would thus seem that A is at least guilty of attempted murder.

READINGS

Cohen, Daniel. "Putting Paradoxes into Pedagogical Use in Philosophy." *Teaching Philosophy* 8 (1985): 309-317.

Smullyan, Raymond. *What Is the Name of This Book?* New York: Prentice, 1978.

SOCIALISM, PARADOX OF. This paradox is discussed together with the PARADOX OF LIBERTARIANISM

SOCRATIC PARADOXES. These are the paradoxes of Socratic optimism and Socratic rationalism. See also MENO'S PARADOX.

Formulation. Some of the more paradoxical doctrines espoused by Plato's Socrates include:

(1)   No one does evil willingly.
(2)   Evil is the result of ignorance.
(3)   To know the good is to do the good.

Statements (1) and (2) are closely related: no one does evil of one's own free will, but rather evil is done by those who lack knowledge of the good. If one knew the good, one would not do evil. Something of this sort is connected with Socrates's demon, which warned him to desist when he was on the verge of doing something wrong. Statement (3) is a somewhat stronger claim: he who knows the good would not only avoid evil but would moreover do the good unhesitatingly.

Explanation. Statements (1) - (3) fly in the face of our everyday experiences of people doing evil of their own free will, and of knowing what is right but doing what is wrong.

Resolution. There are basically two ways to respond to these fundamental Socratic paradoxes. On the one hand, Socrates's claims can be reconciled with our intuitions by seeing them as an attempt to specify a very strong sense of the word "knowledge," one in which acting from one's knowledge is a criterion of having the knowledge in the first place. On the other hand, one can attribute his claims to his pre-Christian intuitions which did not envision the possibility of daemonic despair, or of knowingly and willingly contradicting the will of God. For this second alternative, the paradoxical character of Socrates's claims is the result of his relatively impoverished understanding of the concept of evil.

READINGS

King, James. "Elenchus, Self-Blame and the Socratic Paradox." *Review of Metaphysics* 41 (1987): 105-126.

Vlastos, Gregory. "The Paradox of Socrates." *Socrates*. Notre Dame: Notre Dame UP, 1980.

SOLIPSISTIC PARADOX, THE. "This was our paradox: no course of action could be determined by a rule, because every course of action can be made out to accord with a rule. The answer was: if everything can be made out to accord with the rule, then it can also be made out to conflict with it. And so there would be neither accord nor conflict here" (Wittgenstein, *Philosophical Investigations*, 201). See the PARADOX OF RULE FOLLOWING.

SOPHISM. A sophism is defined as a plausible but nevertheless fallacious argument. Sophisms are thus a type of paradox (see DEFINITION OF PARADOX). Even in the appropriately restricted sense of paradox, however, we would hesitate to affirm the complete synonymity of "sophism" and "paradox". This is because "sophism" connotes duplicity, whereas "paradox" tends to connote wonder at the marvelous or, at least, at surprising results.

SORITES, RECENT. Recent sorites are somewhat more narrow in focus than traditional sorites, insofar as they bear principally on questions of the identity of beings rather than on causal relations. The jury is still out on whether certain recent sorites are veridical or falsidical paradoxes so they may well be genuine antinomies in Quine's sense.
Formulation. There is a variety of Sorites arguments in the recent literature. Among the predicates that have been argued to be incoherent are: beauty (Goldstein), gizzle gicks (Grim, "Is This a Swizzle Stick I See Before Me?"), justice (Quest, thus challenging Nozick's theory of justice; see also Sorensen), people (Unger, "Why There Are No People"), Peter Unger (Unger, "I Do Not Exist"), redness (Travis, "Vagueness, Observation and Sorites"), swizzle sticks (Unger, "There Are No Ordinary Things"), stones (Unger, "There Are No Ordinary Things"), tables (Unger, "There Are No Ordinary Things").
Explanation. If a something is a so-and-so if it has n such-and-suches, then it is also so-and-so if it has $n - 1$ (or $n + 1$) such-and-suches, and so, by induction, it will also be a so-and-so when it has one or no (or $n + m$, where m is as large as one likes) such-and-suches, but that is absurd! Yet since "such-and-such" is such an embarrassingly vague predicate, it just won't do to say that there are any such-and-suches in the first place.
Resolution. The Sorites argument has lead philosophers to drastic conclusions: that language is incoherent (Dummett), that the world is vague (Peacocke), that *modus ponens* is an acceptable principle only in small doses (Parikh). There are various responses to the challenge of the Sorites. First, one can take them as veridical and hence as revealing a fundamental vagueness or underlying incoherence in the predicate in question (*e.g.*, Unger; Wheeler). Second, one can assign the principle of bivalence to specialized languages and believe that it does not apply to everyday discourse in a systematic manner (Rolf). Third, one can reject mathematical induction, or restrict it to specialized contexts (Weiss; Napoli; Trapp). Fourth, one can conclude that the Sorites reveal truth value gaps and adopt supervaluational logic, thus rejecting bivalence in metalogic (Fine). Fifth, one can adopt a many-valued or a fuzzy logic approach according to which each application of induction has a high degree of truth but there is enough doubt introduced to circumvent counterintuitive conclusions (King; Sanford). Sixth, one could adopt the epistemic approach according to which there is an unknowable counterexample to the induction step (Cargile; Campbell). See also the SLIPPERY SLOPE PARADOX and WANG'S PARADOX.

READINGS

Abbott. W. R. "A Note on Grim's Sorites Argument." *Analysis* 43.4 (1983): 161-164.

Barnes, J. "Medicine, Experience and Logic." *Science and Speculation.* Ed. J. Barnes *et al.* Cambridge: Cambridge UP, 1982: 24-68.

Black, Max. "Reasoning with Loose Concepts." *Dialogue* 2 (1963): 1-12.

Burnyeat, M. "Gods and Heaps." *Language and Logic.* Ed. J. L. Schofield and Martha Nussbaum. Cambridge: Cambridge UP, 315-338.

Campbell, R. "The Sorites Paradox." *Philosophical Studies* 26 (1974): 175-191.

Cargile, James. "The Sorites Paradox." *British Journal for the Philosophy of Science* 20 (1969): 193-202.

Fine, K. "Vagueness, Truth and Logic." *Synthese* 30 (1975): 265-300.

Goldstein, Laurence. "The Sorites as a Lesson in Semantics." *Mind* 97 (1988): 447-455.

Grim, Patrick. "What Won't Escape Sorites Arguments." *Analysis* 42.1 (1982): 38-43.

— —. "Is This a Swizzle Stick Which I See Before Me?" *Analysis* 43.4 (1983): 164-165.

Jacquette, Dale. "The Hidden Logic of Slippery Slope Arguments." *Philosophy and Rhetoric* 22 (1989): 59-70.

Kamp, Hans. "The Paradox of the Heap." *Aspects of Philosophical Logic.* Ed Uwe Monnich. Dordrecht: Reidel, 1981. 225-277.

King, J. L. "Bivalence and the Sorites Paradox." *American Philosophical Quarterly* 16 (1969). 17-25.

Lederkramer, David. "Quest on Entitlement Theory." *Analysis* 39.4 (1979): 219-222.

Moline, Jon. "Aristotle, Eubulides and the Sorites." *Mind* ns 78 (1969): 393-407.

Napoli, Ernesto. "Is Vagueness a Logical Enigma?" *Erkenntnis* 23 (1985): 115-121.

Parikh, R. "The Problem of Vague Predicates." *Boston Studies in the Philosophy of Science: Language, Logic and Science.* Vol. 31. Dordrecht: Reidel, 1983. 241-261.

Peacocke, Christopher. "Are Vague Predicates Incoherent?" *Synthese* 46 (1981): 121-141.

Putnam, Hilary. "Vagueness and Alternative Logic." *Erkenntnis* 19 (1983): 297-315.

— —. "A Quick Read Is a Wrong Wright." *Analysis* 45.4 (1985): 203.

Quest, Edward. "Whatever Arises from a Just Distribution by Just Steps is Itself Just" *Analysis* 37.4 (1977). 204-208.

Quine, W. V. "What Price Bivalence?" *Journal of Philosophy* 77 (1981): 90-95.

Read, S., and C. Wright. "Hairier Than Putnam Thought." *Analysis* 45.1 (1985): 56-58.

Rolf, Bertil. "Sorites." *Synthese* 58 (1984): 219-250.
Sanford, D. H. "Nostalgia for the Ordinary: Comments on Papers by Unger and Wheeler." *Synthese* 41 (1979): 175-184.
Schwartz, Stephen P. "Intuitionism and Sorites." *Analysis* 47.4 (1987): 179-183.
Sorensen, Roy A. "Slipping off the Slippery Slope: A Reply to Professor Jacquette." *Philosophy and Rhetoric* 22 (1989): 195-202.
— —. "Nozick, Justice and the Sorites." *Analysis* 46.2 (1986): 102-106.
Thorpe, Dale A. "The Sorites Paradox." *Synthese* 61 (1984): 391-421.
Trapp, Rainer W. "Sinking into the Sand: The Falsity of All Sorites-Arguments." *Erkenntnis* 23 (1985): 123-125.
Travis, Charles. "Vagueness, Observation, and Sorites." *Mind* ns 94 (1985): 345-366.
— —. "On What Is Strictly Speaking True." *Canadian Journal of Philosophy* 15 (1985): 187-229.
Unger, Peter. "I Do Not Exist." *Perception and Identity*. Ed. G. F. MacDonald. Ithaca: Cornell UP, 1979. 235-251.
— —. "There Are No Ordinary Things." *Synthese* 41 (1979): 117-154.
— —. "Why There Are No People." *Midwest Studies in Philosophy* 4 (1979): 177-222.
— —. "Skepticism and Nihilism." *Nous* 14 (1980): 517-545.
Wheeler, Samuel C. "Reference and Vagueness." *Synthese* 30 (1975): 367-379.
— —. "On That Which Is Not." *Synthese* 41 (1979): 155-173.
Weiss, S. E. "The Sorites Fallacy: What Difference Does a Peanut Make?" *Synthese* 33 (1976): 253-272.
Wright, Crispin. "On the Coherence of Vague Predicates." *Synthese* 30 (1975): 325-365.
— —. "Language Mastery and the Sorites Paradox." *Truth and Meaning*. Ed. G. Evans and J. McDowell. New York: Oxford UP, 1976. 223-247.
— —. "Further Reflections on the Sorites Paradox." *Philosophical Topics* 15 (1987): 227-290.

SORITES, TRADITIONAL. Also known as the Heap, this family of paradoxes was introduced by EUBULIDES. Long of scant philosophic interest, there has been a cottage industry in sorites arguments since 1975, for which see RECENT SORITES. The famous Sorites of Themostocles, to the effect that his baby son ruled the whole world, goes as follows.

> My infant son rules his mother.
> His mother rules me.
> I rule the Athenians.
> The Athenians rule the Greeks.

> The Greeks rule the Europe.
> And Europe rules the world.

A sorites is an argument in which a series of incomplete syllogisms is arranged so that the predicate of each premise forms the subject of the subsequent one, until the subject of the first is joined with the predicate of the last in the conclusion. Here is another old example.

> All men who believe shall be saved.
> All who are saved must be free of sin.
> All who are free of sin must be innocent in the eyes of God.
> All who are innocent in the sight of God are suitable for heaven.
> All who are suitable for heaven will be admitted into heaven.
> Therefore, all who believe will be admitted into heaven.

There is another causal sorites in the old saw that for want of a nail the shoe was lost, for want of a shoe the horse was lost, for want of a horse the rider was lost, for want of a rider the battle was lost . . . until it is concluded that for want of the nail the empire was lost. Blaise Pascal presents a truncated version of this argument called Cleopatra's nose: "If the nose of Cleopatra had been shorter, the whole face of the earth would have been changed" (Pensées, viii, 29). The paradoxicality of the conclusion of a Sorites is usually that a seemingly insignificant cause has enormous effects; other Sorites make one class a subclass of another in contrast to our expectations.

STADIUM, THE. See the MOVING BLOCKS.

STONE, THE PARADOX OF THE. A particularized version of the PARADOXES OF OMNIPOTENCE, this medieval paradox seems to threaten the characterization of God as all-powerful.
Formulation. Everyone has asked himself what would happen if an irresistible force meet an immovable object. In Greek myth, Zeus himself once posed such a question when a hound that was fated always to catch whatever it pursued was sent out after a fox that was fated never to be caught. In the event, Zeus turned both the hound and the fox to stone. The question of the title paradox is whether, when God makes a stone, He can make one too heavy for Himself to lift.

Explanation. If God can create such a stone, His potency is limited by His inability to lift it; and if He cannot, that limitation does not speak well of His powers either. In either case, it would seem that God is not all-powerful. **Resolution.** J. L. Mackie initiated the modern vogue in this problem, suggesting that the paradox requires us to dispense either with the concept of omnipotence or with that of God. G. B. Keene, however, argues that "God cannot create a stone that He cannot lift" is equivalent to "Every stone that God can create, He can lift." According to Keene, the equivalence dissolves the second horn of the dilemma and actually reinforces the conception of God as all-powerful since He can in fact lift all stones that can be created. Bernard Mayo contends that Keene's analysis implies that no "cannot" statement could be construed as asserting a limitation and suggests that the paradox might be resolved by treating it as one would the problem that God cannot create a square circle: since there is no such thing as a square circle, there is nothing in the case that God cannot create. Another approach is that taken by Alfred R. Mele and M. P. Smith who recast the paradox as a competition between a pair of omnipotent beings and conclude that the omnipotence of these beings does not guarantee that they will be able to do all they intend to do. For Mele and Smith, however, the problem is not in the beings's omnipotence, but in their intentions.

READINGS

Anderson, C. Anthony. "Divine Omnipotence and Impossible Tasks: An Intensional Analysis." *International Journal for Philosophy of Religion* 15.3 (1984): 109-124.

Chisholm, Roderick. *Person and Object.* La Salle: Open Court, 1976. Chapter 3.

Cowan, J. L. "The Paradox of Omnipotence." *Analysis* 25.1 (1964): 102-108.

— —. "The Paradox of Omnipotence Revisited." *Canadian Journal of Philosophy* 3 (1974): 35-45.

Hoffman, Josua, and Gary Rosenkranz. "What an Omnipotent Agent Can Do." *International Journal for Philosophy of Religion* 11 (1980): 1-19.

— —. "Omnipotence Redux." *Philosophy and Phenomenological Research* 49 (1988): 283-301.

Keene, G. B. "A Simpler Solution to the Paradox of Omnipotence." *Mind* ns 69 (1960): 74-75.

Londey, David, Barry Miller, and John King-Farlow. "God and the Stone Paradox: Three Comments." *Sophia* 10 (1971): 23-33.

Mackie, J. L. "Evil and Omnipotence." *Mind* ns 64 (1955): 200-212.

Mavrodes, G. I. "Some Puzzles Concerning Omnipotence." *Philosophical Review* 72 (1963): 221-223.

Mayo, Bernard. "Mr. Keene on Omnipotence." *Mind* ns 70 (1961): 249-250.

Mele, Alfred R., and M. P. Smith. "The New Paradox of the Stone." *Faith and Philosophy* 5 (1988): 283-290.

Savage, G. Wade. "The Paradox of the Stone." *Philosophical Review* 76 (1967): 74-79.

Schrader, David E. "A Solution to the Paradox of the Stone." *Synthese* 42 (1979): 255-264.

Wierenga, Edward. "Omnipotence Defined." *Philosophy and Phenomenological Research* 43 (1983): 363-375.

Wolfe, Julian. "Omnipotence." *Canadian Journal of Philosophy* 1 (1971): 245-247.

ST. PETERSBURG PARADOX, THE. This paradox of probability theory is concerned with a coin flipping game.

Formulation. "Suppose that a man tosses an ideal coin until heads appears. Then the game is over. He receives $X = 2^n$ cents, where n is the number of tosses of the coin. Thus, if heads appeared for the first time on the third toss, he collects 8 cents. It is to his advantage to get a very long run of tails before heads appears. With probability one, heads will eventually appear and he will collect some money. What is the expectation of the amount of money he will receive? In other words, how much should he pay for the privilege of playing this game to make it a 'fair' game" (Chernoff and Moses, 104).

Explanation. If we toss a coin there are two equiprobable results: heads and tails. Hence, the probability of obtaining tails is 1/2. If the coin is tossed twice, the possibilities are (heads, heads), (heads, tails), (tails, heads), and (heads, heads). Thus, the probability of obtaining two tails is 1/4. Similarly, if the coin is tossed i times, there will be 2^i possibilities, only one of which consists of all tails. Hence, the probability of obtaining i tails on i tosses of the coin is $1/2^i$. The expectation is the product of the payoff by the probability of obtaining that payoff. Thus, the expectation of receiving two cents is $2(1/2) = 1$, since the probability of obtaining tails on one toss is 1/2. Similarly, the expectation of receiving four cents is $4(1/4) = 1$ and the expectation of receiving 2^i cents is $2^i(1/2^i)$ 1. The total expectation of the game is the sum of all these partial expectations:

$$E = 2(1/2) + 4(1/4) + \ldots + 2^i(1/2^i) + \ldots$$
$$= 1 + 1 + \ldots + 1 + \ldots$$
$$= \text{infinity.}$$

The game is quite favorable to the player since he can always win more than any finite amount that he has to pay for playing. The paradox is that few would be willing to pay more than a few dollars to play the game. **Resolution.** The infinite expectation of the game is predicated on the assumption that the player can play an indefinite number of times. In fact, one can only be reasonably sure of averaging more than twenty cents a game by playing a very large number of games.

READING

Chernoff, Herman, and Lincoln E. Moses. *Elemental Decision Theory.* New York: Wiley, 1959. 104–106.

SUBJECTIVISM, PARADOX OF. See PARADOXES OF COGNITIVE RELATIVISM, AND HUSSERL'S PARDOX OF SUBJECTIVITY.

SURPRISE AIR RAID DRILL, THE. See the PREDICTION PARADOX.

SURPRISE QUIZ, THE. See the PREDICTION PARADOX.

TAOIST PARADOXES. These are historically related to, and thus are treated with, the BUDDHIST PARADOXES; but see also HUI SHIH'S PARADOXICAL APHORIMS..

TASTE, THE PARADOX OF. This paradox goes back to Kant and Hume before him. We follow the Kantian version.
Formulation. The thesis is that judgments of taste are not based on conceptions, because if so, judgments of taste would elicit controversy and allow for proof. The antithesis is that the judgments of taste are based on conceptions, because if not, there would be none of the controversy that arises from the our insistence that other agree with our judgments.
Explanation. On the one hand, one cannot establish the judgment, say, that an object is beautiful through an argument based on concepts, so it appears that the judgment of taste does not have the objective universality of any judgment that is based on rules. On the other hand, the judgment that something is beautiful is unlike the judgment, based on individual

inclination, that something is pleasing, for while we accept that others do not find the same things pleasing as we do, the judgment of beauty is universal in the sense that it demands the accent of others. **Resolution.** Kant resolves the paradox of taste by distinguishing between two kinds of conception. There are determinate conceptions, such as the concepts of the understanding, which ground knowledge of objects, and there are indeterminate conceptions, such as the idea of the supersensible, that have objective validity. The idea of the supersensible, which underlies both the object judged and the judging subject, has nevertheless a subjective validity. The universality of the judgment of taste is based precisely on this idea of the supersensible, which is that of "purposiveness without a purpose."

READINGS

Cassier, H. W. *A Commentary on Kant's Critique of Judgment.* New York: Barnes, 1938. Sec. 70.

Kant, Emmanuel. *The Critique of Judgment.* Trans. J. H. Bernard. New York: Hafner, 1951. Part 1, Division 2.

Mothersill, Mary. "Hume and the the Paradox of Taste." *Aesthetics: A Critical Anthology.* Ed. George Dickie, Richard Scalfani, and Ronald Roblin. 2nd ed. New York: St. Martin's, 1989. 269-286.

TERTULLIAN'S PARADOX. Quintus Septimus Florens Tertullian (c. 160-220) was an African patriarch of Christianity who loved paradox and contradiction. In his "On the Body of Christ," Tertullian argued that the Incarnation of Christ "is certain because impossible." He was evidently pushing to an absurd extreme Aristotle's idea (*Rhetoric*, II, xxiii, 22) that it is likely that unlikely things should happen. Various Christian apologists, such as G. K. Chesterton, have reiterated the argument by claiming that the whole idea of God becoming man in order to be crucified is so absurd that it could never be the product of the human imagination and so must be true.

READING

Williams, Bernard. *Tertullian's Paradox.* London: SCM, 1955.

THINKING BEHAVIORIST, THE PARADOX OF THE. By this paradox, Arthur O. Lovejoy seeks to show that the behaviorism of J. B. Watson is internally inconsistent.

Formulation. The behaviorist makes cognitive claims, but when he makes these claims he contradicts himself unless he denies that he knows anything.

Explanation. Watson identifies the awareness of things distant in space and time with certain muscular or bodily movements, but no description of internal bodily events can explicate intentional reference to external objects.

Resolution. In response to Lovejoy, Gilbert Ryle recommends that knowledge of external realities be understood dispositionally: that someone is aware of something in his environment just means that if that something is present in his environment and if such and such conditions obtain, then he will behave in such and such manner with regard to it. In this way, we can refer to external objects while limiting these objects to behavioral processes.

READINGS

Lovejoy, A. O. "Paradox of the Thinking Behaviorist." *Philosophical Review* 31 (1922): 135-147.

Ryle, Gilbert. *The Concept of Mind*. London: Hutchinson, 1949.

THE THIRD MAN ARGUMENT. This paradox arises in Plato's Theory of Forms.

Formulation. "When several things seem large to you, it seems perhaps that there is a single Form which is the same in your view of all of them. Hence you believe that Largeness is a single thing . . . What then if you similarly view mentally Largeness itself and the other large things? Will not a single Largeness appear once again, in virtue of which all these (*sc* Largeness and the other large things) appear large?" (Plato, *Parmenides* 132a1-b2; Vlastos's translation 320-321).

Explanation. According to Plato's Theory of Forms, large things, for example, are large by virtue of their participation in the Form of Largeness; also, it is because of this that the single word "large" can be applied to the many large things. The Form of Largeness is, so to speak, the essence of largeness and so must itself be large. Hence, there must be another Form in which both the Form of Largeness and all large things participate and which makes both large; that is, we can predicate the one word "large" of both the Form of Largeness and large things only if there is a single new Form that both the Form of Largeness and large things participate in. This argument, however, can be iterated indefinitely, resulting in an infinite regress. Even worse, large things are large not by virtue of their participation in a single Form, but by virtue of their participation in an infinite number of Forms.

Resolution. According to Gregory Vlastos, Plato himself could not refute the argument but nevertheless formulated it with great force, thereby revealing his intellectual honesty. Aristotle thought the argument valid and used it to argue against the Theory of Forms. Vlastos contends that the argument is actually invalid because it depends on the following contradictory presuppositions:

(1) The Form has the property that it imparts to things (Largeness is large);
(2) That which has a property cannot be that by virtue of which it has the property (Largeness cannot be large because of Largeness).

K. W. Rankin argues that Plato could not have distinguished the extensional and the intensional aspects of the Forms and, thus, "it is unlikely that he could have at any stage used the Forms as explanations in an unequivocal way" (196). Thus, Plato would not be forced to distinguish properties from Forms, which would defuse the paradox. According to Rankin, Plato's understanding of the logical structure of the argument was confused but, in fairness to Plato, he was wrestling with problems that are still "front-line" today.

READINGS

Rankin, K. W. "The Duplicity of Plato's Third Man." *Mind* ns 78 (1969): 178-197.
Vlastos, Gregory. "The Third Man Argument in the *Parmenides*." *Philosophical Review* 63 (1954): 319-349.

TIME, PARADOXES OF. Paradoxes involving the character of time include the ACHILLES, the ARROW, the CLOCK PARADOX, the DEVIL'S OFFER, GOODMAN'S PARADOX OF CONFIRMATION, KANT'S COSMOLOGICAL ANTINOMIES, the LAMP PARADOX, McTAGGERT'S PARADOX, PASCAL'S WAGER, the PRECESSION OF THE EQUINOXES PARADOX, PARADOXES OF TIME TRAVEL, the TWIN PARADOX.

TIME TRAVEL, PARADOXES OF. Not to be confused with the TWIN PARADOX, these paradoxes seem to confute the conceptual possibility of traveling backward in time. Like the Twin, they arise in the context of Einstein's Special Theory of Relativity.

Formulation. Paul Horwich formulates five paradoxes resulting from the claim that it is possible to travel backward in time:

(1) A temporal interval would have to be traversed in an amount of time less than that of the interval.

(2)   Backwards time travel is incompatible with Leibniz's
       law of the Identity of Indiscernibles.
(3)   The past cannot be undone, but backwards time travel
       would make it possible to undo what is already done.
(4)   The time traveler would be forced to hold inconsistent
       beliefs stemming from conflicts in his memories and in
       his intentions.
(5)   A rocket is programed to fire a probe unless a safety
       switch is on. But the switch is on if, and only if, the
       probe's return is detected by a sensing device. Hence,
       the probe will be fired if, and only if, it is not fired (see
       Earman 231-232).

Explanation. According to Horwich, the first four of these paradoxes are easily resolved sophisms. The first, for example, relies on an illicit absolutist conception of time. Thus the paradoxicality of the argument disappears once we realize that the time in the reference frame of the time traveler is not the same time as that in the reference frame of the interval to be traversed. We will therefore refrain from further consideration of these arguments here. The fifth argument, however, seems to be a genuine paradox. It was formulated by John Earman entirely in terms of mechanical operations in order to avoid considerations of human agency which vitiated earlier versions of the paradox. Thus a rocket is equiped with a probe that will be sent backwards in time and also with a device with which to detect the probe's return to the rocket's present. Furthermore, the probe will be fired whenever a safety switch is off; it cannot be fired when the switch is on. Yet the necessary and sufficient condition for the switch being on is that the rocket has detected the probe's return. Suppose, then, that the probe has been fired. Then, the switch must be off and, hence, the return has not been detected. But since the probe returns to the rocket's present, the only way that the return could not be detected is for the probe not to have been fired, which contradicts our supposition that it has been fired. On the contrary supposition that the probe was not fired, the switch must be on. Hence, the return of the probe has been detected. Yet if the probe has returned, it must have been fired, which again contradicts the supposition.

Resolution. Earman argues that it follows from the paradox that we must give up one of two things: (1) backwards time travel or (2) the supposition that the rocket can be programed in the manner delineated above. There seems to be no logical reason to favor one over the other of these two options but we do have solid empirical evidence for the possibility of executing the desired program in the existence of similar programs. Hence, we have empirical evidence for denying the possibility of backwards time travel. P. Horwich, however, argues that Earman has committed a subtle, but fatal, modal fallacy. Perhaps more importantly, he suggests that the paradox may be avoided by observing that if backward time travel is possible, it would still be the case that not all causal chains would be possible. One criterion for the existence of such causal chains would be consistency and this is enough to eliminate the paradox.

READINGS

Earman, John. "On Going Backwards in Time." *Philosophy of Science* 34 (1967): 211-222.

— —. "Implications of Causal Propagation Outside the Null Cone." *Australasian Journal of Philosophy* 50 (1972): 222-237.

Harrison, J. "Dr. Who and the Philosophers or Time-Travel for Beginners." *Aristotelian Society Supplement* 45 (1971): 1-24.

Horwich, P. "On Some Alleged Paradoxes of Time Travel." *Journal of Philosophy* 72 (1975): 432-444.

Lewis, David. "The Paradoxes of Time Travel." *American Philosophical Quarterly* 13 (1976): 145-152.

Meiland, J. W. "A Two-Dimensional Passage Model for Time Travel." *Philosophical Studies* 26 (1974): 153-173.

Smith, Joseph Wayne. *Reason, Science and Paradox: Against Received Opinion in Science and Philosophy.* London: Helm, 1986. Ch. 2.

Stein, H. "On the Paradoxical Time-Structures of Gödel." *Philosophy of Science* 37 (1970): 589-601.

TRAGEDY, THE PARADOX OF. The paradox of tragedy is an AESTHETIC PARADOX like the PARADOX OF THE UGLY. Like other works of art, tragedy provides us with aesthetic beauty and pleasure, but tragedy depicts happenings that are not pleasurable to witness, that are painful and traumatic to witness, and which may even border on the ugly.

TRINITY, THE PARADOX OF THE. The paradox is expressed by the Athanasian Creed: "We worship one God in Trinity, and Trinity in Unity; Neither confounding the Persons, nor dividing the Substance." Various manners of avoiding the paradox of three persons in one substance have led to the following heresies: Apollinarianism (Christ's divinity and humanity are the same and, hence, there could be no moral development in His life), Arianism (Christ is not divine but created by God expressly for the creation of the world), Euthychianism (the denial of Christ's humanity), Jacobitism (a type of Monophysitism), Monophysitism

(Christ's nature is wholly divine), Nestorianism (there are two separate persons in Christ), Sabellianism (the persons of the Trinity can only be distinguished by their functions), and Unitarianism (the rejection of both the divinity of Christ and the Trinity).

TRUST, THE PARADOX OF. This is a practical problem in salesmanship, similar to the PARADOX OF SINCERITY. In order to maximize his chances to complete most sales, a salesman must establish his trustworthiness to the prospective client; his assertions and his actions must be consistent. The sales process, however, requires that the salesman do whatever may be necessary in order to control the situation and close the sale. These necessities often include submission to indignities and the performance of acts that violate good taste and/or moral principles. Since the client is aware of these exigencies, he is unlikely to believe that the salesman is trustworthy. While not formally contradictory, the salesman does find himself in an impossible situation since, in order to make the sale, he must be trustworthy and he must also perform acts that impugn this trustworthiness.

READING

Oakes, Guy. "The Sales Process and the Paradox of Trust." *Journal of Business Ethics* 9(1990): 671-679.

TRUTH-TELLER VARIANTS OF THE LOGICAL PARADOXES. One of the most conspicuous aspects of the LIAR and other paradoxes of the same ilk is that it predicates falsity of itself. The result is paradoxical in the strong sense of being contradictory. What happens, however, when a statement predicates truth of itself? Mackie (298) collects the following list of examples of truth-teller variants:

(1)   What I am now saying is true.
(2) $S =_{def}$ 'S' is true.
(3)   [The sentence printed in brackets on this page is true.]
(4)   'Yields a truth when appended to its own quotation' yields a truth when appended to its own quotation.
(5)   Obey this order.
(6)   Carry out the next instruction: carry out the previous instruction.
(7)   Is 'autological' autological?
(8)   The largest number named in this book.
(9)   [The only successfully referring phrase printed in brackets on this page.]

(10) If the instruction in Richard's paradox had read 'If the *n*th figure in the *n*th decimal is *p* , let the *n*th figure in *N* be *p* ', would *N* have been a member of *E* ?

(11) 'I am not going to be hanged on yonder gallows.'

(12) Is the class of all classes that are members of themselves a member of itself?

(13) In a certain village the barber shaves all, and only, the men who do shave themselves; is the barber bearded or cleanshaven?

Consider the sentence S defined above. If we suppose that S is true, no contradiction results; likewise, if we suppose that S is false. Nevertheless, many logicians still consider S paradoxical because it fails to assert anything at all. This is perhaps more obvious in the imperative variant

Obey this order!

Here we have a sentence that purports to command us to do something, but there is not anything that it commands us to do. We do not know what actions would count as compliance (or noncompliance) to the order and, hence, it seems that the order cannot place any obligation on us.

READINGS

Mackie, J. L. *Truth, Probability and Paradox: Studies in Philosophical Logic.* Oxford: Clarendon, 1973.

Mortenson, C., and G. Priest. "The Truth Teller Paradox." *Logique et Analyse* 24 (1981): 381-388.

Yablo, Stephen. "Truth, Definite Truth, and Paradox." *Journal of Philosophy* 86 (1989); 539-541.

TWIN PARADOX, THE. A PARADOX OF TIME TRAVEL, like the CLOCK PARADOX, of which it is a graphic illustration, the Twin Paradox is a puzzle in relativity theory about asymmetry in an apparently symmetrical situation.

Formulation. An astronaut says farewell to his twin brother before leaving in a space ship for a star some light years away. The space ship travels near the speed of light, and when it reaches its destination, turns around and returns to earth at the same speed. On returning, the astronaut finds that, while his clocks show the journey to have taken a certain amount of time, the clocks on earth show a rather larger elapsed time, and his twin brother is now considerably aged.

Explanation. The result is paradoxical because the motion of the earth relative to the spacecraft is just the same as the motion of the spacecraft relative to the earth. From the astronaut's perspective, the twin on earth went away and came back at a velocity close to the speed of light. So why has the astronaut not aged more than his terrestrial sibling?

Resolution. According to the theory of relativity, the astronaut is first accelerated, then turned and accelerated in the opposite direction. This "non-inertial" motion is thus in two directions. In contrast, the earthbound twin has no significant motion other than that provided by the inertial passage of the earth around the sun. It is this asymmetry, when incorporated into the equations of the special theory of relativity that results in less time measured and experienced by the astronaut.

READINGS

Kroes, Peter. "The Clock Paradox, Or How to Get Rid of Absolute Time." *Philosophy of Science* 50 (1983): 159-163.

Little, E. M. "Two Simpler Relativity Twin Paradoxes." *American Journal of Physics* 33 (1965): 747-748.

Lowry, E. S. "The Clock Paradox." *American Journal of Physics* 31 (1963): 59.

Marder, L. *Time and the Space Traveller*. London: 1971.

Muller, R. A. "The Twin Paradox in Special Relativity." *American Journal of Physics* 40 (1972): 966-971.

Schlegel, R. "The Clock Paradox: Some New Thoughts." *Philosophy of Science* 44 (1977): 306-312.

UGLY, THE PARADOX OF THE. Like the PARADOX OF TRAGEDY, this is an AESTHETIC PARADOX. The ugly, whether found in works of art or in ordinary experience, is presumably distasteful and unappealing, but under certain circumstances, the ugly is associated with an appealing aesthetic fascination and pleasure.

UNEXPECTED EGG, THE. This is a version of the PREDICTION PARADOX.

UNEXPECTED HANGING, THE. See the PREDICTION PARADOX.

UNNOTICED MAN, THE. See EUBULUIDES' PARADOXES.

UNSUCCESSFUL INTERVENTION, THE PARADOX OF. Proposed in 1986 by Robert M. Gorden, this is a paradox about an individual fighting against his own desires.

Formulation. An agent "intervenes against his desire to X and yet, because his intervention is *unsuccessful*, X's all the same. Assuming that there were desires (or reasons, or whatever) that motivated him *to intervene against his desire to X*, why were they not sufficient to move him simply *not to X*, making intervention unnecessary?" (Gorden 222).

Explanation. Suppose that an individual who has a craving for cream pies also has a desire to lose weight and, therefore, a desire to abstain from eating the pie his wife just baked. The individual is equiped with a machine that will quell his desire for the pie — all he has to do is to press a button. Unfortunately, the machine's battery is dead, so that, when he presses the button, the machine does not work and he ends up eating the pie. Since he pressed the button, however, his desire not to eat the pie must be stronger than his desire to eat it (otherwise, he would just have eaten the pie and left the button alone). But if his desire not to eat the pie was stronger than his desire to eat it, why did he need to push the button in the first place? Observe that the story line admits of various "psychological" or temporal explanations; these explanations do not, however, address the paradox, which focuses on the individual's motivation.

Resolution. Gorden argues that in addition to our normal desires, there are second order desires that one or other of our conflicting (primary) desires win out over the competition. The second order desires are generated by primary desires, but not all primary desires generate second order ones. In particular, only stable desires — roughly, those that are based on generalizable principles — motivate second order desires. Thus, according to Gorden, the individual's desire to eat the pie is actually the stronger of the competing desires, but it is inherently instable and, thus, generates no second order desire. The desire not to eat the pie, however, is really a desire for good health, which is a stable desire; this desire generates a second order desire which motivates the agent to intervene against his desire to eat the pie. This intervention, then, may be either successful or unsuccessful.

READING

Gorden, Robert M. "Desire and Self-Intervention." *Nous* 20 (1986): 221-238.

UTILITARIANISM, A PARADOX OF. Closely related to Singer's PARADOX OF EXTREME UTILITARIANISM, this ethical paradox, proposed by Frederick Kroon, turns on the introduction of telepathic students to moral evaluation.

Formulation. "A person I am observing, Jones, is inflicting pain on someone. Call this action 'A'. I, a confirmed utilitarian, am about to pass moral judgment on action A. Under normal circumstances I would classify A as terribly wrong, but on this occasion I know that others are aware of the fact that I am about to pass moral judgment on A, and I also know that these others, who are in some ways superior to me (they can directly intuit, by a kind of mental telepathy, a person's emotional responses, including his moral approval or disapproval of actions), will learn from my moral stance: if I evaluate A as wrong, that will reinforce their hatred of such acts (a *very* good thing, as there are many of these 'witnesses' to my act of evaluation), while if I evaluate A as right, that will reinforce their admiration of such acts (a *very* bad thing). Suppose I know that there are no other morally relevant consequences, and suppose that I cannot communicate with these 'witnesses'. Suppose, in fact, that this is the final moral 'training' that I, or anyone else, can provide for these witnesses, who are due to spend the rest of their lives on a desert island, applying the moral lesson they will presently learn from me (with horrendous consequences, should I approve of cruelty like Jones'). What should I do?" (Kroon 107).

Explanation. Since on the act utilitarian view, an action is right or wrong depending on the consequences of the action, and since no available alternative will have better consequences than A (because only by observing A, together with my disapproval of A, will the witnesses receive an extremely valuable lesson), A must be judged a right action. Yet if Kroon judges A to be right, it will have very unfavorable consequences (in the cruelty the witnesses will inflict on each other on the desert island), and hence A will not be right after all. Nor can Kroon remain neutral or noncommittal with regard to A because this reaction (a further stipulation) will also encourage the witnesses to perform actions similar to A.

Resolution. Kroon rejects as inadequate several manners of "drawing the paradox's sting": first, denial of the existence of beings such as the witnesses who recognize approval and disapproval without understanding the intellectual background of these actions; second, assertion that the act of evaluation should not count as a casual consequence of the act evaluated; third, restriction of the evaluation of an action to its intended consequences; and fourth, developing a theory of the context of moral evaluation. Unlike in Singer's discussion of his quite similar paradox, Kroon suggests that this sort of paradox applies equally to at least some versions of rule utilitarianism. We may observe here that there does seem to be an ambiguity in Kroon's formulation of the paradox. Let B be Kroon's disapproval of A. Then it is not A alone which has the good consequences, but rather the conjunction of A and B. Thus, it would seem that Kroon could judge A to be wrong and yet judge the conjunction of A and B to be right. The paradox then fades into the non-utilitarian truism that good consequences often follow from bad actions (it is indeed this circumstance that has always been troublesome for utilitarianism). Perhaps the paradox can be resurrected by stipulating that Kroon have the power to stop A before it occurs. On the one hand, since it is better for A not to occur than for it to occur, Kroon should prevent A from happening. On the other hand, if he stops A from occurring, the conjunction of A and B will not occur; but it is better for this conjunction to occur than not to occur, so Kroon should allow A to occur. Presumably, the utilitarian would have to decide whether the nonoccurrence of A or the joint occurrence of A and B has the preponderance of desirable consequences, but this calculus would seem to be confounded if the witnesses understand Kroon's allowance of A as a mitigation of B (his disapproval of A).

READING

Kroon, Frederick. "A Utilitarian Paradox." *Analysis* 41.2 (1981): 107-112.

VERBAL PARADOXES. See LITERARY PARADOXES, OXYMORON, and RHETORICAL PARADOXES.

VERIDICAL AND FALSIDICAL PARADOXES. This dichotomy is due to W. V. O. Quine. According to Quine, a veridical paradox sustains "prima facie absurdities by conclusive argument" (2), whereas a falsidical paradox "is one whose proposition not only seems at first absurd but is also false, there being a fallacy in the purported proof" (3). Whereas a falsidical paradox always contains a fallacy, not all fallacies are paradoxical. As examples of veridical paradoxes, Quine cites the fact that a man may be twenty years old and yet have had only five birthdays (if he was born on February 29th) and the BARBER PARADOX. Falsidical paradoxes are exemplified by a purported proof of "2 = 1," in which division by zero surreptitiously occurs. Quine's notion of paradox as an argument purportedly sustaining an at least seemingly absurd conclusion is especially appropriate to the LOGICAL PARADOXES, but does not quite capture all the nuances of the term. See DEFINITION OF PARADOX.

READING

Quine, W. V. O. "Ways of Paradox." *The Ways of Paradox: And Other Essays.* Rev. enl. ed. Cambridge: Harvard UP, 1976.

VERIFICATION PRINCIPLE, THE PARADOX OF THE. Logical positivism sought to establish a clear demarcation between true science and nonsense-that-might-otherwise-pass-itself-off-as-science. The means of achieving this not ignoble goal was to be the so-called "verification principle," to the effect that statements that were not associated, at least in theory, with a rule or a procedure for their verification were to be accorded nonsense. In the issue, the unverifiability (and hence nonsensicalness) of this very principle proved the petard upon which logical positivism hoist itself.

READING
Ayer, A. J. ed. Logical Positivism. Glencoe, Ill.: Free P, 1959.

VIA NEGATIVA, THE. From Dionysus the Areopagite to Meister Eckhart, Christian mystics have used the *via negativa*, or apophatic path, to affirm God's divinity as a superlogical reality. By saying what God is not, the apophatic path awakens our appreciation of God's radical otherness. In everyday life, men lose their sense of God's incomprehensibility. In order to lead men to confront the inadequacies of the conventional formulas for the divine essence, St. John of the Cross once described God as "dung." This "negative theology," which seeks the "unknown God," is the closest the occidental mind reaches to the sense of nothingness found in eastern mysticism and especially in Zen Buddhism with its paradoxical *koans* (see BUDDHIST PARADOXES).

READING
Hopkins, Jasper. *Nicholas of Cuza's On Learned Ignorance: A Translation and an Appraisal of De Docta Ignorantia.* Minneapolis: A. J. Benning P, 1981.

VICTIM'S PARADOX, THE. This PARADOX OF DEONTIC LOGIC contravenes the intuitive principle that the consequences of obligations should also be obligatory.
Formulation. If a victim bemoans his fate at being robbed, a robbery has occurred. But robbery is forbidden. Therefore, the victim is forbidden to bemoan his fate.
Explanation. Given the two premises

(1)   If a victim bemoans his fate at being robbed, a robbery has occurred.

(2)   A robbery has occurred.

we may conclude by *modus tollens* that

(3)   The victim does not bemoan his fate.

Moreover, robbery is forbidden; that is, (2) is obligatory. Since (3) is a consequence of (2) — and the fact (1) — by the principle cited above, (3) is also obligatory; thus, the victim is forbidden to bemoan his fate. **Resolution.** Azizah al-Hibri argues that this paradox is easily resolved by introducing a dyadic obligation operator into the deontic formalism. She also points out the essential similarity between the present paradox and that of the GOOD SAMARITAN.

READING

Al-Hibri, Azizah. *Deontic Logic.* Washington: UP of America, 1978. 24, 43.

VOTER'S PARADOX. See ARROW'S PARADOX OF SOCIAL CHOICE.

VOTING, PARADOXES OF. This class of paradox concerns matters of democratic procedure. The paradoxes arise when one or another technique of determining the outcome of a vote or election issues in results that are intuitively unfair. The class includes ANSCOMBE'S PARADOX, ARROW'S PARADOX OF SOCIAL CHOICE, CONDORCET'S PARADOX, OSTROGORSKI'S PARADOX, and the PARADOX OF NEW MEMBERS.

READINGS

Fischer, D, and A. Schotter. "The Inevitability of the 'Paradox of Redistribution" in the Allocation of Voting Weights." *Public Choice* 31 (1978): 49-67.

Fishburn, P. C. "Paradoxes of Voting." *American Political Science Review* 68 (1974): 537-546.

Niemi, R. G., and W. H. Riker. "The Choice of Voting Systems." *Scientific American* 234 (1976): 21-27.

Petit, J. L., and E. Terouanne. "A Stormy Assembly: Electoral Paradoxes." *Theory and Decision* 22 (1987): 271-284.

WANG'S PARADOX. One of the best known RECENT SORITES is Wang's Paradox proposed by Hao Wang. Here the predicate "large" or "small" is applied to ever decreasing or increasing numbers: "Consider being a small

number. 1 is surely small. In fact, since it cannot make much difference
to size, if n is small, then so is $n+1$, for any n. But then mathematical
induction applies. Conclusion: all numbers are small" (Travis 347).
READINGS
Dummett, Michael. "Wang's Paradox." *Synthese* 30 (1975): 301-324.
Travis, Charles. "Vagueness, Observation, and Sorites." *Mind* ns 94 (1985):
345-366.

WINE AND WATER PROBLEM, THE. See the BEAKER PARADOX.

WOLGAST'S PARADOXES OF KNOWLEDGE. Elizabeth Hankins
Wolgast has formulated seven paradoxes of knowledge, which she takes
to spring from several untenable assumptions about knowledge. Since
most of these are equivalent or similar to paradoxes addressed elsewhere
in this volume (one of the seven, for example, is Moore's Paradox), we
will not consider them further here.
READINGS
Fetzer, James H. "Wolgast's Paradoxes of Knowledge." *Philosophia* [Israel]
12 (1983): 403-421.
Wolgast, Elizabeth Hankins. *Paradoxes of Knowledge.* Ithaca: Cornell
UP, 1977.

ZALCMAN'S PARADOX. Lawrence Zalcman observes that most
questions are not their own answers, but then asks

> Is the question "What is an example of a question which is
> not its own   answer?" its own answer? (160).

This is a PARADOX OF SELF-REFERENCE similar to the LIAR.
READING
Zalcman, Lawrence. "I'm Glad You Asked Me That Question." *Analysis*
48.3 (1988): 160.

ZENO'S ARGUMENTS AGAINST PLURALITY. Zeno authored a
number of paradoxes against plurality. The argument discussed below is
cited by Simplicius, *In Physica* 141, 6-8, and was propounded in support
of the Eleatic philosophy.

Formulation. If there are many things, they must be both infinitely small and infinitely large.

Explanation. Zeno seems to have argued that whatever has size is divisible into parts and, thus, does not possess the unity characteristic of a single thing, as opposed to many things. Hence, none of the supposed plurality of things can have any size. In contrast, no amount of sizeless things could produce a body with any size. Hence, the parts of any given body must have some size. Now, since each part is sizable, each part must be divisible into parts having some size. By reiterating the argument for each new part, the body is found to be composed of an infinite number of parts having some size and, therefore, the body must be infinitely large.

Resolution. Gregory Vlastos points out that though the premise that a thing cannot be a single thing if divisible into parts is undoubtable from the standpoint of Eleatic doctrine, it is in fact false. An apple, for example, has many parts — skin, core, seeds, and what not — but remains for all that but a single thing. Thus, Zeno's conclusion that the many are infinitely small does not follow. Vlastos then invalidates the conclusion that the many are infinitely large by appealing to the modern notion of convergent series Thus the sum of an infinite number of nonzero sizes may be a finite size and again Zeno's conclusion does not follow. See ZENO'S PARADOXES.

READING
Vlastos, Gregory. "Zeno of Elea." *Encyclopedia of Philosophy*. Ed. Paul Edwards. New York: Macmillan, 1967. Vol. 8, 369-372.

ZENO'S DILEMMA. One of Zeno's Paradoxes, mentioned by Aristotle at *Physics* 209a23-25 and again at 210b22-24.

Formulation. Either place does not exist or, existing, must have a place in which it exists.

Explanation. Zeno was presumably motivated by a desire to show that the very concept of place is contradictory. He argued that whatever exists must exist in some place. Hence, if place exists, place exists in some place. By reiterating the argument for each newfound place, an infinite regress is obtained.

Resolution. Aristotle resolved the paradox by distinguishing among the various senses of "to be" (there was no separate word for "to exist"). Gregory Vlastos, however, points out that Aristotle's solution could not have been advanced in Zeno's time because the required distinctions had not yet been made. Thus the paradox must have been genuinely puzzling to Zeno's contemporaries. See ZENO'S PARADOXES.

READINGS

Aristotle. *Physics.* IV, VI.

Vlastos, Gregory. "Zeno of Elea." The *Encyclopedia of Philosophy.* Ed.
Paul Edwards. New York: Macmillan, 1967. Vol. 8, 369-372.

ZENO'S PARADOXES. Zeno of Elea (born c. 490 BC), a disciple of
Parmenides, is the most famous paradoxer of all time. Zeno's basic strategy
was to disprove positions contrary to the Parmenidean insight that since
only the unchanging One exists nothing in reality can change. He proposes
a series of arguments purporting to show that the concepts of the many
(plurality), motion (change), and place (space) were inherently
contradictory and led to absurdities. Aristotle's Physics attributes to Zeno
four mind-boggling paradoxes against motion: the Arrow, the Moving
Blocks (the Stadium), the Achilles and the Dichotomy (the Race Course).
The Arrow and the Moving Blocks are generally interpreted to be
predicated upon the assumption that space and time are composed of
finitely sized indivisibles or atomic quanta. The Achilles and the
Dichotomy, in contrast, presuppose that space and time are composed of
infinitesimal "points." Thus, whatever may be one's pleasure in regard
to the philosophy of space and time, the very concept of motion will
purportedly still land one in inextricable difficulties. Less well known
than the paradoxes against motion are Zeno's paradoxes against plurality
and against place. The latter is called Zeno's Dilemma by Aristotle. Zeno's
Paradox of the Millet Seed, which attempts to discredit sense knowledge,
is, in contrast to his more subtile paradoxes, an easily controverted pseudo-
paradox. It was because of these arguments that Aristotle calls Zeno the
inventor of dialectics. See the ACHILLES, the ARROW, the DICHOTOMY, the
MILLET SEED, the MOVING BLOCKS, ZENO'S ARGUMENTS AGAINST PLURALITY,
AND ZENO'S DILEMMA.

READINGS

Aristotle. *Physics.* Bk. IV, VI.

Bendegem, Jean Paul van. "Zeno's Paradoxes and the Tile Argument."
Philosophy of Science 54 (1987): 295-302.

Booth, N. B. "Zeno's Paradoxes." *Journal of Hellenic Studies* 77 (1957):
187-201.

Bouwsma, O. K. *Toward a New Sensibility.* Lincoln: U of Nebraska P,
1982. 213-240.

Brochard, Victor. *Études de Philosophie Ancienne et de Philosophie
Moderne.* Paris: 1912. 7-9.

Cajori, F. "The History of Zeno's Arguments on Motion." *American*

Mathematical Monthly 22 (1915): 1-6, 39-47, 77-82, 109-115, 143-149, 179-186, 253-258, 292-297.

Dejnozka, Jan. "Zeno's Paradoxes and the Cosmological Argument." *Philosophy of Religion* 25 (1989): 65-81.

Gale, Richard M., ed. *The Philosophy of Time*. New York: Anchor, 1968. 387-494.

Grunbaum, A. "Messrs. Black and Taylor on Temporal Paradoxes." *Analysis* 12.6 (1952): 144-148.

— —. "Modern Science and the Refutation of the Paradoxes of Zeno." *Scientific Monthly* 81.5 (1955). 234-239.

— —. *Modern Science and Zeno's Paradoxes*. Middletown, CN: Wesleyan UP, 1967.

Knorr, Wilbur R. "Zeno's Paradoxes Still in Motion." *Ancient Philosophy* 3 (1983): 55-66.

King, H. R. "Aristotle and the Paradoxes of Zeno." *Journal of Philosophy* 21 (1949): 657-670.

Lee, Harold N. "Are Zeno's Paradoxes Based on a Mistake?" *Mind* ns 74 (1965) 563-70.

Lee, H. P. D. *Zeno of Elea: A text with Translation And Notes*. Cambridge UP, 1936.

McKie, John R. "The Persuasiveness of Zeno's Paradoxes." *Philosophy and Phenomenological Research* 47 (1987): 631-639

Mill, J. S. *System of Logic*. 5th ed. 389-390.

Owen, G. E. L. "Zeno and the Mathematicians." *Proceedings of the Aristotelian Society* 58 (1957-58): 199-222.

Ross, W. D. Aristotle's *Physics*. Oxford: 1936. 81-82.

Rossetti, Livio. "The Rhetoric of Zeno's Paradox." *Philosophy and Rhetoric* 21 (1988): 145-152.

Russell, Bertrand. *Our Knowledge of the External World*. New York: Norton, 1929. Lectures V and VII.

Salmon, Wesley. *Space, Time and Motion*. Encino, CA: Dickenson, 1975.

— —, ed. *Zeno's Paradoxes*. Indianapolis: Bobbs, 1970.

Sherry, David M. "Zeno's Metrical Paradox Revisited." *Philosophy of Science* 55 (1988): 58-73.

Simplicius. *In Physica*, IV, VI.

Székely, Laszlô. "Motion and the Dialectical View of the World." *Studies in Soviet Thought* 39 (1990): 241-255.

Tannery, Paul. *La Géometrie Grecque*. Paris: Gauthier-Villars, 1877. 124-125.

— —. *Pour l'Histoire de la Science Hellène*. Paris: Félix Alcan, 1887. 247-261.

— —. "Le Concept Scientifique de Continu: Zénon d'Élée et George Cantor." *Revue Philosophique de la France et de l'Éstranger* 20 (1885): 385-410.

Te Hennepe, Eugene. "Language Reform and Philosophical Materialism: Another Round With Zeno." *Analysis* 23 [Suppl.] (1963): 43-49.
Ushenko, A. "Zeno's Paradoxes." *Mind* 55 (1946): 151-165.
Vlastos, Gregory. "Zeno of Elea." *Encyclopedia of Philosophy*. Ed. Paul Edwards. New York: Macmillan,1967. Vol. 8, 369-379.
Whitrow, J. G. *The Natural Philosophy of Time*. London, 1961. 135-137.
Zart, Paulus Johannes. *About Time: A Philosophical Inquiry into the Origin and Nature of Time*. Oxford: North-Holland, 1976. Ch. XI.

ZERMELO-KÖNIG PARADOX, THE. According to Zermelo's Well-Ordering Theorem, every set can be well-ordered. This result was itself highly surprizing, though it turns out to be equivalent to the Axiom of Choice. By definition, two ordered sets are similar if there is a one-to-one order preserving function from one of them to the other. The Well-Ordering Theorem then allows the formation of the family of sets similar to a given set and the derivation of a result that contradicts Cantor's Theorem, namely: the cardinality of the power set of this family is less than or equal to the cardinality of the mentioned family. The paradox may be blocked by imposing certain conditions on set formation. See RUSSELL'S PARADOX.

ZERMELO'S PARADOX. This paradox in statistical thermodynamics is essentially similar to that of MAXWELL'S DEMON.

GLENN W. ERICKSON, Ph.D.
Professor Adjunto
Departamento de Filosofia
Universidade Federal do Rio Grande do Norte, RN, Brasil

JOHN A. FOSSA, Ph.D.
Professor Adjunto
Departamento de Matemática
Universidade Federal do Rio Grande do Norte, RN, Brasil

DTP Beth Camara